The Poetics of Appropriation

The Literary Theory and Practice of Huang Tingjian

The Poetics of Appropriation

The Literary Theory and Practice of Huang Tingjian

David Palumbo-Liu

Stanford University Press
Stanford, California • 1993

Stanford University Press
Stanford, California
© 1993 by the Board of Trustees
of the Leland Stanford Junior University
Printed in the United States of America

CIP data are at the end of the book

Acknowledgments

This book derives from my doctoral dissertation at the University of California at Berkeley, and I thank the members of the committee that supervised it—Cyril Birch, James Cahill, Bonnie Isaac, and the two members from outside institutions, Earl Miner and Stephen Owen. I am especially grateful to Professor Owen, who offered close readings of my translations, checked my critical thinking, and honed my perceptions of the subject matter.

Of those who at various times read and commented on parts of the manuscript, I thank in particular Michael Fuller, Jonathan Kowallis, and Pauline Yu. Encouragement and advice from Peter Bol and Stuart Sargent in the early stages of the project were very helpful. Finally, I am especially grateful to Professor Chow Tse-tsung for his advice and suggestions on the entire manuscript. Any errors or inaccuracies that remain are solely my responsibility.

Part of the research for the dissertation was aided by a grant from the Joint Committee on Chinese Studies of the American Council of Learned Societies and the Social Science Research Council, and I thank them for providing me with the opportunity to work in East Asia, particularly at Kyoto University. I am grateful to Professor Shimizu Shigeru for sponsoring me as a Research Fellow on the Faculty of Letters at Kyoto University; Professor Arai Ken for facilitating my work at the Research Institute for Humanistic Studies; and Professor Ōno Shusaku, who shared his work on Huang Tingjian with me.

On my return to the United States, the Mabelle McLeod Lewis Memorial Foundation provided a grant that helped in the completion of the dissertation, and grants from the Walsh Fund of Georgetown University and the Center for East Asian Studies at Stanford University assisted me in the revision process. I am also grateful to the Department of Comparative Literature at Stanford for its support.

In revising the manuscript, I benefited greatly from the meticulous comments and suggestions of the Press reader and the painstaking and elegant work of my copyeditor, John Ziemer. I especially thank Helen Tartar, humanities editor for the Press, for her enthusiasm and help. I also thank Ben Huang and Derek Lim for their research assistance.

To my mother I owe acknowledgment for introducing me to Chinese culture. Finally, I wish to express my gratitude to my wife, Sylvie Palumbo-Liu, for constantly helping me reformulate my thoughts on literature and having faith in my efforts, and to my son, Fabrice, whose youthful pleasure in life always refreshed me when energy ebbed—this book is dedicated to them.

D. P.-L.

Contents

	Preface	ix
	Abbreviations	xiii
	Critical Introduction	1

Part I: Huang Tingjian as a Northern Song Poet

ONE	Confronting the Tang	25
TWO	The Mediated Poem	47
THREE	The Illusion of Immediacy	69

Part II: Huang Tingjian's Theory and Practice

FOUR	Extending Verse	91
FIVE	Words and the Shaping Will	117
SIX	Allusion: Writing and Reading	148
	Conclusion: Signing the Palimpsest	173

Appendixes

A	Short Biography of Huang Tingjian	195
B	On Translating Huang Tingjian	197

Reference Matter

Notes	201
Bibliography	227
Character List	239
Index	251

Preface

The culture of ancient China is often regarded as tradition bound, always reverent of its past and anxious to preserve it, yet the Northern Song dynasty (960–1126) witnessed a radical reinterpretation of many facets of traditional culture—history, philosophy, art, and literature. Those who performed these reinterpretations legitimized their re-reading of the past first by assimilating it and then by asserting that they were the proper extension of past tradition in the present day. This was the age of the great encyclopedias, compendiums, imperial anthologies, and catalogues; however, while promoting the collection, classification, and preservation of traditional texts, a group of literati created new ways to interpret and create cultural objects that transformed the representation of the past.

In literature, this revision of the past had specific ramifications. Northern Song poets confronted what they themselves acknowledged as the Golden Age of Chinese poetry, the Tang dynasty (618–907). Many Northern Song poets, particularly those writing during the last century of the dynasty, were haunted by a deep sense of self-consciousness, an awareness of the challenge to emerge from the shadows of the greatest poets of the tradition even as they claimed an affinity with their predecessors. The effort to surpass prior poetry was part of the larger act of reinterpretation—poets strove to find a way to situate themselves within the cultural tradition while declaring themselves distinct.

The poetry produced under such historical contingencies and cultural imperatives has often been compared unfavorably to that of the Tang. Critics, from the Northern Song to today, have charged that the Northern Song lyric poet profoundly failed to meet the challenge he sensed for himself. Both traditional and modern critics agree on two reasons for this failure. First, they see in the Northern Song lyric a strong and dominating discursive strain of "philosophizing"—the poet is too absorbed in reasoning out ideas, too little concerned with conveying feeling. Second, they find Northern Song verse too allusive, too "bookish." Both critiques are informed by the same aesthetic—both argue against *mediation*. For these critics, the Northern Song lyric is too opaque, too dense: it demands an intellectual investment precisely at the moment that the primary values of lyric poetry call for an immediate emotional response.

Discussions of the negative aspects of the Northern Song lyric frequently mention Huang Tingjian (1045–1105). He, more than any other poet of his time, openly acknowledged and actively exploited the mediated quality of lyric poetry in his poetic theory and practice. Huang regarded the past as an inescapable presence. In response, he engendered a poetics that recognized and incorporated the textual histories of words in order to create new meanings, meanings with his imprimatur.

Critics chide Huang most for expounding a theory that they see as a platform for plagiarism, an excuse for acts of poetic appropriation. The perception of Huang's verse as a pastiche of allusions, coupled with the criticism that for Huang poetry is simply an opportunity to display his erudition, leads to a reading of Huang's verse that is itself only an exercise in erudition. The reader seeks to identify the source of recondite allusions as a way to dissipate the density of the poem and discovers that once he has excavated those sources, the poem is but an empty form, a pretext for a game of wit. But this hermeneutic strategy ignores the historical forces that occasioned Huang's poetics and consequently misses the reasons why in many respects Huang is an *exemplary* (not anomalous, or marginal) Northern Song poet.

This study is aimed at providing the background for understanding why Huang was so greatly admired, especially by outstanding literati of his age such as Su Shi and why later scholars claim Huang is the characteristic Northern Song poet. In this work, I relate his poetics to both the larger context of traditional Chinese poetry and specific changes in late Northern Song material history. Huang Tingjian's was an extremely complex intellect—he discoursed freely on art and calligraphy, philosophy and literature, and he was deeply influenced by Buddhism (although his perception of Buddhism is highly syncretic, and his application of it highly metaphoric). A comprehensive study of Huang's poetry would thus involve a more profound exploration of the interrelationships among these discourses than I provide here, as well as an analysis of his *ci* poetry. Our understanding of Huang Tingjian, his literary theories, and his poetic practices is impeded by the facts that one of his central pronouncements comes to us only through the records of another and that his various collections contain poems that scholars claim were written by others.[1] In this monograph I confine myself to the particular task of elucidating a specific element of his theory and practice that provides a logic uniting all his comments on poetry and a way of identifying the salient characteristics of his verse. It also offers a particularly compelling point of comparative study.

Huang's poetics reflects a basic rethinking of the key issues of the classical Chinese poetic tradition and allows us to sense both the salient characteristics of classical Chinese lyric poetry and their relation to Western notions of poetry. In his heavily allusive and intellectually complex rereading and rewriting of the past, we have a crucially important set of observations on the nature of literature and culture and the relation of the past to the present, as well as a daring transformation of the literary canon.

In the first part of this study, I locate Huang within the context of Northern Song letters and focus especially on the manner in which that age, and others, have defined the Northern Song against the backdrop of the greatest age of classical poetry—the Tang. How did Northern Song poets respond to their uncomfortable proximity to such impressive predecessors, and how did their response shape their literary art? In the second part, I examine the theories and poetic practice of Huang Tingjian to see how he both incorporated the response of his contemporaries in his own works and developed that response into a highly individual program of composition.

This study is bracketed by a consideration of how Huang's poetics can be related to Western literary concerns. It is not my intent to fit Chinese literature into the frame of Western literary discourse, far from that; rather, I wish to use my analysis of Huang Tingjian to scrutinize that frame in a comparative critique. The introduction thus surveys important documents of Western literary criticism that remark on issues with which Huang was deeply concerned: imitation, technique, and spontaneity of composition. I point out ways that these discourses grapple with the contradiction between craft and nature, a contradiction that informs Huang's poetics to a great extent. I then discuss Huang's particular response and how that response was determined in large part by Huang's position as a classical Chinese poet writing at a historical moment that articulated these issues as explicit questions.

In the conclusion I return to the consideration of how Huang's literary project resembles, but ultimately differs from, Western literary theories of influence and intertextuality. My main argument is that radically different notions of textuality separate classical Chinese poetics from the basic presumptions of Western literary composition. In Huang Tingjian's poetic theories and practice, we have an extremely important set of tools to view the classical Chinese lyric tradition and its relation to the Western tradition.

Abbreviations

For complete publication data on the books cited in the following list, see the Bibliography, pp. 227–38.

CLEAR	*Chinese Literature: Essays, Articles, Reviews*
HJAS	*Harvard Journal of Asiatic Studies*
LDSH	He Wenhuan, ed., *Lidai shihua*
NHZJ	*Zhuangzi: Nanhua zhenjing*
SBBY	Sibu beiyao ed.
SBCK	Sibu congkan ed.
SHSG	Huang Tingjian, *Song Huang Shangu xiansheng quan ji*
Shi	Huang Tingjian, *Shangu shi zhu*
SKQS	Siku quanshu ed. (Taipei: Yingshu, 1978)
SRYX	Wei Qingzhi, comp., *Shiren yuxie*
SWGS	Su Shi, *Su wenzhong gong shi bianzhu jicheng*
TX	Hu Zi, comp., *Tiaoxi yuyin conghua*
WJ	Henzō Kinkō, *Wenjing mifulun*
WX	*Wen xuan*
WXDL	Liu Xie, *Wenxin diaolong*
XLDSH	Ding Fubao, *Xu lidai shihua*
YZ	Huang Tingjian, *Yuzhang Huang xiansheng wenji*

The Poetics of Appropriation

The Literary Theory and Practice of Huang Tingjian

Critical Introduction

If there is one thing that allows us to employ the word "lyric," derived from a particular poetic form in the West, to the *shi* poetry of traditional China, it is the primacy accorded by poets in both traditions to the notion of spontaneous composition and originality. In the course of this study, I will exert some critical pressure on both these concepts and tease out the differences in their articulations in the West and traditional China. I begin by quoting three exemplary passages, the first by Khakheperresenb (ca. 2000 B.C.) and the next two by Huang Tingjian (1045–1105), that variously show a shared investment in the image of poetry coming forth afresh and immediately from an emotional response to the world.

Would I had phrases that are not known, utterances that are strange, in new language that has not been used, free from repetition, not an utterance which has grown stale, which men of old have spoken.

In Du Fu's [712–70] composing of verse and Han Yu's [768–824] composing of essays, there is not one word that does not come from somewhere else. Probably, because later generations do not read enough, they say that Han Yu and Du Fu made these expressions up themselves. Those of old who were able to compose literature were able to mold the myriad phenomena. They took the expressions of the ancients and entered them into brush and ink—it was like a pill of Spirit Cinnabar, which spots iron and turns it to gold.

The meaning of poetry is inexhaustible, yet the talent of men is limited. In pursuing inexhaustible meaning through the use of limited talent, even Tao Yuanming [365–427] and Du Fu could not achieve mastery in capturing it.[1]

The mournful echoes of the voice of an Egyptian scribe dead some three thousand years have been used by two twentieth-century critics of

Western literature as an emblem of a key motif in literary history. Their combined remarks bracket nearly all of neo-classical, modern, and postmodern English literature. W. Jackson Bate, in *The Burden of the Past and the English Poet*, uses Khakheperresenb's words to remark on a theme that he traces from Restoration England to the Romantic age—a writer's constant awareness that his language is not his alone, that his art is always haunted by the art of others. John Barth, addressing the question "Is postmodernist fiction an art form to take seriously?" uses the passage to assert the "exhaustion" of "the aesthetic of high modernism" and the legitimacy of a new form of writing.[2] The questions this topic raises form a major set of concerns in both ancient and modern Western literary criticism and deeply shape our understanding of literary art.

It is tempting to draw a simple correlation between all three quotations to form a smooth consensus bridging time and cultural space, bringing the classical Chinese poet within our horizon of understanding. I will forestall that moment, however, in order to probe more deeply the differences between Western ideas on the use of past texts and those of classical Chinese poets. Perhaps precisely *because* these quotations seem so complementary it is important to see how they ultimately reflect very different presumptions about what poetic language *is*. At the same time, this differentiation allows us to perceive on what grounds the two traditions share similar concerns.

The question of language's "exhaustibility" is inextricably linked to the production of literature: the assertion that language is *not* exhaustible is a solace of latter-day writers—it leaves open the possibility of "true" literary creation. If language *is* exhaustible, then all latter-day writers can do is attempt to mask their work's secondary nature—the art of revision becomes synonymous with art itself.

In both China and the West, meditations on these questions take form in discourses on the art of composition. Such discussions implicitly or explicitly link the issues of imitation and originality to a questioning of the very nature of art, counterposing spontaneous, pre-reflective composition (originality) to imitation (the use of literary models); the freedom of "pure" creation against the necessity of writing in/to a tradition. The possibility that poetic language is prescribed leads to both a heightened sense of the importance of revision and a rethinking of the relationship between past and present poets.

On the one hand, one recognizes prior greatness in order to master one's craft; on the other hand, one must go beyond such models to emerge as distinct. Yet the questions remain: Is verbal art limited to simply revising the works of others? Is one's work always haunted by the ghosts of previous articulations?

The range of the texts I survey in this introduction covers the ancient period to the modern age. In this comparative analysis it becomes clear that not only a sense of the abiding nature of the contradiction but also the *discursive responses* to such a dilemma are shared by a wide range of critics in Western literary history. Only after recognizing and comparing certain key elements of the responses of writers in the West and classical China to this dilemma can we gauge the validity and usefulness of transposing Western theoretical concepts such as the "anxiety of influence" and "intertextuality" to the classical Chinese tradition.

By the same token, making these distinctions will give us a more accurate sense of how both traditions conceived of the basis of literary art. Most specifically, Huang Tingjian's poetics will mean more to us if we see how writers and critics in the classical Chinese tradition articulated concepts similar to those in the West yet founded them on very different notions of literary composition—if we see the affinities between the two traditions and at the same time use their differences to better understand their distinctness.

Here I trace the basic and profound vacillations in the strategies of Quintilian, Longinus, Edward Young, Schiller, and T. S. Eliot as they seek to evade the central contradictions in their arguments on imitation and originality. Despite Khakheperresenb's early pronouncement on belatedness, writers in the West felt the threat of literary exhaustion differently in different times. Yet the primary issue is not so much exhaustion as the fear of repetition. It is this fear that serves as a subtext for all discourses on imitation and originality, for repetition cancels the basic value of the lyric—it negates the ideal of a speaking subject's autonomy and authenticity.

Longinus on Imitation

Aristotle suggests a relationship between the individual and the collective and between innate and acquired literary skill: "Ordinary people do this [practice some form of rhetorical argument] at random or through practice and from acquired habit. Both ways being possible, the subject can plainly be handled systematically, for it is possible to inquire the reason why some speakers succeed through practice and others spontaneously; and everyone will at once agree that such an inquiry is the function of an art."[3]

Later Quintilian introduced a tension between these two notions in his discussion of imitation:

> From these [great authors of the past] ... is to be derived a supply of words, varied figures of speech, and the principle of verbal arrangement; by them, too, the mind is to be directed towards examples of every good quality in writing—for there can be no doubt that the greater part of art lies in *imitation*. Discovery clearly came first, and is of first importance. But it is none the less profitable to follow up other people's successful discoveries. And every technique in life is founded on our *natural desire to do ourselves what we approve of in others.* [Italics added][4]

It is interesting how Quintilian straddles the issues of invention, discovery, and imitation. He mentions discovery, the thing of "first importance," only briefly, as if it went without saying. The rhetoric of this passage implicitly diminishes the stature of discovery, for which we may read "originality," and elevates the topic at hand, *imitation.*

Quintilian gives only one reason for the primary importance of discovery: it *came* first. The valorization of the idea of origin stands out clearly here, but the text in which this statement is embedded argues in another direction. Quintilian first borrows Aristotle's claim regarding our imitative nature ("Imitation is natural to each man from childhood, one of his advantages over the lower animals being this, that he is the most imitative creature in the world, and learns first by imitation") and extends it to the realm of literary composition.[5] Although the rhetoric of the passage suggests it is "natural" to award discovery primacy, imitation is nonetheless *equally* "natural" and, most important, the only way that we progress. If we pair Aristotle's statement with Quintilian's, it becomes clear that imitation is the very thing by which culture (ethics, art, science) perpetuates itself, the only way that society retains cohesion and longevity.

But no sooner does Quintilian set up this argument than he makes it a foil for another, different, assertion. The hinge of this transition lies in the lines: "Yet this very principle [imitation], which makes every accomplishment so much easier than it was for men who had nothing to follow, is dangerous unless taken up cautiously and with judgement." The judgment that Quintilian proceeds to elaborate is an account of discovery that argues a much stronger case than simple temporal priority. The significance of the notion that the originals of antiquity confronted a much harder task than do the moderns because those first poets had to create things *ex nihilo* gradually changes; it becomes clear that what is of real importance to Quintilian is setting up an argument that will allow the moderns equal, if not greater, status than the ancients. Discovery, and the assertion of individuality that is concomitant with discovery, returns to center stage in Quintilian's discourse, but this resuscitated type of discovery is qualitatively different from the first.

Quintilian recalls the notion of the naturalness of imitation from his opening remarks and twists it in a direction that reconciles imitation with discovery. He encourages poets to imitate the originals *in being original*:

> What would have happened in those times which lacked models if men had thought that they should do and think nothing that they did not already know? Obviously nothing would have ever been discovered. How, then, can it be wrong for us to discover something that did not exist before? Those untutored men of old were led by sheer natural talent to bring so much to fruition: are we not to be inspired to search by the very fact that we know that those who have sought in the past have found? Can we not make use of our experience in one set of facts to dig out another? Shall we have nothing except by someone else's courtesy—like painters whose only ambition is to copy pictures by a process of guidelines and measurements?

Quintilian goes on to further modify the pristine image of the ancients—he asserts that "among the orators whom so far we know as masters, no one has appeared who cannot be found lacking, or open to criticism, in some respect or another." In this case modeling one's writing on one's predecessors is to mimic the imperfect. Quintilian's final move away from imitation is to declare that "the greatest qualities of an orator—talent, facility of discovery, force, fluency, everything that art cannot supply—these things are not imitable."

This passage is the first articulation of what becomes paradigmatic in discourses on imitation: a proclamation or concession of the value of models, a call to imitate those models, and then a gradual inversion that allows the modern to equal and eventually surpass the ancient; the original inevitably gains ascendancy over imitation. Models are first set up for emulation, then competition, and as the contest is announced, the argument, which was at first weighed heavily in favor of those who will always retain temporal primacy, is balanced by pointing out the imperfection of originals: since they are not perfect, they are imperfect models for imitation. Finally, the nature of the discourse switches from prohibition to fatalism—one *cannot* imitate the things of greatest value. The discourse on imitation thereby sets its own limitations while pointing out the ultimate value of what lies beyond it.

The tension between art and something whose greatness transcends art is intensified in Longinus. Again this issue is inextricably linked to questions of originality and imitation. At some point, individual talent must surpass what it can gain from traditional models.

> The question from which I must begin is whether there is in fact an art of sublimity or profundity. Some people think it is a complete mistake to reduce things like this to technical rules. Greatness, the argument runs, is a natural product, and does not come by teaching. The only art is to be born like that. They believe moreover that natural products are very much weakened by being reduced to the bare bones of a textbook.[6]

Longinus goes on to defend his project:

> What Demonsthenes said of life in general is also true of literature: good fortune is the greatest of blessings, but good counsel comes next, and the lack of it destroys the other also. In literature, nature occupies the place of good fortune, and art that of good counsel. Most important of all, the very fact that some things in literature depend on nature alone can itself be learned only from art. (2.3; 463)

Longinus attempts to balance the two aspects and rationalize his project, but even in this rationalization, art necessarily comes second. The last, and "most important," reason he lists has, in fact, little to do with the technique of composing—it is rather a consciousness of what technique *cannot* do.

Longinus' treatment of the subject of imitation, like Quintilian's, contains a movement that elevates the ancients only to deflate them. His first move is to gather both ancients and moderns into a commonality that effaces difference. He begins by evoking his famous analogy—the model of divine inspiration is transferred onto a model wherein latter-day poets receive the spirit of prior poets. What is of particular note, however, is that this transference is both unbidden and unproblematic: "Many are possessed by a spirit not their own.... The genius of the ancients acts as a kind of an oracular cavern, and effluences flow from it into the minds of their imitators" (13.2; 476).

From this analogy Longinus speaks of emulation: "These great figures, presented to us as objects of emulation and, as it were shining before our gaze, will somehow elevate our minds to the greatness of which we form a mental image" (13.2; 476). The commonality implicit in the analogy of oracular possession is lessened in the practice of emulation. The ancients are no longer represented by the metonymy of disembodied spirits that infuse the spirit of the latter-born poet. (And the extension of this model creates a vision wherein poets throughout the ages can share this common locus/spirit.) In the second image, the ancients are now more *objectified*—they stand apart from latter poets even as they aspire to join in the ancients' greatness. And this graphically portrayed otherness allows Longinus to speak of competing with the ancients.

Longinus makes explicit the rivalry that is only implicit in Quintilian (where Quintilian calls on the latter poet to match the powers of discovery of former poets):

Plato could not have put such a brilliant finish on his philosophical doctrines or so often risen to poetical subjects and poetical language, had he not tried, and tried wholeheartedly, to compete for the prize against Homer, like a young aspirant challenging an admired master. To break a lance in this way may well have been a brash and contentious thing to do, but the competition proved anything but valueless. (13.4; 476)

This brand of emulation evokes a strategy of writing that occurs, as it were, under the gaze of the ancients, a neat inversion of Longinus' prior image of the latter-day poets gazing on past masters: "It makes a great occasion if you imagine such a jury or audience [consisting of great orators of the past] for your own speech, and pretend that you are answering for what you write before judges and witnesses of such heroic stature" (14.2; 476). This rather intimidating image is, however, immediately converted in the closing passage of Longinus' discourse on imitation: "Even more stimulating is the further thought: 'How will posterity take what I am writing?'" (14.3; 476) The focus of Longinus' discourse emphatically shifts from the collective past—from the poet's predecessors—to the poet's *own* legacy.

In the famous Chapters 33–36, Longinus further lowers the stature of imitation. Like Quintilian, Longinus notes that the great masters of the past were not without technical flaws, but Longinus even argues that some of the most valued parts of their works display imperfections:

The universe ... is not wide enough for the range of human speculation and intellect. Our thoughts often travel beyond the boundaries of our surroundings. If anyone wants to know what we were born for, let him look round at life and contemplate the splendor, grandeur, and beauty in which it everywhere abounds....

So when we come to the great geniuses in literature—where, by contrast, grandeur is not divorced from service and utility—we have to conclude that such men, for all their faults, tower far and above mortal stature. Other literary qualities prove their users to be human; sublimity raises us towards the spiritual greatness of god. Freedom from error does indeed save us from blame, but it is only greatness that wins attention. Need I add that every one of those great men redeems all his mistakes many times over by a single sublime stroke? (35.2–36.2; 495–96)

The argument here against the absolute value of technical perfection emphatically shifts the focus from style to something that transcends style and is profoundly inimitable—the sublime.

This passage performs two important functions. First, it argues against the technical imitation of models; instead of sharing a *technique* with past masters, the latter-day poet is urged to share an *apprehension* of grandeur with them. Second, the stance toward the other source of imitation, nature itself, is radically altered. To merely represent nature is not enough: one has to grapple with something that surpasses nature—something that overflows the confines of the physical. Most significantly, just as Longinus subsumes both predecessors and nature in the same notion of imitation, he transfers his notion of competition with one's predecessors onto nature. This shift, from the mimetic representation of reality to the representation of a transcendent vision, has nothing to do with Platonic ideals, which correspond to lesser embodiments in the real world, but refers to something in the natural world that gestures beyond itself. (This shift is echoed in a similar manner in Schiller's treatise on the naive and sentimental; see below.)

Like Quintilian's, Longinus' discourse undercuts the concept of imitation even as it argues for it. Their qualified endorsements of imitation are important indexes of the paradox that even as technique and imitation are rendered indispensable, they are placed in a position secondary to discovery and invention; yet the prospects of being truly original seem impossibly remote. The corollary to this problematic relation of poet to predecessor is that although we owe reverence and respect to those who came before and to the tradition that they embody, we also value differing from those prior poets. Neither Quintilian nor Longinus is able to resolve this paradox, which abides as well in Edward Young's treatise on originality.

Young's *Conjectures*: An Eighteenth-Century Formulation

The impact on Romantic aesthetics of Longinus' treatise was enormous—it was interpreted as an endorsement of individual expression, spontaneity, and freedom from rules and method. The beginnings of this characterization have been traced to the mid-eighteenth century.[7] Two central texts that encouraged and argued for such a characterization were Nicolas Boileau's preface to his translation of Longinus (1674) and Edward Young's *Conjectures on Original Composition* (1759). Boileau is responsible for the argument that Longinus had something other than technique in mind when he spoke of the Sublime:

> It is thus necessary to know that by the Sublime Longinus did not mean what orators call "sublime style" [*le stile sublime*], but this extraordinary and marvelous thing that strikes in discourse and that makes it a work which elevates, ravishes, and transports. Sublime style constantly desires great words, but the Sublime can be found in a single thought, a single figure, a single turn of phrase. Something may be written in the sublime style but not be Sublime; that is to say, it may not have anything that is extraordinary or astounding about it.[8]

Boileau thus gestures toward something that is beyond style, something that cannot be confined by or defined through the analytic discourse of technique, but resides apart from such a critique. This interpretation falls solidly on one side of the dichotomy that Longinus attempts to balance and reconcile: the side beyond artifice and technical training. Samuel Monk notes the significance of this distinction: "The idea that the sublime is not a matter of style opened the way for investigations into the inner quality of great art, into the experiences of artist and reader when the one perceives a sublime object and the other experiences a great work of art."[9]

Edward Young's treatise is not alone in arguing for originality, but it is the most emphatic and comprehensive text of mid-eighteenth-century England to do so. Here it is important to trace Young's use of and departure from the notions of Greek and Latin literary criticism mentioned above. He echoes Aristotle and Quintilian—all poets imitate; he also distinguishes the imitation of nature and the imitation of works of other poets. But Young immediately relegates the latter to inferior status:

> *Imitations* are of two kinds; one of nature, one of authors: The first we call *Originals*, and confine the term *Imitation* to the second. I shall not enter into the curious enquiry of what is, or is not, strictly speaking, *Original*, content with what all must allow, that some compositions are more so than others, and the more they are so, I say, the better.[10]

From this calculatedly simple distinction, Young moves to deflate the notion of imitation in even more explicit and pejorative terms. Whereas Aristotle and others speak of the naturalness, and even the moral necessity, of imitation, Young sees its appearance in literary composition as nothing less than an affront to nature:

> By a spirit of imitation we counteract nature, and thwart her design. She brings us into the world all *Originals*: No two faces, no two minds, are just alike; but all bear nature's evident mark of separation on them. Born *Originals*, how comes it to pass that we die *Copies*? That meddling ape *Imitation*, as soon as we come of years of *Indiscretion* (so let me speak) snatches the pen, and blots out nature's mark of separation, cancels her kind intention, destroys all mental individuality; the lettr'd world no longer consists of singulars, it is a medly, a mass; and a hundred books, at bottom, are but One. (19–20)

The issue here is nothing less than a question of Self. Young goes far beyond pointing out the artistic ramifications of slavish imitation mentioned by Quintilian; he gives a moral imperative against imitation and even conceives of it as a threat to the ontological status of the individual.

His countermodel to imitation's perversion of nature is natural creation: "An *Original* may be said to be of a *vegetable* nature; it rises spontaneously from the vital root of genius; it *grows*, it is not *made*. *Imitations* are often a sort of *manufacture* wrought up by those *mechanics*, *art*, and *labour*, out of pre-existent materials not their own" (7).[11] The original, and its manifestation in nature, is sufficient unto itself, neither requiring nor admitting external matter. This construct is both a discrete and an unapproachable area of privilege.

Young next attacks imitation on yet another front; he proceeds to debunk prior poets, *even the originals*. To begin with, he (condescendingly) invents a class of "accidental *Originals*," those who most likely imitated but, because their models are not extant, are given credit for being original (8). Young then makes an astounding point that extends this notion. Just as we may have misplaced credit for originality on some predecessors, we may give the very first originals too much credit—they after all had no other choice. This assertion calls attention to itself for its absolute refutation of Quintilian's claim that the first originals had a more difficult time discovering things because they had no models. Young completely inverts that notion and, in doing so, diminishes the value placed on those original poets: "After all, the first ancients had no merit in being *Originals*: They could *not* be imitators. Modern writers have a *choice* to make; and therefore have a merit in their power" (10).

More than any previous discourse on the subject, Young's posits the *will* of the latter-day poet as a determining factor in the relationship between ancients and moderns. This issue enters into his treatise again as he speaks of the stature alloted to the ancients. Young maps out a battlefield for a contest between ancient poets and latter-day poets, where the stakes are of high ethical and aesthetic value and the moral ramifications of the later poet's actions abundantly clear. He must stand strong against the weight of the tradition; yet he is, in a sense, his own worst enemy:

> [But] why are *Originals* so few? not because the writer's harvest is over, the great reapers of antiquity having left nothing to be gleaned after them; nor because the human mind's teeming time is past, or because it is incapable of putting forth unprecedented births; but because illustrious examples *engross, prejudice,* and *intimidate*. They *engross* our attention, and so prevent a due inspection of ourselves; they *prejudice* our judgement in favour of their abilities; and they *intimidate* us with the splendor of their renown, and thus under diffidence bury our strength. (9)

Although the ancients are here portrayed as instigating this intimidation, the only thinly veiled subtext (which extends in several directions throughout the *Conjectures*) implies that the moderns themselves, through a failure of will, have themselves let this awesome image of antiquity stifle both their better judgment and their creative powers.

Young is not so blind as not to see the danger of dogmatism, nor can he sustain this absolute stand against literary models. He concedes the usefulness of imitation in a rather clever displacement, setting up a scapegoat that embodies the critical blindness of which he wishes to preclude being accused:

> He that admires not ancient authors, betrays a secret he would conceal, and tells the world, that he does not understand them. Let us be as far from neglecting, as from copying, their admirable compositions.... Let our understanding feed on theirs; they afford the noblest nourishment; But let them nourish, not annihilate, our own. (10)

Young's point here is that the ancients are of use only if they are *used* in a judicious manner. A careful guard must be kept against "apeish" imitation. To secure this viable ground for emulating the ancients, Young puts forth his notion of *proper* imitation:

> Imitate them [ancient authors]; but imitate aright.... Imitate; but imitate not the *Composition,* but the *Man*. For may not this paradox pass into a maxim? *viz*. "The less we copy the renowned ancients, we shall resemble them the more." ... Let us build our Compositions with the spirit, and in the taste, of the ancients; but not with their materials. (11)

The way out of the paradox described by Young derives in part from Quintilian's advice to model (judiciously) one's search for discovery after the ancients' search; Young also draws on Longinus' words on emulation. The proper object of imitation for Young, as it was for Quintilian and Longinus, is not technique, but spirit. (Young, however, adds a rather more specific dimension to the object of emulation. It is something more precise than a will to discover or a shared apprehension of the sublime, something closer to poetic sensibility.)

But Young even admits that *technical* imitation is of use to a "lesser genius," one still in the "infantile" stage of genius:[12]

> By the praise of genius we detract not from learning; we detract not from the value of gold, by saying that diamond is greater still. He who disregards learning, shows that he wants its aid; and he that overvalues it, shows that its aid has done him harm. Overvalued indeed it cannot be, if genius, as to *Composition*, is valued more. Learning we thank, genius we revere. (17)

This compromise seems to settle the tension and balance the one-sidedness of Young's initial proclamations regarding the primacy of originality. And yet the treatise continues for more than twice the length covered thus far, continually alternating between the author's initial stance against imitation and his attempt to account for the value of technique as found in compositional models.

Although Young's discourse may rightly be taken as a central document in the move away from imitation, Young never resolves the paradox of originality. In the *Conjectures*, the complexities of the paradox, the wide-ranging ramifications of either stance, surface in greater clarity, for all of (or *because* of) Young's attempts to evade them. Young's treatise also opens up, via his insistence on the priority of poetic will and its moral dimension, an important link to early Romantic aesthetics as seen in Schiller's *On Naive and Sentimental Poetry*.

The Poetic Will and the Sentimental

Schiller's treatise is compiled from a series of articles in his journal, *Die Horen*, in 1795 and 1796.[13] In these essays Schiller distinguishes naive and sentimental poetry, but the real base of his argument has to do less with poetic composition than with a stance toward the natural world:

> The poets are everywhere, as their very name suggests, the *guardians* of nature. Where they can no longer quite be so and have already felt within themselves the destructive influence of arbitrary and artificial forms or have had to struggle with them, then they will appear as the *witnesses* and *avengers* of nature. They will either *be* nature, or they will *seek* lost nature. From this arises two entirely differ-

ent modes of poetry which, between them, exhaust and divide the whole range of poetry. (183; 106)

The naive poet *is* nature—he is able to perceive it immediately and perfectly in all its plenitude. In contrast, the sentimental poet's observance of the natural world is mediated by "arbitrary and artificial forms," that is, by consciousness, a consciousness of his alienation from nature.

The analogue of this distinction in the realm of poetic composition is easy to perceive: the naive poet creates poetry without awareness of his art, and his poem is perfectly spontaneous; the sentimental poet cannot write in this fashion, aware as he is of the *art* of poetry. The absolute value that Schiller places on the naive is unmistakable, but so too is his effort to allow for, and champion, the sentimental.

By a process similar to Young's debunking of the ancient originals, Schiller deflates the naive precisely on the grounds of will:

Their [natural phenomena, and by extension the naive] perfection is not to their credit, because it is not the product of their choice. They accord us then, the quite unique delight of being our example without putting us to shame. They surround us like a continuous divine phenomenon, but more exhilarating than blinding. What determines their character is precisely what is lacking for the perfection of our own; what distinguishes us from them, is precisely what they themselves lack for divinity. We are free, they are necessary. (163; 85)

Here Schiller performs two operations on the naive. First, like Young, he argues against being awed and blinded by the purity and unity of antiquity (although Schiller does not here contrast antiquity and modernity, it is clear that the naive/sentimental dichotomy is temporal). Second, he emphasizes that the sentimental poet's alienation from nature incites his will to approximate that lost wholeness, whereas the naive *is* nature of necessity and the question of will never arises.

This distinction has immense ramifications for the nature of the poetic work:

Once man has passed into the state of civilization and art has laid her hand upon him, that *sensuous* harmony in him is withdrawn, and he can now express himself only as a *moral* unity, i.e., as striving after unity.... If one now applies the notion of poetry, which is nothing but *giving mankind its most complete possible expression*, to both conditions [of the naive and sentimental], the result in the earlier state of natural simplicity is the completest possible *imitation of actuality*—at that stage man still functions as a harmonious unity and hence the whole of his nature is expressed completely in actuality; whereas now, in the state of civilization where that harmonious cooperation of his whole nature is only an idea, it is the elevation of actuality to the ideal or, amounting to the same thing, the *representation of the ideal*, that makes for the poet.... The former move us by nature, by sensuous truth, by living presence; the latter by ideas. (188–89; 111–12)

The rhetoric of this passage is heavily ironic. The sentimental, expressed in such deprecatory ways ("only as a moral unity," "nothing but giving mankind its most complete possible expression," "only an idea"), is at once diminished before the wholeness of the naive, "the completest possible imitation of actuality." But this valorization of the naive is quickly and surely undercut, as Schiller gives the sentimental a way to surpass what seems to be perfection: he relegates the naive to representations of actuality and gives the whole realm of ideas over to the sentimental poet. Schiller's valorization of the latter is clear:

If one compares the species with one another, it becomes evident that the goal to which man in civilization *strives* is infinitely preferable to that which he *attains* in nature. For the one obtains its value by the absolute achievement of the finite, and the other by approximation to an infinite greatness. (189–90; 113)

Even if the ancient poets are victorious too in the simplicity of forms and in whatever is sensuously representable and *corporeal*, the modern can nonetheless leave them behind in richness of material and whatever is insusceptible of representation and ineffable, in a word, in whatever in the work of art is called *spirit*. (192, 115)

Perhaps Schiller's most emphatic pronouncement along these lines is the following:

But if the naive poet gains on the one hand in reality at the expense of the sentimental, and brings into actual existence what the latter can only arouse a lively impulse to attain, the latter for his part possesses the great advantage over the first that he can give the impulse a *greater object* than the former has supplied or could supply. All actuality, we know, falls short of the ideal; everything existing has its limits, but thought is boundless. (230–31; 155–56)

The naive poet is able to sense nature in its fullest (although he is not aware that he *is* sensing it), but Schiller argues that nature in its fullest is nonetheless finite. Here we have a particular twist on the Longinian argument against technical perfection and for the sublime.[14] By his very alienation from nature, the sentimental poet, fallen from the realm of experience into the realm of idea, finds a greatness of conception denied the naive poet.

Two other notes further compromise the value of the naive. First, the naive is perceptible only through the sentimental; that is, it cannot exist without the latter:

> It is absolutely necessary that the object which inspires it should be *nature* or at least be taken by us as such; second, that it be *naive* (in the broadest meaning of the word), i.e., that nature stand in contrast to art and put it to shame. As soon as the latter is joined with the former, not before, nature becomes naive. (161–62; 83–84)

Second, the naive poet is no longer even a possibility:

> Poets of this naive category are no longer at home in an artificial age. They are indeed scarcely even possible, at least in no other wise possible except they *run wild* in their own age, and are preserved by some favorable destiny from its crippling influence. From society itself they can never arise; but from outside it they still sometimes appear, but rather as strangers at whom one stares, and as uncouth sons of nature by whom one is irritated. (186; 109–10)

Although Schiller makes it clear that these naive poets are victims of society's mooring in the sentimental, there is still a sense that a poet *must* write as part of the collective. It is one thing to be alienated from nature, a common condition of all moderns, but to be alienated from society as well condemns one to a condition that is worse than anonymity.

Indeed, Schiller has so forcefully and rigorously argued for the sentimental that the naive as object of an imaginative (since we cannot ever know what we are missing, such is the absolute disjuncture of our alienation) nostalgia becomes secondary to its function as prompting the sentimental's search for it. Despite the clear primacy of the sentimental, however, Schiller is uneasy about completely dismissing the naive. The priority of origin and nature is simply too deeply entrenched in Western imagination.

Schiller proposes this compromise:

> In the final analysis, we must ... concede that neither the naive nor the sentimental character, each considered alone, quite exhausts that ideal of beautiful humanity that can only arise out of the intimate union of both.
>
> For so long as one exalts both characters as far as the *poetic*, as we have thus far considered, much of the limitation which adheres to them falls away, and their antithesis becomes all the less noticeable the higher the degree to which they become poetic; for the poetic mood is an independent whole in which all distinctions and all shortcomings vanish. (249; 174–75)

The paradoxical nature of this vision with which Schiller seeks to elide the opposite natures of the naive and the sentimental via the esemplastic power of the poetic finds echoes throughout his discourse. These pronouncements are all ramifications of the central paradox of a sentimental that can transcend nature in seeking it: "The opposite of naive perception is, namely, reflective understanding, and the sentimental mood is the reflection of the effort, *even under the conditions of reflection*, to restore naive feeling according to its content" (230; 154–55n). The corollary to this paradox of poetic consciousness in the realm of poetic composition is a style that erases itself and yet can be identified: "The genius must solve the complex tasks with unpretentious simplicity and facility.... And only thus does genius identify itself as such, by triumphing over the complications of art by simplicity" (174; 96). The dichotomy of naive being versus sentimental ideation finds its match in the dichotomy of simplicity and art; just as the sentimental strives to transcend its very identifying mark—the consciousness of alienation—and attain pure being, art seeks to triumph over itself through simplicity, the absence of art.

Yet, to extend the correspondence, we find that the sentimental—prey, as it were, to its own condition of alienation—realizes at every turn that the naive is absolutely irretrievable. Schiller proffers this compensation: that toward which the sentimental moves is necessarily greater than that which it cannot achieve. But what is the corresponding compensation in art?

> It is precisely this mode of expression in which the sign disappears completely in the thing signified, and in which language, while giving expression to a thought, yet leaves it exposed where otherwise it cannot be represented without simultaneously concealing it; and this it is we generally call a gifted style displaying genius. (176; 98–99)

The sign that disappears here is precisely a sign of difference—for art is the only thing that gives evidence of the exertion of poetic will. For it to disappear erases the very thing that Schiller champions: the will to seek what is lost. The stigma of alienation here becomes a mark of moral triumph. Literature should be precisely the representation of the world of ideas that exists beyond simple representation. But a regressive movement, which absorbs and hides art, threatens to destroy literature: once nature is attained, the traces of art are made transparent. Schiller stops short of that, however. He struggles to allow art to remain and evokes a "gifted style displaying genius," an art that withdraws sufficiently so as to allow the object of representation to stand unconcealed and yet an art that abides somehow, so that the object not be taken as mere natural thing.

The logical extension of the disappearance of art is the disappearance of the artist, and the resulting loss of identity negates the effort to individuate oneself from the past. August von Schlegel, for one, was not satisfied with the tenuous compromise of Schiller's model. Responding to the portrayal of Shakespeare as the perfect illustration of natural genius, Schlegel remarks: "To me [Shakespeare] is a profound artist, not a blind and wildly coursing genius. What has been babbled on this subject I hold, in general, to be a mere fable, a blind and extravagant illusion."[15] The paradox Schiller so profoundly feels and so energetically attempts to elide draws together the most problematic strands of Longinus and Young—the double paradox of art and nature; the tradition and the individual. These discourses are particularly concerned with the double role of art. It guarantees entry into the pantheon of the tradition; yet, by showing its traces too heavily, it threatens to be a dense mediation that calls attention to itself too obviously. To be visible, the individual must inscribe a signature predicated on art, yet aesthetic pleasure comes precisely in a (partial) erasure of art, an illusion of Nature that nonetheless reveals the artist's hand at work. The artist must show evidence that he or she has both mastered the craft and transcended "mere" art.[16]

In the twentieth century, T. S. Eliot spoke out against the idea that an individual poet could write outside tradition, yet his revision of a "classic" tradition evinces many aspects of the paradox we have traced from antiquity.

Eliot's Individual and Tradition

Eliot's celebrated essay "Tradition and the Individual Talent" (1919) reacts against much of what he understood as the Romantic values latent in Young and elaborated in Schiller.[17] In this reaction we see the paradox inverted but still unresolved. Eliot's purpose is to debunk the notion of originality and substitute a vision of impersonal composition, one that draws on both the pastness of the tradition and its abiding presence. He begins by attacking the very notion of originality:

No poet, no artist of any art, has his complete meaning alone. His significance, his appreciation is the appreciation of his relation to the dead poets and artists. You cannot value him alone; you must set him, for contrast and comparison, among the dead. I mean this as a principle of aesthetic, not merely historical, criticism. The necessity that he shall conform, that he shall cohere, is not one-sided; what happens when a new work of art is created is something that happens simultaneously to all the works of art which preceded it. The existing monuments form an ideal order among themselves, which is modified by the introduction of the new (the really new) work of art among them.   (49)

Eliot's choice of words is indicative of his stance toward the individual poet: by placing him *among the dead*, he sets the stage for the rest of the essay, which sets out to extinguish the notion of personality and erase the notion of purely individual significance.

The point of view which I am struggling to attack is perhaps related to the metaphysical theory of the substantial unity of the soul: for my meaning is, that the poet has, not a "personality" to express, but a particular medium, which is only a medium and not a personality, in which impressions and experiences combine in peculiar and unexpected ways.   (56)

Poetry is not a turning loose of emotion, but an escape from emotion; it is not the expression of personality, but an escape from personality.   (58)

Eliot's "struggle" is more than rhetoric, for the concept of personality is absolutely entrenched in the notion of lyric poetry. But his alternative vision of a "medium" is problematic. Besides being ill-defined and amorphous, it cannot account for any agent behind it. And yet the extinction of the individual personality is for Eliot an absolute requirement for any poet who, in his eyes, makes the proper choice to join the tradition: "What happens is a continual surrender of himself as he is at the moment to something which is more valuable. The progress of an artist is a continual self-sacrifice, a continual extinction of personality" (52–53). Actually, however, in Eliot's essay personality is not so much extinguished as sublimated into various loci, for example, the "tradition," the "dead," the "continental mind" (51). But with each articulation of a locus of reconciliation, Eliot re-articulates the paradox, which compromises and undermines the promise of this fusion of self with the Other.

For example, the celebrated analogy of the catalyst shows up in several paradoxical arguments:

When the two gases ... are mixed in the presence of a filament of platinum, they form sulphurous acid. This combination takes place only if the platinum is present; nevertheless the newly formed acid contains no trace of platinum, and the platinum itself is apparently unaffected; has remained inert, neutral, unchanged. The mind of the poet is the shred of platinum. It may partly or exclusively operate upon the experience of the man himself; but, the more perfect the artist, the more completely separate in him will be the man who suffers and the mind which creates; the more perfectly will the mind digest and transmute the passions which are its material.   (54)

The notion of impersonality appears here to be more than impassive; beyond that there is a real sense of passivity. The mechanics of the analogy require that the platinum be present in the admixture, yet by what agency are the ingredients placed in the beaker? In quest of annihilating the personal, Eliot seems to have recourse only to the accidental convergence of the individual and the historic moment.

In the preface to *The Sacred Wood*, Eliot appropriates the image of Young's (and others') "vegetable genius" and twists the metaphor to his own purposes. Instead of standing for the expression of the individual's emotions, an expression uninhibited by any concern for prior models (as it does in Young), in Eliot the image is used to convey something severed from personal expression: "We can only say that a poem, in some sense, has its own life; that its parts form something quite different from a body of neatly ordered biographical data; that the feeling, or emotion, or vision, resulting from the poem is something different from the feeling or emotion or vision in the mind of the poet" (x). Nevertheless, Eliot is not entirely comfortable with the implications of impersonality. For example, when he speaks of Donne, he again borrows a mechanical metaphor; but here the *active* presence of a shaping hand is unmistakable: "A thought to Donne was an experience; it modified his sensibility. When a poet's mind is perfectly equipped for its work, it is constantly amalgamating disparate experience."[18]

This "amalgamation" is, a few paragraphs later, elaborated into an act that involves the conscious and forceful manipulation of language: "The poet must become more and more comprehensive, more allusive, more indirect, in order to force, to dislocate if necessary, language into his meaning."[19] The "constant" energy behind such active "amalgamation" and "dislocation" contrasts sharply with the analogy of the catalyst.

A similar contradiction between the active will to forge poetry and the passivity of an impersonal and organically evolved poem is seen in the very articulation of a poet's stance toward the tradition. Eliot suggests that modern poets' knowledge of things is equivalent to their apprehension of past poets: "Someone said: 'The dead writers are remote from us because we know so much more than they did.' Precisely, and they are that which we know" (52). That is, any act of knowing necessarily involves knowing the past. In Eliot's discussion of the relationship between a new work and the body of traditional texts, there is again the sense that to have one's work join the "ideal order" of the tradition is not only unproblematic but unavoidable. In both cases, there is a deceptive seamlessness in the relationship between past and present, between the individual and the tradition.

Yet at the same time, Eliot also claims that tradition "cannot be inherited, and if you want it you must obtain it by great labour" (49). Here it seems clear Eliot wishes to avoid claiming that the poet's attachment to the tradition is a necessary one; to argue that would deprive the writer's entry into the tradition of any moral value. Just as Schiller's sentimental poet must strive for the naive and in that quest surpass it, Eliot's poet confronts a tradition that is not simply an open space habitable at liberty by anyone. But in making this an achievement born only out of a "great labour," Eliot swerves from his initial statements that portray the individual's relation to the tradition as a necessary one.

Another interesting correlation between Eliot's discussion of the tradition as an "ideal order" and his elaboration of the catalytic model is that in the latter the individual poet, of whom at first is demanded nothing less than a sacrifice of self before the temple of the tradition, comes to mimic the very ideal order into which he is to be subsumed. If the beaker represents not some accidental convergence of individual and history but a poetic Self that receives the "gases" and whose meaning-generating mechanism, the mind, causes those gases to react in a particular manner yet remains unchanged by it, then we have an odd replica of the "ideal order" of the tradition.

Like the all-embracing yet never changing flask on the poet-chemist's shelf, the tradition can absorb all manner of texts. Eliot optimistically argues that every new work changes the texts of the traditional order as much as they alter the new entries to the corpus, yet there is, behind all the rhetoric of assimilation and absorption, the shadowy but necessary presence of a meta-tradition that remains identifiable as "tradition," warding off the unorthodox. Eliot cannot admit this entity into his argument, since it would completely dismantle the "ideal," not of the tradition, but of the unproblematic relationship between the collective orthodoxy and the individual work. Eliot cannot posit a test that allows one to judge if the individual work is part of the tradition, since by his model all works automatically belong, but just such a test—just such a meta-tradition—is necessary if one is to distinguish tradition from anything else. On a meta-critical level, then, we re-enact the same paradox of the individual and his predecessors. How can one be absorbed into something and yet have one's work identified as one's own? How can the "tradition" absorb works and yet be defined nontautologically as other than the *un*orthodox? (The most pressing question is, simply, What *is* tradition?)

To this larger entity (which we may pose as an attendant concept encircling Eliot's "tradition") every new work is admitted, but although the tradition may suffer certain modifications, its structural power to differentiate, and therefore identify itself, remains intact and dominant: "We shall often find that not only the best, but the most individual parts of [the poet's] work may be those in which the dead poets, his ancestors, assert their immortality most vigorously" (48). The contradiction in this passage is unmistakable: the dead will not stay dead and are in fact not dead. On the contrary, they are most visible as they argue their immortality. Here Eliot diverges even further from his premises. That the dead poets are arguing *vigorously* (a further intensification of the contradiction) with live poets is evidence that what they are battling, whether it be time or the voice of the individual poet, has some strength. In either case, the fact that they are even arguing seems to contradict Eliot's views on both the nature of a literary work and the unproblematic nature of absorption of the past into the present. The corollary of this in terms of the paradox of originality is clear—Eliot's statements add up to the claim that the part of a poet's work that is most identifiable as that poet's creation is precisely the spot where the struggle with his or her predecessors is most apparent. These are certainly not Eliot's terms—for him the past shows up in the present in a non-contestive manner. But the underpinnings of Eliot's literary criticism belie both the complacency of the living in deferring to the tradition and the resignation of the dead to being simply present. This passage is evidence of the tenacity of the paradox even as Eliot claims that it is a false one.

Indeed, throughout "Tradition and the Individual Talent," the neat model of assimilation/modification is compromised by retreats into relativism, the same weak compromise noted in Longinus, Young, and Schiller: "We say: it [a literary work] appears to conform, and is perhaps individual, or it appears individual, and may conform; but we are hardly likely to find that it is one and not the other" (51).

In each of the texts considered here, the paradox of originality shows up in multifarious ways, each time involving the same pair of dichotomies: nature and art, the individual and the tradition. It is not clear that any of the responses successfully resolves the dilemma, but that very failure may give us a better sense of the relationships (that again enable other, particular discourses on art, literature, individuality, nature) between the two sets of terms.

In reading classical Chinese literary criticism, one is struck by similar pronouncements on the tension between art and nature and in particular the proper relationship between former and latter poets. The paradox of originality is not absent from the Chinese tradition, nor is the double role of art as a sign of craft and a sign of "not nature," but the discussions of these ideas in China are predicated on a very different set of circumstances and resulted in distinctly different responses. Ultimately we find quite different notions of what it is to write poetry and what it is to be a poet.

Although there seems no satisfactory way out of the dilemma in the texts discussed above, in their self-contradiction we find an implicit demarcation of a problem central to the presumptions of poetic composition. In the same way, one derives a more accurate vision of Huang Tingjian's theories by focusing on the vacillations in his discourse. Huang is also caught between ideals of spontaneous composition and craft, originality and imitation. His compromises, his modes of eliding the paradox, his stretching of the very parameters of aesthetics, articulate a remarkable revision of the classical Chinese poetic tradition even as they give us a way to see the classical Chinese tradition, and, by extension, the Western literary tradition, more distinctly.[20]

PART I

Huang Tingjian as a Northern Song Poet

ONE

Confronting the Tang

Those critical of Huang Tingjian's use of prior verse attack him for robbing the original poet, ruining the purity of the original verse, and calling this concoction art. To bolster their claim that what Huang saw as an act of poetic revision actually was one of violent piracy, they attribute to Huang the particular motive of pride and cite this passage:

> My mind has become drunk on the *Classic of Poetry* and the *Chuci*. I feel as though I have obtained something from them, yet I will forever be behind the men of antiquity. As for discoursing on words today, we should let Shaoyou [Qin Guan, 1049–1100], Chao [Buzhi, 1053–1110], Zhang [Lei, 1054–1114], and Wuji [Chen Shidao, 1053–1101] do it. You may ask one or two of these four gentlemen about the subject.
>
> In days past Wang Zhifang [1069–1109] composed two pieces in the style of the *Chuci* and sent them to me. They seem to be presentable. I once told him that [composition] is analogous to the situation of craftswomen of today—their patterned weaving is the marvel of a whole generation. When they plan to make a piece, it is proper for them to study the mechanism behind weaving [i.e., the loom]. Then and only then are they able to form brocade. You should try out this thought [in taking on your literary endeavor].[1]

Every discussion of this passage I have found uses Huang Tingjian's pronouncement as evidence of his deep discontent over his belatedness. The critics, however, tend to note only the first section, but in an important way the second part suggests Huang's reaction to the condition of belatedness articulated in the first. Huang remarks that he has grasped something from the most ancient anthologies of poetry but admits his inability to close the gap between the ancients and himself.[2] He refers the addressee of this letter to the members of the group of scholars around

Su Shi, who he says are better able to explicate words, but this moment of self-confessed inadequacy may be taken as signaling a will to go beyond antiquity. Huang leaves behind the question of recuperating the language of antiquity and turns to another matter.

Huang's analogy, likening literary composition to weaving, may be an allegory for one of the chief components of the late Northern Song project: the effort not to recuperate the past but to correlate present-day action with what latter-day literati understood to be the intent behind the ancient texts. Huang does not praise the weavers of his day for imitating ancient patterns and motifs; rather, he focuses on a more basic, and more essential, matter: the tools of the craft. In like fashion, Huang is interested in exploring the tools of literary art in order to produce literature that will dazzle *his* age. He is interested less in seeking out the precise etymologies of words in an effort to revive their original meaning than in learning how to join words in particular constructs that engender new meanings.

Huang's remarks shift the focus from restoring the past to composing texts based on a particular understanding of those models: we might even infer that this understanding is the "something" Huang has obtained from the classics. In his poetry Huang transforms the curse of belatedness into an imperative to create something different based on a particular understanding of past art and marks his position as a point of origin for a new poetics. We might correlate this movement away from imitation with the more general situation of late Northern Song poets, specifically their changing relationship to their Tang predecessors.

Arguably, more than any previous age in China, the Northern Song was involved in assessing its relationship to its past. In Song poetry one can sense the presence of a tremendous range of prior texts, but the main focus of late Northern Song poets was the Tang dynasty. Northern Song poets have inevitably been compared, both by later critics and by themselves, to the poets all agree were the finest of any age. The Tang greats drew on a lyric tradition over a millennium old and achieved poetry that perfected centuries-old techniques while losing none of (and indeed, adding much to) the lyrical quality of that verse.

In many ways it was the ill-fortune of Northern Song poets to follow the Tang—any effort by any Song poet was necessarily weighed against the most mature works of the greatest Tang masters. The modern critic Qian Zhongshu cites the opinion of many critics that Song poetry is, in a word, worthless. This opinion is reflected in the minimal inclusion of Song *shi* (lyric) verse in anthologies of classical Chinese poetry. Indeed,

Confronting the Tang

Qian cites one modern anthology that moves from the Tang directly to the Ming, bypassing entirely the Five Dynasties, Song, and Yuan periods.³ Another modern critic, Hu Yunyi, goes so far as to claim that *shi* poetry was completely exhausted by the time of the Northern Song. To compound this crippling situation, the political, aesthetic, and literary realms were all, according to Hu, hostile to the development of *shi*.⁴

It was not until the Qing dynasty that interest in Song *shi* poetry was revived by such men as Qian Qianyi (1582–1664) and Huang Zongxi (1610–95) and that Song poetry was again considered seriously. But even then the relative value of Song poetry was hotly debated; the established view was still deeply entrenched in literary opinion. The main issues are outlined in the preface to an important anthology of Song verse compiled in the Qing dynasty, the *Song shi chao*:

From the time of the Jia[qing; 1522–67] and the Long[qing; 1567–73] reigns, critics of poetry have revered the Tang while dismissing the Song, seeing the poetry collections of Song poets as fit for only "covering the sauce jar" or for "papering a wall."⁵

... Those who today dismiss Song poetry have yet to truly see a Song poem [since what has been handed down is biased]. Even though they may have seen a Song poem, they are incapable of assessing its origin and ramifications, and this is no different from not seeing it at all.

The flaw actually resides not so much in dismissing the Song as it does in revering the Tang. Probably what is revered is what those of the Jiaqing reign period and later regarded as "Tang" and not what the men of the Tang and Song eras conceived of as the Tang. Therefore, it follows that if what critics construe as the "Tang" is not the Tang as it was regarded at that time, then neither is their notion of what is "Song" accurate, and thus their assumption that it is decadent is quite understandable.

The Song was close in time to the Tang, and the Song poets' made great efforts to learn from the Tang and became particularly refined and devoted. To skip over the men of old [i.e., the Song] and go past them, claiming that they were simply coarse plagiarists, is like expelling one's father's tablet [from the family shrine] and treating one's grandfathers' tablets as if they were one's fathers'.⁶

This preface contains a number of insights into the way Song poetry has been regarded since its time and gives a sense of the pervasiveness of the Tang versus Song critique. The authors note the perpetuation of what they claim is an incomplete and distorted image of Song poetry. Too much of what is received as Song poetry is, to their minds, framed in a manner ignorant of its spirit. To misunderstand Song poetry as mere plagiarism is to ignore an essential element in the literary development of the lyric tradition and to make literary history discontinuous. It also completely mistakes the revisionary project of the Song.

Hu Yunyi speaks of the Northern Song poets' deep self-consciousness of their position vis-à-vis the Tang, a self-consciousness that led them to probe deeply into the nature of Tang literary art. Behind this effort one can sense a will both to learn from that art and to discover what might be left to do:

> Although in terms of creativity the Song lacks the greatness of the Tang, in terms of the investigation of poetry the Song progressed much more profoundly and penetratingly than the Tang. They performed extremely astute criticisms of each Tang poet and analyzed in great detail each Tang poem. They were able to view each poet's unique character and each poem's strong point. Most of all, for each great Tang poet—Li Bo, Du Fu, Bo Juyi, Li He, Wang Wei, Han Yu, Li Shangyin—no matter if in terms of diction, verse refinement, parallelism, or prosody, they were unwilling to relax the rigor of their examination; rather, they increased the scrutiny of their study.[7]

Song poets were particularly awed by what they considered to be the all-encompassing virtuosity of the great Tang poets. Their ability to assimilate and perfect the varied styles and modalities of the ancients placed them in a seemingly unsurpassable position. Two great Tang masters are described by Song writers thus:

> Delving into the subtleties of the *Liezi* and the *Zhuangzi*, holding close the discriminations of Su [Qin; ?–317 B.C.] and Zhang [Yi; ?–309 B.C.], seizing on the factuality of Ban [Gu; 32–92] and Ma [Sima Qian; 145–90 B.C.], hunting out the blossoms of Qu [Yuan; 4th c. B.C.] and Song [Yu; 3rd c. B.C.], rooted in the *Classic of Poetry* and the *Classic of Documents*, and measuring all by means of Confucius, what Han Yu composed was precisely the accomplished form of all these men's *wen* [literature, cultural discourse].
>
> Han Yu's *wen* is like Du Fu's poetry, which amassed the strengths of the many literati and matched them according to his own time. In previous times Su Wu's [2nd c. B.C.] and Li Ling's [?–74 B.C.] verse was strong in terms of lofty marvelousness; Cao Zhi's [192–232] and Liu Gonghan's [Liu Zhen; ?–217] poetry was strong in untrammeled abandon; Tao Qian's [365–427] and Ruan Ji's [210–63] verse was strong in tranquillity and blandness; Xie Lingyun's [385–433] and Bao Zhao's [414?–66] verse was strong in lofty purity; Xu Ling's [507–82] and Yu Xin's [512–80] verse was strong in refinement and elegance.
>
> Therefore, Du Fu's verse exhausted the style of lofty marvelousness, took to the extreme the vital energy of untrammeled abandon, enclosed the vigor of tranquillity and blandness. He wove together the manner of lofty purity and fully set forth the stance of refinement and elegance. The works of all these literati [of antiquity] could not reach [the excellence of] his verse. Still, without

bringing together the strong points of these great writers of antiquity, even Du Fu could not arrive at this.[8]

In the light of such an understanding of their predecessors, late Northern Song poets found themselves emulating the awesome assimilative powers of writers such as Han Yu and Du Fu and attempting to synthesize the valued aspects of prior texts. What Northern Song poets admired in the Tang greats was the ability to do to their predecessors what they themselves wished to do to their own Tang predecessors.

Many scholars have offered schematic analyses of the filiations of Northern Song poets to their Tang predecessors. Although self-pronounced "schools" (*pai*) of poetry did not appear until much later, such as the Jiangxi *pai* that took Huang Tingjian as its ancestor (with the exception of the loose and short-lived Xikun group of poets), literary critics have traced the influence of one or more Tang poets on groups of Song poets. With some variance, most critics of Song poetry agree to the following groupings for the early and mid–Northern Song periods:[9]

1. *The Late Tang Style*. This style is exemplified by the works of Jia Dao (779–849), specifically, his restrained and intimate landscape poetry and carefully balanced, crafted couplets. Chief among the imitators of this style in the Song dynasty was Lin Bu (967–1028).

2. *The Bo Juyi Style*. Poets such as Wang Yucheng (954–1001) were attracted to both the plain, prosaic diction of Bo Juyi and his group and Bo's concern with social issues, as, for example, in his "New Music Bureau" series.

3. *The Xikun Style*. This style takes its name from an anthology compiled by Yang Yi (974–1020), Li Zonge (965–1013), Liu Yun (971–1031), and Ding Wei (962–1033), the *Xikun chouchang ji*. These poets were admirers of Li Shangyin, and this anthology is characterized by rich, allusive, and idiosyncratically imagistic poems.

In the mid–Northern Song two other groups emerged:

4. *The Changli Style*. This group, led by Ouyang Xiu (1007–72), Mei Yaochen (1002–60), and Su Shunqin (1008–48), held as their model Han Yu. They reacted against what they considered the vacuous floridity of the Xikun group and championed instead the moral seriousness and sharp imagery of Han Yu and Meng Jiao (751–814). In particular, these poets attacked Buddhist and Taoist influence in literature and associated the ornate embellishments of much of Five Dynasties and early Song poetry with this influence.

5. *The Lixue School.* More of an inclination than a school, poets such as Shao Yong (1011–77) used poetry as a vehicle for particular investigations into Neo-Confucian concerns.

As attractively neat as these categories are to the literary historian, and as much as Song poets themselves distinguished between the styles of some groups, as Hu Yunyi notes, such groupings are vague and provisional. Even the members of a relatively defined group such as the Xikun poets wrote poems that are decidedly not like Li Shangyin's, poems with a marked affinity for other Tang models such as Bo Juyi.[10]

The usefulness of such categories becomes most obviously strained when one tries to address the poetics of the Yuanyou era (1086–94). According to Liang Kun's logic, the Jiangxi *pai* (in which Liang anachronistically includes Huang Tingjian) is filiated with *every* Tang model (Bo Juyi, Jia Dao, Li Shangyin, Han Yu, and Du Fu), as well as with the Jin poet Tao Qian.[11] This breakdown of categories amply illustrates the largely syncretic nature of the poetry of the late eleventh century, that of Su Shi and Huang Tingjian being most representative of the period.

Fang Hui notes how Yuanyou poets departed from simply imitating one or another style:

The poems of the Yuanyou era were not made according to the Yang [Yi] and Liu [Yun] [Xi]kun style, nor were they made according to the late Tang style of the Nine Monks,[12] nor even to the Bo Juyi style. Each [Yuanyou poet] used the power of his own talent to rise heroically in poetry. The extraordinariness of [Huang] Shangu was that he had the "transformed nature" of the Xikun style [i.e., had adapted the technical innovations of Xikun poetry], and yet he did not slavishly imitate its method of organizing a poem.[13]

Another critic claims that "Huang Tingjian employed the craft of the Xikun style and transformed the 'naturally forming' [i.e., its seeming spontaneity] character of Du Fu."[14] In both these observations we find the same claim—Huang Tingjian and other Yuanyou poets modified and synthesized elements from several prior "schools" of poetry; they did not rigidly follow any one school. By and large Yuanyou poets were eclectic, seeing past poetry as presenting various sets of possibilities. A "style" could be modified, reinterpreted, or blended with another. Huang borrowed not only from what he saw as the technical advances evident in these styles but also directly from prior poetry.

The ecumenical character of late Northern Song poetry is part of the general intellectual nature of the times, which may be seen in a number of pronouncements by literati. For example, this comment by Wang

Confronting the Tang

Anshi (1021–86):

> If anybody reads the classics alone, it is unlikely that he can really comprehend them. That is the reason why I have read, in addition to the classics, the writings of the philosophers, the manuals of medical doctors, herbalists, story-tellers, not overlooking anything in my quest for knowledge.... Having done these things, I am now in the position to comprehend the major import of the classics.[15]

Peter Bol notes Su Shi's interest in synthesizing elements from a wide range of sources. He speaks of Su Shi's "conviction that any style is achieved through integrating a diversity of interests. We might say that he thinks that integration is the style of all styles. Thus the guiding principle and purpose of style can be the idea of integrating diverse borrowings."[16]

The complexity of the notion of style in this period is also evident in the ways literati traced the influence of prior models. Speaking of Northern Song painting, Alexander Soper notes, "Ch'ao Pu-chih [Chao Buzhi] listed no less than twelve different authorities, ranging in time from Wu Tao-tzu [Wu Daoxuan, ?–792] and Chou Fang [Zhou Fang, ca. 730–ca. 800] to Ts'ui Po [Cui Bo, ca. 1050–80], from whom he borrowed the various parts of his repertory."[17] Not only did literati envisage themselves as synthesizers of models in particular realms of activity, they also saw affinities in style between the arts—the biography of the painter Li Gonglin (1049–1106) says that Li absorbed the "style" of the poet Du Fu.[18]

We may look on the efforts of Northern Song literati to know intimately the poetry of the Tang and other eras as part of a larger project to bring together various facets of antiquity in some coherent manner, a project that was to characterize the Northern Song. Above all, there was the overwhelming desire to make sense out of past culture, especially during the late Northern Song, which was characterized by both a tremendous range of interests and experimentation and the double desire to go beyond the secondary models of the early Song period and the primary models of the past. The past was awesome both in size and in complexity, and during the late Northern Song the implicit problems of cultural transmission became explicit questions.

Northern Song Modes of Identification

From the time of the early Northern Song to Huang's age, we may trace a gradual yet decisive change in poets' stances toward their predecessors. The following anecdote can serve as an example of the attitude of many early Northern Song poets:

Wang Yuanzhi [Yucheng] initially imitated Bo Juyi's poems; in Shangzhou he once composed a poem on being inspired by the spring day:

> A pair of peach and apricot trees cast shadows on the bamboo fence, oblique;
> Ornamenting the household of the Assistant Commissioner of Shangzhou.
> Why will the spring wind not permit this?
> Carrying orioles' voices, it blows and breaks several branches of blossoms.

His son Jiayou said to him, "Du Fu has the lines, 'It is as if the spring wind were taking advantage of me, / It comes at night and blows and snaps off several branches of flowers.'[19] His words and yours seem rather similar; therefore, I suggest you change yours."

Yuanzhi gleefully said, "If the poem achieves this excellence, then have I not been able to unconsciously match Du Fu?"[20] Because of this Yuanzhi went on to write, "Originally I was a follower of Bo Juyi; do I dare hope that Du Fu was my prior incarnation?"[21]

Wang Yucheng's response to the accusation of plagiarizing Du Fu is to take it as a pleasant surprise, even a compliment.[22] He argues that he has unconsciously expressed the intent behind Du Fu's lines in precisely Du Fu's words, thus "according" with both Du Fu's thought and expression. This leads him to "dare" to imagine that this uncanny repetition is a sign he is the reincarnation of the great Tang poet.

His response displays a playful and ironic stance toward the whole issue. Whereas his son is mildly anxious about what readers might think of seeing Du Fu's lines signed by his father, Wang is bemused by the fact that he had thought that Bo Juyi was his master. Had the lines derived from Bo Juyi, then the matter might easily be explained as conscious or unconscious repetition of words he has ardently studied. Drawing forth Du Fu, unconsciously and inexplicably, turns the event into a happy accident in the poetic cosmos. Throughout, however, he evinces no anxiety about having his verses recognized as another's, no sense of displeasure or chagrin that his verse is seen as a borrowing from the Tang poets, no argument for originality or difference.

This attitude is modified in the mid–Northern Song. As poets announce their affinities to prior greats, their mode of identification is overlaid with a firm and serious sense of sharing a moral sensibility with the prior poet—his ethos is now the latter-day poet's torch to bear into the present day, as manifested in both personal action and literary style. The most famous examples of this mid–Northern Song mode of identification are found in the texts of Ouyang Xiu and Mei Yaochen, who often linked themselves as a matched pair to the two great mid-Tang writers Han Yu and Meng Jiao. Mei Yaochen writes:

I have heard that Tuizhi [Han Yu] and Dongye [Meng Jiao] became friends when they were both still unknown. Although Meng's poverty never abated while Han rose higher and higher, there was no change in the two men's feelings for each other. Han was not haughty, nor did Meng experience any shame. They simply based their friendship on moral right.

You and I are like this; you need not yield before the ancients in conduct.[23]

In addition to moral seriousness, Ouyang and Mei found they shared with Han Yu and Meng Jiao an approach to literature and a literary style. Jonathan Chaves paraphrases a poem Mei Yaochen wrote that may serve as an example of a mid–Northern Song literatus working out equivalences between groups of Tang and Song poets:

Han Yu is said to have had universal genius. He swept away opposing views like so much dust. Chang Chi [Zhang Ji; 765–830] and Lu T'ung [Lu Tong; d. 835] vied in the "new and strange." Meng Chiao [Meng Jiao] was praised most of all for being "outstanding." In modern times, Ouyang Hsiu [Ouyang Xiu] is like Han Yu, a vast ocean, or a mighty mountain. Shih Man-ch'ing [Shi Manqing (Yannian); 994–1041] and Su Shun-ch'in [Su Shunqin] are like Lu T'ung and Chang Chi respectively. Mei himself is like Meng Chiao.[24]

Compared with this pronounced desire to identify oneself and one's group meticulously with Tang coteries, writers of the Yuanyou era moved toward identifying oneself by revising the phrases of one's poetic predecessors.[25] Two pronouncements by Su Shi are emblematic of this change in the mode of identifying oneself. In the first, he praises his mentor, Ouyang Xiu:

From the time of the Han to now, those who have practiced a Way [*dao*] that does not come from Confucius and thereby thrown all below into chaos and turmoil have been numerous! The Jin dynasty [265–420] perished because of Laozi and Zhuangzi. The Liang dynasty [502–57] perished because of Buddha. No one rectified this situation.

More than five hundred years passed, and then came Han Yu. Those who study him take him to match Mencius. Han Yu was certainly not far from Mencius. Now, more than three hundred years after Han Yu, we have Ouyang Xiu. His study extends beyond Han Yu and Mencius and reaches to Confucius.

He writes the truths of the rites and music and humane principle and harmonizes them in the Great Way [*da dao*]. His words are simple and yet brilliantly clear, trustworthy and penetrating. He evokes phenomena and places them in categories, discerning all in terms of perfect principle so as to convince the people. Thus all below Heaven are united in revering him as a master.

... Ouyang, in discoursing on the Great Way, resembles Han Yu; in speaking on events, he is like Lu Zhi [754–805]; in recording them, he is like Sima Qian; in verse, he resembles Li Bo. These are not my words alone; they are the words of all on earth.[26]

This is more than simple praise of Ouyang Xiu for reviving the Great Way; the nature of Su Shi's evaluation is directly determined by how he understood Ouyang would have wished to be remembered—as one whose identity was fused with those he himself revered.

But Su Shi exactly reverses the direction of this semblance in his depiction of himself: "The appearance and spirit of [Tao] Yuanming resembles mine; the mind and physiognomy of Letian [Bo Juyi] resembles mine."[27] Here it is not the latter-day poet who is seen in terms of his approximation of his predecessor's identity; rather, the prior poet is seen in terms of the later poet's identity; the father is modeled after his son.[28]

The strategy of calling attention to oneself even in praising one's predecessor is found again in a record by Huang Tingjian. Huang eulogizes the great Tang poet Du Fu, but just as important, Huang sets himself up as the only vehicle for the continuation of Du Fu and what he represents:

The Account of the Hall of the Great Odes

Hearing that I have often wished to copy out Du Fu's series of poems on the East and West Rivers and the Gorges at Kuizhou and to carve them in stone to be stored in Shu in the home of someone who is fond of letters and interested in all manner of things, Yang Suweng, an excellent and great man of chivalrous character, enthusiastically asked me if he could join in the project.[29] He also wished to make a building with wide spaces between the columns to shelter this stone and asked me to give it a name.

I named it the Hall of the Great Odes and told him, "From Du Fu on down to the present, more than four hundred years, this literature [*si wen*] has fallen to the ground.[30] Even those gentlemen engaged in literary composition who have risen in eminence by following their worldly capabilities have yet to enter his hall, much less his room."[31] I have often wished to follow in his steps.

Once I traced out the place where I happily met his intent and noted down some comments in a few words; but in the end I sunk back to the worldly and found no time to carry the project through....

Still, Du Fu's marvelousness lies in the fact that he placed no intention on literary composition. Now with regard to those poems [created] without intent that yet completely achieve their [maker's] intent, if one is not broadened by the Airs of the States, the Odes, and the Elegies or deepened by "Encountering Sorrow" and the "Nine Songs," how can one truly savor their meaning and charge through their gate?

Thus, if one leads later generations to pursue this on their own, they will obtain a profound understanding of it. If one leads later generations to ascend the Hall of the Great Odes and they seek it by means of my words, then their intent will be halfway realized.

As for those who like to bore and pierce through things beyond all reasonableness, they abandon this great intent and take their interest in what they haphazardly encounter in the poem concerning forests and streams, men and beasts, grasses and trees, fish and insects.[32] They believe that everything in the poem has some allegorical significance and are like those who exchange riddles and obscurities. In this way Du Fu's poems have been abandoned.[33]

There are many significant points in this record of Huang's naming of the hall. To begin with, it is a record of Huang's stance toward past, present, and future *wen*. The act of creating a permanent record of Du Fu's verses by carving them in stone is both a testament to Huang's reverence of Du Fu and a mark of his own literary project—he clearly sees himself as a torchbearer of prior values, ethical and literary, not simply the eulogizer of things dead and vanished forever.

The texts copied out exist not only as indexes to a prior age, a prior poet, but as vehicles for an ongoing process of acculturation. Du Fu's poems are not merely the products of their creator; they refer the reader to the great tradition of ancient verse—the *Classic of Poetry* and the *Chuci*. The very name of the hall has roots extending far beyond Du Fu, and when Huang refers to "this literature" falling into disregard, he gestures toward that tradition. It is a tradition embodied not only in Du's verse but, just as important, also in Huang's ability to recognize its presence in Du Fu's poetry and in his gesture of leading others to recognize the same.

Huang's ability to sense the affinities linking the Classics, Du Fu's verse, and his own circumstances derives from his integration of their "intent."[34] He claims his apprehension of this comes spontaneously, paralleling the spontaneity of Du Fu's composition (which in turn repeats the spontaneity of the verse of the ancients); these acts of reading and writing participate in the same project of manifesting a continuum of affinities. Du Fu's verse is composed without prior intent (*yi*): it spontaneously evokes the intent of the canonical texts. A private interest in creating a work that identifies oneself as unique is displaced: the perpetuation of a communal ethos takes precedence.

The emphatic act of carving out the poems in stone complements the tone of despair in Huang's voice. Du Fu's poems have survived and are still read; what Huang is lamenting is, rather, a loss of understanding, his contemporaries' inability to discern the line of transmission between the Classics and Du Fu. They, with their incomplete learning, strain to elide their lack of understanding by randomly applying any and all interpretive tools blindly to everything in the poem.

Huang's act of naming the hall marks the deeper issue—not only preserving Du Fu's verse, but also drawing forth and solidifying the affinities linking the Classics and Du Fu, and, as the one who bestows the name that explicitly joins the two, Huang Tingjian. Again, the ethos is continued by a reading of those texts that preserves and transmits their proper meaning—and the reader of Du Fu is the author of the record—Huang Tingjian, who now appears absolutely necessary to the continuation of Du Fu and the great tradition.

These pronouncements from different periods in Song literary history reveal a shift in the latter-day poet's attitude toward his predecessors—from noting coincidental repetition to claiming a willful affinity to placing oneself at the fore. This mode of foregrounding oneself is evident too in the lyric poetry of late Northern Song writers such as Su Shi and Huang Tingjian.

"To Be Able to Say"

The citation of a prior poet's lines does not, of course, begin in the Northern Song; however, Northern Song and pre–Northern Song poets conceived of the act of citation in very different ways. Although this dichotomy seems to lump together an unwieldy number of pre–Northern Song poets, I believe the late Northern Song mode of addressing one's predecessors is rather distinct. In citing the words of their predecessors, earlier poets "played" the role of those they cited, that is, they adapted their poetic personae; in the Northern Song role-playing, as we shall see, took on an altogether different nature. The following series of poems, which consists of various citations and adaptations of previous poems, provides a good example of the different ways in which Song and pre-Song poets "played" the roles of prior poets. An understanding of this will, in turn, give us a better sense of the difference in their conceptions of what it meant to write verse against the backdrop of the lyric tradition.

Intoned Beneath the Moon atop the West Tower of the Walled City of Jinling	金陵城西樓月下吟
Jinling night, quiet and still, a cool wind rises.	金陵夜寂涼風發
Alone I ascend the high tower, gazing toward Wu and Yue.	獨上高樓望吳越
White clouds reflected in the waters that shake the empty city,	白雲映水搖空城
4 Clear dew, suspended pearls, drip the autumn moon.	白露垂珠滴秋月
Beneath the moon I chanted quietly and stayed for a long time.	月下沉吟久不歸
From ancient times to now, encounters are rarely seen by human eyes.	古來相接眼中稀
To be able to say, "Clear waters, pure as bleached silk,"	解道澄江靜如練
8 These words always make one recall Xie Xuanhui.³⁵	令人長憶謝玄暉

This poem by Li Bo (701–62) begins, as many of his verses do, with a straightforward, quick setting of scene and mood. He depicts the scene from various perspectives and through various means—plain diction, dramatic monologue, rich imagery, allusion, and word play. He also calls on a poetic genre of meditations on lost times, longed after friends, a view of historically significant vistas from atop high places. In his closing couplet, Li Bo draws the dramatic movement of the poem forward, out of a relatively detailed set of meditations. He is moved by a prior poet's line and seems to give the poem over to this other poetic presence, the one in his mind's eye—Xie Tiao (464–99).

Li Bo frames the line from Xie Tiao within his own context, however: "To be able to say, 'Clear waters, pure as bleached silk,' / These words always make one recall Xie Xuanhui." Li Bo is not borrowing Xie's line to describe the scene or to enhance the representation of his natural surroundings. Rather, it refers the reader to an enunication by a prior poet, a reference with specific non-mimetic functions. The natural scene described by the line is secondary to the line's role in evoking another poem and another poet.

Li Bo sighs over Xie Tiao, but most important, he sighs over Xie Tiao's ability to craft a beautiful verse about this scene. Li Bo is announcing his affinity with Xie and his admiration for Xie's skill and poetic sensibility. To sense more precisely what force the line holds, we must turn to Xie Tiao's poem.

Late in the Evening I Ascend "Three Mountains" and Turn to Gaze on the Capital District　　　晚登三山還望京邑

From the shores of the Ba River one may gaze on Chang'an,　　灞涘望長安
And at Heyang one may espy Luoyang.　　河陽視京縣
The brilliance of the sun cleaves to the flying roof tiles,　　白日麗飛甍
4　Jutting in and out, each one may be seen.　　參嵯皆可見
Remnants of rosy clouds scatter, forming patterned lace,　　餘霞散成綺
Clear waters, pure as bleached silk.　　澄江靜如練
Noisy birds cover the spring islets,　　喧鳥覆春洲
8　Varied flowers fill the fragrant suburbs.　　雜英滿芳甸
Depart! I've been held up too long.　　去矣方滯淫
Cherished in my thoughts, the pleasure of feasts now over.　　懷哉罷歡宴
The fine time of returning home, alas, when will it be?　　佳期悵何許
12　Tears fall like drifting sleet,　　淚下如流霰
Whoever has feeling knows to gaze toward home.　　有情知望鄉
For whom is it possible for black hair not to change to white?[36]　　誰能鬒不變

　　Just as Xie Tiao was the source for Li Bo's allusion, Xie Tiao too has his allusions: the first line plays off a couplet by Wang Can (177–217), from one of his "Seven Sorrows Poems" ("Western Capital in Chaos, No Ways or Laws"): "From the south I ascend the high banks of the Ba River and turn my head to gaze back at Chang'an."[37] In Wang Can's poem the poet gazes back on the capital as it lies in ruin and chaos: the poem is a meditation on the disappearance of order, elegance, and righteousness, on the instability of things.

　　Xie Tiao's next six lines describe the natural scene. Viewing the capital with particular clarity, the poet finds everything accessible. Lines 5 and 6 give an even more detailed vision couched in rather ornate couplets, linking the scene to rich fabrics—above, the clouds are like patterned silk, below, the waters are as pure as bleached silk. Both images gesture metonymically to the courtly life of the capital. Nevertheless, even as the poet fills the landscape with dense, rich, and beautiful images, all linked to the elegance of the court, he also gazes beyond the capital. His reverie is broken by the abrupt intrusion of "Depart! I've been held up too long." The change in sentiment is reflected in the rude shift from elegant and ornate diction to exclamatory ejaculations.[38]

　　Line 9 comes again from Wang Can, from another of his "Seven Sorrows Poem," "Jingman Is Not My Village, Why Do I Linger?"[39]

Confronting the Tang

Here the bitterness and frustration of the poet comes to the surface, where before it was hidden beneath his reverie. Line 10 also derives from ancient verse; this time the source is the *Classic of Poetry* (no. 28, "Yang zhi shui")—"I yearn, I yearn, what month shall I return home?" These two allusions give a fuller context for the allusions of the opening lines. The first couplet appeared to be a neutral, general observation; now we know how to read it more profoundly. In his mind's eye the poet observes the beauty of the capitals, but he does so because he has no other view.

The poet meditates on his home, and this meditation supplants the images of the court. The feasts of the capital are now over for him as he returns to his post in the west; he wonders when he will finally return to his own village. The attraction of the present view is taken over by his thoughts on a desired past and a seemingly impossible future. "Tears fall like drifting sleet" is a wonderful inversion of the imagery found in the first section of the poem, which likens the sky and river to the fabrics of the court. Here Xie Tiao's burst of emotion sweeps away that ornate figuration, and instead natural imagery is used to express his feelings.

But we have yet to answer the question posed after reading Li Bo's poem—what about Xie Tiao's line strikes Li Bo as particularly moving? One would expect Li Bo to allude to a less neutral line from Xie Tiao's poem, something more dramatic, explicit, such as "Tears fall like drifting sleet." One might well admire the citation for its craft—the couplet juxtaposes the still river below against the gradually dissipating clouds above, the static image of silk against the slowly forming lace texture. But one might also see Li Bo's appreciation for its function in the development of sentiment in the poem.

The ingenuity of the allusion lies in its citing of a line from a moment when Xie Tiao is quietly gazing at a beautiful view of the capital. Li Bo's allusion counts on the reader's awareness of the dramatic development of Xie Tiao's poem: at any moment this quietude will be recognized as stagnation, the still, crystalline clarity of the river is about to become an image the poet would break away from but cannot. The line is considered particularly beautiful not only because of the serenity of the scene it depicts but also because the effect of the beauty of the line is recognized to be ephemeral. Its transitory beauty, nevertheless, is embedded in the poem and perpetuated precisely by Li Bo's apprehension of it. Li Bo is "playing" Xie Tiao, mimicking his former presence and following his thoughts and feelings by way of a particular poetic medium, stylistic and allusive; but at a particular moment he steps back and lets Xie speak for himself, and Li Bo.

In the Northern Song, Su Shi added his voice to the series of articulations and echoes we have noted. His articulation emblematizes a significant difference in a poet's stance toward and use of his predecessor—rather than defer to Xie Tiao, Su Shi imposes himself at the foreground of the poem in a movement similar to Huang's positioning himself before Du Fu in his "Account of the Hall of the Great Odes."

Sending Off Mr. Zhang of Jiazhou 送張嘉州

When young I was not willing to be a Marquis of the Ten Thousand Households, 少年不願萬戶侯
I didn't even recognize Mr. Han Jingzhou. 亦不願識韓荊州
I would rather be a chief magistrate for the Han at Jiazhou, 頗願身爲漢嘉守
4 Carrying wine, I would skim over lofty clouds. 載酒時作凌雲遊
An empty name is of no use to me now, white-haired. 虛名無用今白首
In a dream I arrive instead at the mouth of Longhong Stream. 夢中却到龍泓口
How are floating clouds and ceremonial caps worth speaking of? 浮雲軒冕何足言
8 There are only rivers and mountains, hard to enter into one's hand. 惟有江山難入手
"The moon above Mount Omei, a half wheel of autumn, 峨眉山月半輪秋
Its shadows enter Pingqiang, the Jiang River flows on." 影入平羌江水流
These words of the Banished Transcendent, who else could compose them? 謫仙此語誰解道
12 I ask you to climb an upper story sometime and view the moon. 請君見月時登樓
Laughingly we'll banter over the myriad matters, how could they really exist? 笑談萬事真何有
We will give ourselves over to East Cliff Wine all the time, 一時付與東巖酒
When you return and get a big bundle of cash, 歸來還受一大錢
16 For all my good advice, don't reject this yellow-haired old man.[40] 好意莫違黃髮叟

We do not have to wait until the direct citation of Li Bo in lines 9–10 to find Su Shi evoking Li Bo and calling forth his own entry into the chorus. The first couplet is a direct response to and negation of the opening of Li Bo's "Letter to Mr. Han Jingzhou": "I would not employ my life as a Marquis of the Ten Thousand Households; I would rather come to know Mr. Han Jingzhou." Su Shi paraphrases Li Bo's first statement

Confronting the Tang

and thereby draws attention to the comparison, but then he rejects Li Bo's alternative. Instead, Su Shi proposes his own alternative, substituting his object of praise for Li Bo's. But Su quickly drops his moralizing stance and begins a journey beyond such concerns—a wine-inspired poet now discourses on strange and marvelous things. Here Su Shi is again following the rhetorical exposition of Li Bo's letter, which goes on to suggest that Han set up a banquet to showcase Li Bo's poetic talent, his ability to compose impromptu verse.

Lines 5–6 introduce the second quatrain, and their tone of resignation and passivity contrasts sharply with the opening quatrain's energetic bravado. Drunken cavorting in the clouds has turned to vague, somnambulant wandering. The poet dismisses the pseudo-debate introduced by the first couplet of the poem.[41]

"Now" (*jin*), Su Shi, white-haired, has no use for courtly fame, that which most men take to be their intent. His dismissal of such concerns as "not worth speaking of" recalls this phrase in the biography of Li Guang in the *Records of the Historian* (*Shiji*) and connects with the thought of the poem's opening couplet: "A Marquis of Ten Thousand Households, how is it worth speaking of?" Su Shi is breaking off his discourse on such matters and closes the first half of his poem with a reference to all that is worth speaking of: "Rivers and mountains," hard to make enter one's hand (*ru shou*), hard for any one, much less a poet, to control.

The biography of Zhang Yue (667–730) in the *Tang History* (*Tang shu*) posits this relationship between rivers and mountains and poetic creation: "After he was banished to Yuezhou, his poems became increasingly plaintive and mournful, people said he had obtained the aid of the rivers and mountains."[42] Here Su Shi inverts that relationship: rivers and mountains are providing resistance rather than aid, his poem is frustrated by the scene before him, and thus he gives the poem over to another poet—Li Bo.

In the next line, the moon of Su Shi's homeland near Mount Omei is already signaling its disappearance into the season of death; its shadows slide into the plains. The difficulty of making Nature enter one's grasp is contrasted with the frightening ease with which it slips away. And it is here that Su Shi seems to deliver the poem to another poet, the very one he one-upped in the opening couplet. The lines, "The moon above Mount Omei, a half wheel of autumn, / Its shadows enter Pingqiang, the Jiang River flows on" are the opening couplet of Li Bo's "Song of

Mount Omei's Moon."[43] Su Shi then adds yet another reference to Li Bo's verse, this time introducing his praise of Li Bo's lines with the very phrase Li Bo used to praise Xie Tiao. Su is thus admiring Li Bo for the same poetic talent that Li admired in Xie Tiao—the talent not only to compose lines but also to capture a particular poetic sensibility just so, and in so doing Su Shi offers Li Bo the highest compliment possible.

Su's praise of Li Bo's line on Mount Omei is particularly touching because Omei is Su Shi's homeland—he admires Li Bo for capturing a sense of his own land, a sense that escapes his ability to articulate it. These six lines thus move from an acknowledgment of the difficulties of poetic composition to a citation of one poet's successful control of his craft to a kind of praise giving that at once bestows praise and indicates that, for Su Shi at least, Li Bo has matched the rare poet Li felt could masterfully compose verse—Xie Tiao. Indeed, this movement echoes Li Bo's poem precisely in its reflection on the art of poetry and poetic sensibility.

But Su Shi also extends the topic opened by Li Bo. Li sees no difficulty in the immediate evocation of Xie Tiao's intent behind "Clear waters, pure as bleached silk": one simply has to repeat the line for it to have effect. Su Shi, on the other hand, poses a question—"Who knows how to compose these expressions?"—and then passes on the task to himself.

Li Bo's poem is supposed to have been "intoned" in exactly similar circumstances, beneath the moon atop the West Tower of Jinling. Su thus calls on his friend to join him in replicating Li Bo's act and thereby participate in a kind of poetic ritual. But even as Su Shi denies that he can compose lines as well as Li Bo, he attempts to do exactly that.

His invitation to his addressee, a Mr. Zhang of Jiazhou, to imbibe the wine, to spend his cash, and sing the verses of prior poets conspicuously plays on the persona of Li Bo. Zhang is going to Jiazhou, and to its east is Fu Gorge, atop which East Cliff lies. Fu Gorge was famous for its wine, and from the Tang onward, the subject of wine in a poem never fails to evoke Li Bo. Su Shi adds this element to his poem to complement not only the evocation of Li Bo begun with his citation of Li Bo's letter and later his allusion to Li Bo's reference to Xie Tiao, but also to complement three other oblique references to Li Bo's persona. There are as well allusions to both Yang Xiong and Sima Xiangru's biographies in the line "Carrying wine, I would skim over lofty clouds."[44]

Both Yang and Sima Xiangru were famous poets with whom Li Bo

Confronting the Tang

felt a special affinity. Yang Xiong is said to have commented, "Sima Xiangru's prose-rhapsodies do not seem to come from the human world. This is precisely because he had attained the ultimate in 'divine transformation.'" It is exactly this notion of a transcendent poet that Li Bo adopted for himself, a "banished transcendent," the name Su Shi uses to refer to Li Bo.

As the person of Li Bo is referred to, his poetic persona is evoked through Su Shi's verse; the invitation to spend one's cash on wine strongly echoes Li Bo's verse, particularly the last section of his poem "Urging Forth the Wine" 將酒進:

From ancient times the sages and worthies are silent,	古來聖賢皆寂寞
There are only great drinkers to leave behind their names.	惟有飲者留其名
In days of old the King of Chen[45] feasted in the Pingle Hall.	陳王昔時宴平樂
4 Dippers of wine worth ten thousand cash, unrestrained pleasure and jest.	斗酒十千恣歡謔
Why does our host say there is little cash?	主人何爲言少錢
Go directly and buy wine, we'll pour you a cup!	徑須沽取對君酌
Take my Steed of Five-Flowered Hues, the Fur Garment worth a thousand cash,	五花馬千金裘
8 Call the boy to fetch them and exchange them for fine wine!	呼兒將出換美酒
And we'll dissipate the myriad ancient sorrows together.[46]	與爾同銷萬古愁

Su borrows the bravado, energy, careless abandon, the easy colloquialism, and diction of Li Bo, as well as his wine-imbibing persona. But perhaps the most compelling parallel lies in the gesture both poets make to their own craft. Li Bo announces that even wise men and worthy ministers are forgotten; there are only (*wei you*) drinkers to leave their names to posterity.

In lines 7 and 8 of Su Shi's poem, Su follows the same formula, but explicitly inserts a tone of seriousness missing in Li Bo's poem. He too dismisses concerns for officialdom and says the "only thing" (*wei you*) of concern to him is trying to frame the eternal things of nature in his poetry. Su Shi, however, brings forth the truly problematic nature of poetic composition, and after raising the possibility of poetic failure, of being unable to make Nature enter his grasp, Su takes up his own challenge. At the moment that he seems to relinquish the reins of the poem, Su Shi snaps them back in Li Bo's spirit. Su Shi recalls Li Bo's style, manner, and understanding of prior poetry; just as important, however, he is "playing" Li Bo in a distinctive manner, reinterpreting that former poet in a particular and identifiable manner.

Su Shi feigns weakness only to reverse it, to enact its negation via poetic writing that clearly sets the emulator as primary. In fact, he imitates the strategy of Li Bo's letter (alluded to in the first couplet of Su Shi's poem), which begins by praising Han Jingzhou but quickly turns into a proud declaration by Li Bo of his own poetic greatness.[47] The telling difference is that Han is not Li Bo's poetic predecessor, but a prospective patron; there is no question of poetic competition. Su Shi manipulates Li's rhetorical strategy to serve as an allegory of poetic relationship.

Xie Tiao's original phrase has passed through the hands of two of the greatest poets of China, each one playing off echoes of the original and adding his own touches in significantly different ways so as to identify himself in the midst of praising others. With characteristic wit, Huang Tingjian twists the line to make his own utterance while relying on the accreted meanings of the line.

In "Respectfully Sending off Zhou Yuanweng to Close up the Jizhou Judiciary Hall and Attend the Examinations of the Ministry of Rites,"[48] Huang varies Xie Tiao's line after first removing Xie from the poem: "Custodian Xie does not see the empty and pure water, / Pure waters like bleached silk, bright oranges." Huang is near Xuancheng, where Xie once served as chief magistrate. Huang evokes Xie negatively: "He cannot see these things any more, yet I see them as he must have." Huang removes the adjective "clear" from the original line and adds the "bright oranges," to his own line, perhaps a partial allusion to another poem by Xie Tiao, "In the South, Blossoming Oranges."[49]

Huang's invention relies on his occupying the space left empty by Xie's absence, of synthesizing two visions and claiming them as a sensibility he shares with the prior poet. Seven years later, Huang again approaches Xie's line, but with a very different point of view:

On Chao Yidao's Painting of Wild Geese in Snow	題晁以道雪鴈圖
Flying snow sprinkles reeds like silver arrows,	飛雪灑蘆如銀箭
In the foreground a wild goose flies up in alarm, and looks back.	前鴈驚飛復回盻
Who can I rely on to tell Xie Xuanhui,	憑誰說與謝玄暉
"Don't say, 'Clear waters, pure as bleached silk' "?[50]	莫道澄江静如練

Yan Youyi claims that to avoid an accusation of plagiarism, Huang turned Xie's line around, an example of "employing the allusion while reversing its meaning."[51] Ronald Egan points out that Huang is punning on Xie Tiao's simile—the painting is on silk and furthermore depicts an active rather than a tranquil scene.[52]

Both criticisms of Huang's use of Xie Tiao are apt, but when this poem is read in the context of Huang's earlier use of the line, there may be another level of significance—one pertaining to the composition of verse, and in fact continuing Li Bo's and Su Shi's explicit manner of using the citation as a way to remark on poetic capability. Huang voices the desire to negate Xie's pronouncement and consequently uproot the series of latter-day articulations of it. He seems to play off Su Shi's rhetorical question, "Who can say these words?" by asking instead, "Who will tell Xie *not* to say these words?" We may ask, "How can Huang's articulation be a manifestation of Xie's sensibility?"

Huang was, if anything, a master ironist. We may see in his quest to deny the existence of a prior line his own acknowledgment of its power and, since there is no one to perform the task, his recognition of its impossibility. He seems to remember (and even gesture toward) his own effort to efface Xie Tiao, to displace his predecessor and replace himself as a point of view, and to sense his failure. Yet Huang has also succeeded in reviving Xie's line.

The line is a symbol of the deep-rootedness of prior verse; in acknowledging this, Huang has succeeded better than he did before—the line now unmistakably carries not only Xie Tiao's identity but also Huang's particular statement about its role in the contemporary world of poetry. Nevertheless, there is frustration in Huang's voice for all its playfulness—a recognition that one cannot rewrite or silence the past. One's only alternative is to manipulate it well. This recognition is precisely that which informs his famous pronouncements on poetic revision.

These poems contain a distinct set of responses. The great Tang poet Li Bo shows his appreciation of Xie Tiao's line by framing it in a compelling context of his own that draws out its implications; the Northern Song poets make an explicit gesture of differentiation. Su Shi's response is to challenge Li Bo at his own game—to appropriate his voice but announce his act as piracy, to step into the dialogue between Li Bo and Xie Tiao and subsume them both. Huang's first response is to slyly attempt to elide Xie Tiao's voice and substitute his own—"I will say these words for him; he cannot see these things now." But the words, after all, are Xie Tiao's and without that identity (and its further manifestations in later verse) Huang's line would simply be flat. Huang's next response is to attempt to confront Xie Tiao directly and transform what has been deadened by usage, to extend the significance of the line.

In the Northern Song there is an overwhelming recognition of the presence of past poets, but the great poets of the time firmly believed that presence should be placed within their own mastery. And, as the poems presented above suggest, the evidence of this mastery largely depended on the explicit reformulation of former texts. It is this foregrounding of prior verse that contributes importantly to the mediated quality of late Northern Song verse. But the mere presence of prior verse is not in itself striking; more important are the ways in which it appears and the purposes to which the late Northern Song poets put it.

TWO

The Mediated Poem

The foregrounding of past texts in Northern Song lyric verse is doubly determined—first, by the particular relationship Northern Song poets held to the Tang; and second, because of eleventh-century China's project of reassessing the nature of the Way, by the demand for a new poetics that could address these specific cultural issues. As Hu Yunyi notes, because its intellectual and aesthetic milieu differed radically from that of preceding ages, Northern Song poetry is accused of being anti-lyrical.[1]

This key mode of distinguishing Tang and Northern Song poetry helps to explain why, for many critics, Huang's heavily allusive and intellectually demanding poems characterize his age. The charge of intellectualism is inextricably tied to that of allusiveness—both are seen to run counter to the primary value of poetry as spontaneous emotional response. In this chapter I examine these related criticisms and explore how such mediation was part of the larger project of Northern Song literati culture and how these two modes of mediation come to characterize the poetics of the Northern Song.

Against the Grain: The Philosophical Strain in Northern Song Poetry

If we were to sum up [the] differences that set Song poetry apart from the poetry which precedes it, we might say that for the men of the Song a poem was not simply an expression of feeling, a delineation of an emotional state; it was an expression of feeling, to be sure, but at the same time it was also an expression of intellect.[2]

This comment by Yoshikawa Kōjirō is a rather neutral version of one of the most common ways of distinguishing the verse of the Song dynasty from previous verse. Neutral, because Yoshikawa is using the Tang as the point of comparison and grants the Song some expression of feeling.

Other critics are not so moderate. Either implicitly or explicitly they charge that Northern Song poetry directly contradicts the very nature of traditional Chinese lyric poetry. Yan Yu's (1180–1235) *Canglang shihua* gives one of the strongest of the early condemnations of Song verse for being too intellectual: "The various gentlemen of recent generations produce idiosyncratic understandings. They take diction, erudition, and logical discourses to be poetry. How is it that this is not well-crafted? And yet in the end they will never match the poetry of the ancients."[3] Other critics concur: "The poets of the Tang stressed emotion, their distance from the *Classic of Poetry* is very small; the poets of the Song stressed principle [*li*], their distance from the *Classic of Poetry* is very great."[4]

Both these criticisms hold that Song poetry is separated from the tradition by its emphasis on "inherent principle" (*li*) and its incorporation of prosaic diction in the expression of that concern.[5] Although "philosophical" poetry (or at least poems that contained philosophic elements) was part of the Chinese lyric tradition long before the Song dynasty, Northern Song verse does tend to be more discursive than previous verse not only in terms of its sustained meditations on the multifaceted nature of things but also in the way in which philosophical speculation was integrated into poetic forms. Northern Song poetry synthesized elements from disparate sources and integrated them with prosodic, rhetorical, and stylistic techniques either traditional or particular to the Song.

The dominant element in the "philosophical" quality of the Northern Song poetry is what critics have termed a "narrative" or prosaic manner of presentation that accommodates lengthier treatments of philosophical issues.[6] One example is this poem by Huang Tingjian written in 1071.

Rising at Dawn in Linru　　　　　　　　　　　　　　曉起臨汝

A partial moon just now precipitously shining;　　　缺月欲崢嶸
The crowing fowl believe it is time.　　　　　　　　鳴雞有期信
The distant traveler presses for an early harnessing,　征人催夙駕
4　The lodger's dream not yet completely started awake.　客夢未渠盡
In the desolate wilds are many broken bridges,　　　野荒多斷橋
The Yellow River is frozen, no cracks as in jade.　　河凍無裂璺
A thin horse treads and falls over on the ice;　　　　羸馬踏冰翻

8	A worried fox cuts across the grove and escapes.	疑狐觸林遁
	A pure wind cleanses, shakes, the day's first sun;	清風蕩初日
	The tall trees warble with secluded tones.	高木囀幽韻
	Mount Song's height is suddenly before my eyes,	嵩高忽在眼
12	Its lofty peaks connect several prefectures.	岌峨連數郡
	Murky clouds silently hang in the void;	玄雲默重空
	Thinking to dampen ten thousand *li* [Chinese miles].	意有萬里潤
	But the cold darkness does not produce any rain,	寒暗不成雨
16	So they wrap it to their bosoms, pressing it into a tiny space.	卷懷就膚寸
	Looking at these configurations, I think of the Ancient One	觀象思古人
	Who moved or stood still in rhythm with the movements of the heavens.	動静配天運
	Things come at one time;	物來斯一時
20	But when nothing is obtained, that is also in perfect accord.	無得乃至順
	The cool and warm only follow the cycle;	涼暄但循環
	Use and Rejection, how can one be joyous or angry over them?	用捨誰喜慍
	How can I get one who has forgotten words	安得忘言者
24	To discuss the "Discourse on Making Things Equal" with me?[7]	與講齊物論

Several things in this poem call attention to its departures from what might be considered a common exercise in the subgenre of "early rising" poems. Such poems begin with the poet rising before others, gazing out onto the roads, and urging an early departure. The environment offers him signs that it is indeed early, and these signs prompt a reflection on the cause of his journey and his general situation and an emotional response.

One thing that immediately sets "Rising at Dawn in Linru" apart is its diction. The first line uses the binom *zhengrong* (high and precipitous) to describe the moon and its light. The term is usually applied to tall and jagged mountain peaks, but here Huang, in a kind of metonymic transfer, uses it to describe what is up there next to the mountains. The term calls attention to itself and to one notable precedent: Du Fu's first "Poem on Qiang Village," which begins with the same binom, "Lofty and craggy, red clouds in the western sky / Rays of the sun fall on the level ground."[8] This kind of bold allusion to another poet's distinctive use of language is unusual in an opening line of poems of this genre. In the first line of his poem, Huang thus signals both his reworking of a prior form and his awareness of the tools of the craft; the poem immediately shows the markings of this self-consciousness.

In line 2, the roosters, from the peculiar quality of this light (which is not, after all, that of the rising sun), believe that it is time to start crowing. The sense of uncertainty begun by the ambiguous image of line 1, engendered by its unusual semantic character, is carried over to this line. The motif of uncertain and unstable signs runs throughout the poem: the hoary moonlight carries with it associations of intense cold and death; the road seems impassible—the bridges are broken, the river frozen. The movement of the horse is frustrated; the eerie atmosphere causes the fox to seek escape.

In the next segment of the poem (lines 9–12), the "pure wind" seems to sweep away the images of foreboding and anxiety; the warbling of the birds differs qualitatively from the crowing of the roosters. The roosters crow only because they have read a (false) cue in the precipitous moon, but the birds here sing spontaneously, without "believing" in a fixed time. With the skies clearing, the poet suddenly finds a real mountain peak before his eyes, replacing the image of the figured moon of the first line. Its solidity stands forth as the faltering moon disappears, and this physical presence seems to act on the landscape, forming connections and continuities where before there were only broken bridges.

This movement from instability and discontinuity to stability and continuity is echoed in the next two couplets (lines 13–16). Again, as in the beginning of the poem, a strange psychologizing of nature is correlated with our attempt to read nature. Before, the poet thought that the roosters must have believed that it was dawn from the strange light of the moon.[9] Here he attributes an intent (*yi*) to the clouds overhead. He continues his projection of mentality onto nature by claiming that the rain clouds are biding their time.[10] But the existence of either intent can never be proved. Reading nature is problematic, and it calls attention to itself as an act of will.

Huang begins to parallel the reading of nature with readings of texts. "Looking at heavenly configurations" is used in the *Classic of Changes* with reference to the legendary Fu Xi, a sage who read the signs of heaven and thus, as Huang says, moved in perfect accord with natural cycles.[11] The next line is taken from the *Zhuangzi*, this time from the "Discourse on Nurturing Life": "Your master came because it was naturally suitable; when he departed, it was also suitable for him to go, and followed smoothly [the workings of Heaven]."[12]

The Mediated Poem

"Use and Rejection" is a common phrase in poetic diction by this time; its ultimate source is *Analects* 8.11: "If employed, then carry out matters; if rejected, then store up [your talent]." The final couplet alludes to the famous passage in the *Zhuangzi*:

The fish trap exists because of the fish; once you've gotten the fish, you can forget the trap. The rabbit snare exists because of the rabbit; once you've gotten the rabbit, you can forget the snare. Words exist because of meaning; once you've gotten the meaning, you can forget the words. Where can I find a man who has forgotten words so I can have a word with him?[13]

The allusions at the end of the poem alternate between Confucian and Daoist texts; Huang uses the *Classic of Changes*, the *Zhuangzi*, and the *Analects* to support the general "philosophy" of the poem: one should not be discouraged at being ill-used; rather, one should attune oneself with the natural cycles and remain unperturbed. The lesson to be learned is supposedly to read the "configurations of heaven," yet the signs presented in the poem are problematic. It is one thing to say that things shift and change and that one should recognize that mutability and achieve a detached view of things. But the poet seems trapped in *exactly* the kinds of reading that ignore that larger view. His anxiety at "early rising" and his interest in projecting mentality on nature betray the intensity of his desire to read what might be called the "lesser" signs. He opts for philosophy in the end and sees in it an escape from reading the lesser configurations, and from words altogether. Yet, in the paradox of Zhuangzi, he feels compelled to speak of the uselessness of speech.

The poet wishes to discuss the "Discourse on Making Things Equal," which contains a sustained discussion of words. "Words are not just blown out like wind. Words have something to say. But what if what they have to say specifically is not fixed, then do they really say something? ... What do words rely on, that we have right and wrong?"[14] Words, Zhuangzi goes on to say, rely on binary oppositions that lack any definition in and of themselves. "The Way has never known boundaries; speech has no constancy. But because of [the recognition of a] 'this,' there came to be boundaries."[15] Huang accentuates the inescapable desire of man to read, write, and speak words, words that may well be unstable things. Huang could thus be vulnerable to the charge that his desire to read (both texts and natural signs) might overflow the wisdom he has just spoken to comfort himself. What should have been a neat Daoist tag resists closure and remains open to speculation.

We can get a clearer sense of the "philosophizing" nature of the Song lyric by comparing two poems on the same topic from the Tang and the Song. First, like "Early Rising in Linru," this next poem by Huang Tingjian is about discriminations, about consciousness.

Setting off at Early Morn 早行

As my stone headrest fell I started, the first to wake. 失枕驚先起
The other households half in the midst of dreams. 人家半夢中
Because I hear the roosters I know it is early morning, 聞雞憑早晏
4 Divining the Dipper I discriminate west and east. 占斗辨西東
My horse's reins are moist, I know the road has dew on it; 轡濕知行露
My clothes simple and thin, I can feel the dawn wind. 衣單覺曉風
The autumn sun plays with the light and shadows, 秋陽弄光影
8 Suddenly it spits forth half a forest of red.[16] 忽吐半林紅

Next, a poem by the mid-Tang poet Bo Juyi:

Early Rising 早興

The dawn light comes shining forth, the rafters of my room brighten. 晨光出照屋梁明
As the men first strike on the gate at dawn, it lets forth a single sound. 初打開門鼓一聲
The dogs climb the stairs to sleep, I know the ground is still damp, 犬上階眠知地濕
4 The language of the birds perched by the window announces the sky has cleared. 鳥臨窗語報天晴
The fogginess of last night's wine is half-cleared, yet my head is still heavy. 半銷宿酒頭仍重
Newly casting off winter clothes, my body is suddenly light. 新脫冬衣體乍輕
Waking from sleep my mind is empty, longings and fancies depleted; 睡覺心空思想盡
8 Lately dreams of home don't often form.[17] 近來鄉夢不多成

Both poems share many conventions of the "early rising" subgenre. In both, the poet is isolated from the rest of humanity, rising early and observing from various signs that the night has barely ended. Unlike Huang's poem, however, the second half of Bo Juyi's poem moves into a personal reflection on the poet's life and a different set of discriminations. He rises early, half groggy and sluggish after a mild bout of drinking. His body seems lighter, however, for the winter has ended; the poet is still marking cause and effect, but this is not cause for rejoicing. His sleep is empty of dreams, particularly dreams of home. He attributes this to his drinking, but that is a mask for a deeper despair—even his half-conscious mind has given up hope of returning. The sound of the gate being opened only increases his sense of isolation, for the journey that so often accompanies an "early rising" poem is for him a moot point, for what he desires to move toward is denied him. The poem moves smoothly from the scene to the poet's identification with it.

This emotional movement is absent from Huang's poem. Instead, Huang dwells on abstract discriminations. Whereas Bo Juyi moves from the scene to a response, Huang lingers in observing nature, on reading it. Where Bo Juyi says his body feels lighter its new summer clothes, indirectly signaling the change of season (and with that information we know he has been residing there for some time and also that the spring, a time for returning home, holds nothing for him), Huang's light clothes lead only to his being able to better feel the immediate scene. Unlike Bo Juyi's line, the image is not a vehicle toward a deeper understanding of the poet's emotional response but another piece of information that tells us how well Huang intellectually senses the scene itself.

Huang adds up these discriminations, yet the sum of the parts is a static description of early morning, and it is precisely because of this absolute stasis that the final couplet, mimicking the sunrise, is so impressive. Nature suddenly becomes active. The penultimate line subtly introduces the sun, idly toying with light and shadows. Then, in the last line, it absolutely transforms the scene. The force of this transformation is underscored by the repetition of the word "half" (*ban*). Things seem to be split between one state and another; the scene is static, but awaiting change.

The last line attracts even more attention because of its imagery; the verb "to spit out" (*tu*) rarely has seen such usage. Again, as with the unexpected use of the binom *zhengrong* in the first couplet of Huang's "Rising at Dawn in Linru," this unusual usage has a precedent in Du Fu, this time his "Poem on the Moon": "At the fourth watch the mountains spit out the moon,/In the dwindling night, the waters illuminate the loft."[18] Whereas Du Fu uses the verb to construct a startling opening image, Huang uses it to provide an unexpected twist at the end of his poem. The image is integrated into the carefully structured syntax of the poem, contributing to the sudden shift in mood.

Huang has imitated yet modified the subgenre to answer the question "What is early morning like?" Unlike Bo Juyi's earlier treatment, his scene is not a backdrop for lyric introspection but an object of examination as a phenomenon in itself. Huang's poem unfolds as a corollary to the sunrise—it is a sudden awakening, and our understanding of it is matched by the abrupt change in the poet's perceptions.

Another example of Huang's adaptation of prior forms to accommodate Song "philosophizing" is the following poem in praise of a recluse.

From Baling on a Calm Yangtze, I Approached the Xiang Tributary and Passed Through the City. There Was No Day Without Rain. I Arrived at Mount Huanglong and Paid My Respects to the Teacher of Pure Zen. I Continued Until Late That Day, When It Cleared. I Unexpectedly Met the Zen Traveler Dai Daochun and Chatted with Him. I Made These Lines and Presented Them to Him.	自巴陵略平江臨 湘入通城無日不 雨至黃龍奉謁清 禪師繼而晚晴邂 逅禪客戴道純欵 語作長句呈道純
Traveling in the mountains for ten days, the rain dampens my clothes.	山行十日雨霑衣
I stand in front of Mofu Peak, facing the light of the setting sun.	幕阜峰前對落暉
The waters of the plains spontaneously add to the filling of the paddies.	野水自添田水滿
4 The cuckoos under the cleared part of the sky summon their comrades still in the rain to return.	晴鳩却喚雨鳩歸
The Gentleman of the Spirit Source, the man with the Eye of Heaven,	靈源大士人天眼
The Teachers of the Paired Pagodas were the instruments of the Buddhas.	雙塔老師諸佛機
White-haired, hoary countenance, I have again arrived here.	白髮蒼顏重到此
8 I ask you whether you are still the man of old.[19]	問君還是昔人非

As in both "Setting off at Early Morn" and "Rising at Dawn in Linru," this poem in praise of one who has left the trammels of the common world to pursue spiritual enlightenment is immediately concerned with observing the relationships among phenomena. The lyric voice is withdrawn; the voice of the first line seems rather removed from the pronouncement, as if it were a casual observation. In the second line the poet has joined in the landscape—by occupying a position in front of the mountain, he is inscribed into the theme of the reciprocal relationships of nature. Ten days of rain have soaked his clothes; the setting sun strikes both the front of Mofu Peak and the poet on Mofu Peak, who participates in its meeting the rays of the setting sun. This integration of the poetic voice into the natural scene is in keeping with the occasion of the poem—a welcome to a fellow traveler in Zen. The quatrain closes with a continuation of reciprocal relationships—ten days of rain have spontaneously replenished the waters of the fields; cuckoos under a clearing sky summon their comrades to return.[20] The rainfall brings about these things as a matter of course, the simple and almost banal fact that the poet's garments are soaked becomes part of a larger sphere of meaning that joins him to the scene.

The "Gentleman of the Spirit Source" is a name taken by the Zen master Weiqing; the "Eye of Heaven" is one of the Five Eyes of Buddhism: it symbolizes the acuity with which one may penetrate the mysteries of all things. The next line refers to the monks Huinan and Zuxin, his son. Both were Zen monks who resided on Mount Huanglong. When Huinan died a pagoda was built for him on the mountain; when Zuxin died, a pagoda was erected for him next to that of his father. The two were referred to as the "Teachers of the Paired Pagodas." An "instrument of the Buddhas" is someone who has mastered Zen.

This couplet follows the preceding couplet in form, but whereas the former couplet sets forth causal relationships, here the formula is name/attribute. Nevertheless, this is a superficial difference—a deeper similarity is that the two couplets make the same sort of statement regarding the correlation of things and the nature of things. The man who called himself the Gentleman of the Spirit Source had the nature of one who could penetrate the nature of the myriad phenomena. The two items of the sentence are inextricably linked.

In like fashion, the Teachers of the Paired Pagodas were masters of Zen, their identity bound with the knowledge they had absorbed and perpetuated. The formula of having parallel terms within each of the two lines (that is, the terms are parallel both in inter- and intra-sentence structures) of a parallel couplet is a familiar High Tang technique. Here Huang uses it to reinforce a particular philosophical observation on the relationship between nature and things. It is not exactly a causal relationship; rather, it points to the manifestation of natural principles, and here the teachings of Zen take their place amid those same natural principles.

The final couplet addresses Dai Daochun directly. The question posed in the last line is from the "Discourse on Things Not Transforming" ("Wu bu qian") by the Jin dynasty monk Seng Zhao (d. 415): "Fanzhi left home and returned white-haired. His neighbors asked, 'Are you still the man of former times?' Fanzhi replied, 'I am still the man of former times; I am not the man of former times.'"[21] Fanzhi's response is taken to mean that physically he is the same man, despite his aging, but spiritually he is now enlightened. Huang is thus asking Dai if he too has obtained enlightenment. Throughout the poem there have been observations of particular relationships, and here the doubling continues. Weiqing takes another name and has the Eye of Heaven; his identity is manifested in a higher sphere of enlightenment. The father leads his son; together their pagodas serve as double indexes to their followers. The poet comes once more to Huanglong and asks if Dai has learned anything since first coming to the mountain.

These doublings have their corollary in the observations made in the first quatrain, where the poet sets up a series of relationships within the natural world. The poem implies that recognition of these relationships and the recognition of deep spiritual relationships are linked by similar workings of the mind. He regards the natural world as presenting a set of discriminations for his interpretation. This process ultimately reflects back on the poet himself—his ability to sense the change in the person he addresses is correlated with the change in understanding enacted in the process of coming to know the world of the poem.

The philosophical nature of Song poetry may thus be seen to lie not simply in its use of philosophical ideas but also in the manner in which those ideas determine the larger structuring of the poem (in contrast, in earlier poetry philosophical statements often have the quality of an aside, a comment subordinate or complementary to the dominant "scene" and emotional "response"); in the poet's use of traditional devices such as narrative style, allusion, and parallelism to support and nuance that speculation; and finally, in the poet's ironizing of that very discourse. Philosophical discursiveness was one major criticism against Northern Song poetry; the other, related, one was the mediation of prior texts. Both were seen to rob the lyric of immediate comprehension. Northern Song poets could not evade the fact that in their age prior texts were distinct and nearly necessary components of a poem; the question was how to mute their presence while using them.

Poems Made of Books

The term often used to describe the mediation of prior texts in Northern Song lyric poetry is "bookishness." For example, the Qing critic Wang Fuzhi (1619–92) claims that Su Shi's and Huang Tingjian's verse

The Mediated Poem

is wholly dependent on books: "If you take away the books [that they allude to in their verse], then there is no poetry."[22]

Why did Northern Song poets so emphatically foreground the presence of the past? One response has been given above: the Northern Song's fondness for philosophical speculation was not simply a brief affectation or isolated dalliance with discursive erudition. Rather, it was intimately linked to the intellectual character of the period, with its emphasis not only on an encyclopedic knowledge of the past as viewed in texts, paintings, calligraphy, and music but also on a firm awareness of how those cultural objects were created and on the application of the knowledge derived from those objects to the present day.

Another response links that more general answer to the possibility that Northern Song poets were acknowledging two obvious conditions: first, they needed to recognize the stature of the past, particularly the Tang. To do so openly, explicitly reworking those texts in their own works, was one way of showing their mastery over their predecessors. Second, the Tang had, after all, raised all that had preceded it in poetry to an insurmountable height—one of the few areas left open for the Song was precisely the area of intellectual inquiry. In order to understand more fully the unique character of Northern Song lyric poetry, we must consider how late Northern Song poets approached the tradition of learning from texts and used it to foster a program of what they claimed to be spontaneous composition.

The first step in learning to write poetry is learning how to apprehend the significance of texts; only after that can a kind of composition be affected that transcends technique. Bookishness can then be seen as an instrument for a more complex and contemporaneously relevant kind of composition, without hindering the free expression of emotion.

Learning to Read

"There is not one day that the Gentleman does not study. How can it only be one day! There is not one moment that he does not study. How can it be a moment! There is not one instant that he does not study. Study! It is the same as Self! Self is the same as study!"[23] Urging one's friends to study nearly becomes a subgenre of poetry in the Northern Song. Goyama Kiwamu traces the beginnings of the Northern Song's particular love of learning to the new examination system, which gave more men the opportunity to better their position. Also, the proliferation of classical texts made possible by advances in printing allowed many of the newly wealthy to build private libraries and claim learned status.[24] Arai Ken argues that poets such as Huang took to writing "bookish," "obscure" verse in order to distinguish themselves from those newcomers, whom they considered unlearned and vulgar poetasters.[25] We should therefore correlate this new poetics with a change in material culture.

Even during the Northern Song we can find an intimation of the charge of intellectualism. Zhang Zai (1020–77) claims:

> Of those who were capable of understanding poetry in ancient times, only Mencius "turned back and met the intention of the poet." The intent of that poetry was perfect evenness and ease, it was not necessary to stringently seek after it. Those who stringently seek after poetry today are thus completely ruining its basic intent; how can they perceive the intent of the poet by reading this way?[26]

This passage is significant in three ways: first, it asserts that the proper way to read poetry, specifically the *Classic of Poetry*, is not to bore and pierce through it;[27] second, it implies that the kind of verse that solicits such reading is removed from the nature of poetry; and third, a Northern Song intellectual already had a perception of the very critique posterity would use to characterize the poetry of his age.

The criticism against straining to compose poetry suggests its opposite—the virtue of spontaneous emotional response.[28] The problem, then, for Northern Song poets was how to write poetry that accommodated the intellectual issues of concern to them in a construct that both met the aesthetic demands of the lyric tradition *and* effaced the labor of understanding complex issues. Their solution can be found in a paradoxical vision predicated on both the craft of the poet and the understanding that the poet could expect of his reader. If the poet could compose verse in accord with the principles of the tradition, and if the reader had the sensitivity and learning to perceive immediately the nuances of the tradition in the poem, then the poem, however mediated by allusion to prior texts, might successfully transmit the intent of the poet as if that mediation were not present. The immediacy of an emotional response to things would thus be not approximated but equaled.

The basic purpose accorded to lyric poetry, to "speak the intent" of the poet (*shi yan zhi*), is complicated in the Northern Song by an understanding of that intent as consisting of a number of coinciding and coexisting intents: that of the poet, of his reader, and of the prior writers whose words are employed by the later poet. Nevertheless, Northern Song poetry had to fulfill the conditions placed on all lyric poetry despite its complexity and multifacetedness—its "intent" was to be immediately perceived. To both convey and perceive the intent of the poet, the intellect of the man of letters had to be so firmly grounded in the texts of the culture that working with those texts had become second nature.

There evolved a community of literati whose discourse was guaranteed efficacy by what might be called a "cultural competence" (to use an analogy to Chomskyan linguistics) in the understanding and communication of cultural principles. This competence, as in Chomsky's use, was pre-reflective—spontaneous, "natural." Literature, however complex, had to be made natural, authentic, and spontaneous in order for its powers of transmission to be perfectly employed; the aesthetic and moral value of *wen* depended on sincerity and spontaneity.

Ouyang Xiu makes explicit the relationship between reading the intent of the ancients, taking the Classics as one's source, and creating *wen*:

In study, one should take the Classics as one's teacher. In doing so, one must first seek its sense. If this sense is obtained, then one's mind will be settled; if one's mind is settled, then the Way will be pure; if the Way is pure, then the center will be fully realized; if the center's fulfillment is real, then in bringing forth *wen* it will be as a glimmering radiance.[29]

With thorough knowledge of the Classics, one's own writing could achieve the same unblocked reading as the Classics: "The *wen* of the Sages is the beauty of the Way. The *wen* is not difficult, but perfect of its own accord."[30]

Ouyang Xiu draws on a well-established vision of the continuity of *wen*,[31] but such an ideal image of an apparently seamless continuum between past and present came with an inherent skepticism. From the beginning of written texts in China, commentaries and discourses on them point out that the proper focus of reading should be achieving a sense of the ancients' intent, not simply gaining a bare competence in reading. The number of conditionals in Ouyang Xiu's piece is more than stylistic finesse; it points to the real contingencies that the Northern Song, above all previous ages, felt with regard to the nature of cultural transmission via texts.

In his study of Ouyang Xiu, James T. C. Liu claims that newly critical perspectives on the classic texts arose because of developments in printing in the Northern Song. Whereas before only the "official" version of any particular text was generally accessible (through rubbings from the canonized version carved in stone under governmental auspices), there became widely available not only this one version but also contending versions and commentaries arguing the correctness of various interpretations: "The learned scholars who checked into the other sources that were becoming increasingly available to them found many apparent shortcomings in the official versions, such as dubious texts of non-Confucian origin, misleading interpretations, and possible textual errors, all beclouding the real meanings of the classics."[32] This rise in the rate of the production and dissemination of different texts, along with expansion of the book-buying public and their claim to be literati, greatly contributed to the Song project ascertaining *true* learning and its relation to the Way.

Thus the reader had to attempt to fill two basic gaps in reading the Classics. First, he had to overcome the absence of the ancients not simply by reading their words but by reanimating their intent. Second, in tracing that intent, he had to contend with a general skepticism regarding both the text scrutinized and possible alternative interpretations. Thus, in addition to the newly complicated expressive perception of "intent" noted above, the ideal of immediate and accurate apprehension of texts was complicated by an intensified skepticism regarding the texts themselves.

The challenge was imposing, but the reward was great, for if the reader could bridge these gaps and authentically grasp the intent of the Classics, then he would dispell the opacity and obliqueness of what was hidden or dimmed by time and assimilate the intent of the ancients into his own. In writing, the poet might then speak forth his intent while simultaneously speaking the intent of the tradition. This ideal rendering of the acts of reading and literary composition would render the salient values and principles of past and present whole and viable.

It was in approaching and obtaining knowledge through texts that the moderns could model themselves after the ancients; the focal point became the "spot where the ancients employed their minds," an ambiguous locus that exceeded mere textuality.[33] The following essay by Huang Tingjian addresses all these issues:

It is essential that in the study of all things under heaven one have a revered master. After that, one may penetrate the subtleties and enter the marvelous. Although one may not thoroughly understand the intent of the former kings, as least one has its source, and thus one will not be far removed from the model of the Classics.

Now the intent of the Six Classics is profound, but there are the writings of

The Mediated Poem 61

the scholar of the two Han dynasties, those of Mengzi and Xunzi, and in recent times those of Liu Chang and Wang Anshi. Study them, and you will penetrate more than half the sense of the ancients.

As for the craft of literary composition, it is difficult. We have Zuo Qiuming, Zhuangzi, Dong Zhongshu, Sima Qian, Sima Xiangru, Liu Xiang, Yang Xiong, Han Yu, Liu Zongyuan, and this generation's Ouyang Xiu, Zeng Gong, Su Shi, and Qin Guan. Their method and principles are brilliant and can be discussed and studied.

As for the writings of Shen Nong, Huang Di, Qi Bo, and the Lord of Thunder,[34] the men of Qin and Yue were pure in understanding their intent, but scholars rarely studied Huangfu Mi or Zhang Ji's *Discourse*.[35] Even if they did study them, they were not able to reach their source.

In recent times, Gao Ruona was acclaimed to be adept in medicine, yet after he died his formulas were not passed down.[36] I have a Daoist friend named Yang Jie who once spoke to me of the *Ben cao* and the *Su wen*.[37] He went on to talk of carefully observing the Five Turnings of Fate and the Six Vital Energies and thereupon made the Medicinal Stone.[38]

Because my worldly attachments were many, I was not able to follow Yang Jie and study with him. In old age I hid myself among the barbarians. A disease of their miasmal vapors overtook me. I was almost lifeless, and I regretted not following the teachings of Master Yang early on. Today, on account of official business I have come to Qing Shen.[39]

Now I take Master Yang's discourse on medicine; being earnestly entrusted with it, I have conscientiously studied it. His argument is deep and extensive.

The land of Shu is secluded and distant; there was no one to ask about what he did not understand. Yang Zijian closed his door, reading books and piercing through the works of Huang Di and Qi Bo. How can it be easy to obtain such a thing, studying without a master? Nevertheless, his "Flowing Secretions" had an intent setting them forth; one cannot be without some direction.

When these two wise men were marvelously dexterous with regard to the myriad phenomena, only then did they produce these formulas, only then were they truly skilled. They described the nature of the myriad things, and it was passed down from generation to generation. Now Yang Zijian explicates the Five Turnings of Fate and the Six Vital Energies, marking down illnesses and weighing the register of medicine comprehensively as a means to probe the prescription of moxa to give to the people. This is indeed a case of a humane man employing his mind.[40]

After first emphasizing the necessity of having a "revered master," Huang opens the possibilities of study and learning much wider: the revered master may be encountered through the text. Secluded and sequestered from the world and removed temporally from prior masters, Yang Zijian has somehow, on his own, successfully read the intent behind the discourses of the past. (The concept of "intent" is central to Huang's poetics, for it is a guarantor of internal coherence and affinity to the larger, external cultural tradition.) Two things aid Yang in his project: first and foremost, his extensive and earnest study; and second, his intent, which has through Yang's particular act of reading found its corollary in the intent of the ancients. Huang points out an instance of learning without present masters and makes the problematic relationship between absent master / text / student explicit.[41]

But learning to read well, learning to read the correct texts, is not enough. One must perceive the quintessence of the text: the spot where the ancients "employed their minds." More than any discrete fact conveyed by a text, this "spot" was conceived to be the real informing locus. Learning was not pursued merely to accumulate passive knowledge: the ancients' employment of their minds was to be matched in the present-day reader's employment of his mind in a like fashion.

Huang's essay on the *Analects* describes the process of learning as one in which the student makes connections between the intent of the text and its ramifications, ramifications specifically related to the situation of the student.

The *Xunzi* says: "Those who love study penetrate the ever-constant categories. Thus they hear one and know one [thing]." This is the defect of those who have come to study lately. Hearing one and knowing two, this is what might be called loving study. From this, one may, by advancing his intellect, arrive at hearing one and knowing ten. From this one may, advancing his knowledge even further, arrive at taking one and connecting it, and taking [that] one and connecting it; this is the enterprise of the sage. From the student's gate one arrives at the mysterious room of the sage.[42]

For Huang, the Classics do not exhaust all knowledge; rather, they direct the conscientious reader to the proper kinds of speculation, guiding him as he formulates his ideas. In another essay he likens the Classics to a road map. One would not embark on a long journey without either a map or someone to ask directions from: "The art of the Classics leads men to know which direction to take. Broad learning enables one to explicate even extreme disorder and hasten its resolution; this is the art of gazing on texts."[43] Huang again makes this point in the first of his letters to Xu Shichuan: "There is a necessary way to learning: in reading books, you must seek out your own affairs with every word and every sentence. Only then will you see where the men of the past brought their true mind into play."[44]

The Mediated Poem

If one has truly identified and penetrated the intent of the ancient text, then that text becomes part of one:

> Although one might [after thoroughly reading the text] set it aside and go off and relax and wander, the text's flavor will still reside in one's bosom. Retaining it, one may see the spot where the ancients employed their mind. If [your learning] is like this, then [you may] completely employ your mind in one or two books, and all else will be like breaking joints of bamboo; each one will welcome the knife blade and split apart.[45]

Goyama points out that only by integrating learning into the self did Song intellectuals (and here he is speaking specifically of Su Shi and his group) feel it was possible to engender a "live usage" (*huoyong*), a usage that has a relevant application to the present and is not simply a nostalgic repetition of past acts.[46]

The image of splitting bamboo is a common symbol of perfect effortlessness and spontaneous action—the final product of learning to trace the intent of the ancients' through their texts. This same process is articulated by Cheng Yi (1033–1107):

> In reading the *Analects* and the *Mencius*, do so thoroughly and get the real taste of them. Apply the words of the sage to yourself earnestly. Do not treat them as so many words. If people will but look on these two books as being meant for concrete application to themselves, they will derive much benefit throughout life.
>
> There are people who have read the *Analects* without having anything happen to them. There are others who are happy after having understood a sentence or two. There are still others who, having read the book, love it. And there are those, who, having read it, *unconsciously dance with their hands and feet.* [Italics added][47]

The result of this kind of understanding of the Classics and their relation to one's own circumstances is an integration of what was formerly other, a state wherein one might act pre-reflectively in accord with the traditional ethos.[48] The image evoked at the end of Cheng Yi's statement is precisely the image of the highest aesthetic/expressive response to outward stimuli evoked in the Great Preface to the *Classic of Poetry*—the very defining image of poetic composition:

> Poetry is where the intent of the mind goes. Lying in the heart, it is "intent"; when uttered in words, it is "poetry." When an emotion stirs inside, one expresses it in words; finding this inadequate, one sighs over it; not content with this, one sings it in poetry; still not satisfied, one unconsciously dances with one's hands and feet.[49]

This discussion of the "anti-lyrical" nature attributed to Song poetry seems to have come full circle: classical texts now have a place alongside outer stimuli as inspiring an aesthetic response. Most important, the classical texts are not seen as evoking any less of an authentic and immediate response than do natural phenomena.

One can find similar pronouncements on the value of learning in early Chinese literary criticism. In the early sixth century, Liu Xie writes:

> One has [also] to acquire learning in order to maintain a store of precious information, and to contemplate the nature of reason so as to enrich one's talents; one must search deeply and experience widely in order that one exhaustively evoke the source of light; one must master literary traditions in order to make one's expressions felicitous and smooth. It is only then that he commissions the "mysterious butcher" to write in accord with musical patterns; and it is then that he sets the incomparably brilliant "master wheelwright" to wield the ax in harmony with his intuitive insight.[50]

The crucial difference in the Northern Song is the value of integrating the *intent* of the prior writers with one's own. As we have noted above, the Northern Song view of this process of perceiving and integrating intent raised it to the status of an explicit and ongoing questioning. The connections drawn between the intent of the prior writer and that of the latter-day poet stressed the *interpretive* act of the latter.

This act of interpretation and assimilation directly influences the ability of the reader to become a writer. Perfectly integrating past texts into one's own present usage erases the difference between the ages. The spontaneous appreciation of past texts is correlated to the spontaneous composition behind the *Classic of Poetry*. In the realm of poetry, this kind of learning provided the poet with a set of precedents and expressive devices germane to his own writing; he made the connection between the intent of the ancients and his own practice.

Learning to Write

The following comment by Fan Xiwen (fl. 1266) distinguishes between merely using prior texts to form a pastiche of citations and applying one's perception of those texts to the spontaneous composition of poetry:

> The line from Du Fu says, "Reading books, I have gone through ten thousand volumes. / When the brush descends, it is as if it were possessed by spirit."[51]
>
> In reading books and achieving "breaking through ten thousand volumes,"

one may thus plunge to the depths and ascend to the heights; what act is not possible? This is not what is called taking the texts of ten thousand volumes to make [or, to be] poetry.⁵²

These lines of Du Fu appear nearly every time Northern Song literati speak of the relationship of learning and composition. One of the greatest poets of the High Tang provided Northern Song poets with what seemed to be an absolute endorsement of learning.

Still, Fan Xiwen feels compelled to *explain* Du Fu, and this explication is based on a particular interpretive strategy—the Northern Song effort to explain its premises. Fan Xiwen tells us Du Fu's lines imply that learning should not turn prior texts into mere grist for the poetic mill or block an immediate response to outer stimuli; rather, it should enable the poet-scholar to move freely and easily in both understanding and creating verse.

If one can integrate past texts and spontaneously embody them as one's Self, then, by a similar process, past poetry may be made into one's own. In recognizing the significance of prior verse, one could see (and call forth) the larger significance of one's own work. On the other hand, the failure to read the texts of the past properly nullifies the effort to compose well in, and for, the present. Huang Tingjian notes:

As for meaning, if in study one has yet to penetrate ten thousand volumes, then in looking on the compositions of the ancients one will not be able to use them fully as models.

All the new poems you sent me convey your inspiration and are lofty, far-reaching. But the language is raw and stiff and does not harmonize well with prosodic rules. Often the vital energy of the phrasing does not reach that moment when the meaning was first conceived. Is this malady not due to the fact that your learning is not yet essential and broad?⁵³

Here Huang points to the failure to assimilate the lessons of prior works so well that the intent behind the present work is perceptible in its full force. As a sensitive reader of poetry, Huang is able to discern the intent of the poet, but the poem that would serve as its vehicle is blocked and deficient precisely because the poet has not read well enough to express his ideas properly. This is the "lesser learning," the "bookishness" so antithetical to lyric values, that obstructs the immediate expression of authentic emotion.

Huang's essay "Lun zuo shi wen" (On composing poetry and prose) brings together several of these ideas:

Each day your new[ly written] poems contain surpassing verses; they may truly be enjoyed. If they do not perish, then it is because they have reached the spot where the ancients put down their brushes. As for my own verse and prose, how can they be good enough to be called well crafted? Yet you are now attempting to leave behind your ideas, and thus I will respectfully speak to you on the matter.

For phrases and intent to be lofty and surpassing, they must come from study. Those who have lately come to study verse sometimes hit on marvelous phrases, [but] they are like a man who closes his eyes and feels an elephant. He will follow along the parts of its body he comes in contact with and may reach a place where all is not what it seems it should be, but where what it seems to be cannot be. If he opens his eyes, then he will see the whole body. To meet the ancients, one does not wait for such evidence....

If in the examination hall your writing is slow and muddled, it is because when you study you do not pierce through the subject. It is proper to exert one's strength in study. The years and months seem to flow by, and one reaches the years when one's essential strength is weak. So in study do not value the miscellaneous and broad, but value the essential and profound. In making literary expressions, you must copy the ancients.[54]

Those who have not adequately integrated past models can achieve only groping, accidental writing. This is more than a question of aesthetics and poetic conventions—it bears on the idea that craft allows language to participate in a greater scheme of things: the perpetuation of culture.

To read words without sensing the resonances of *wen* is to misread, to take the enunciation out of proper context. Words are imbued with layers of meaning as they are used in time; each layer implies an accretion of readings and interpretations, but this accretion should enhance rather than obfuscate its identity as a manifestation of culture.

Huang raised the issue of the relationship between learning and the true understanding of poetry again in his famous remark that latter-day scholars cannot appreciate great verse because they cannot understand how such verse is a unique invention that exploits the semantic history of the words employed:

In Du Fu's composing of verse and Han Yu's composing of essays, there is not one word that does not come from somewhere else. Probably, because later generations do not read enough, they say that Han Yu and Du Fu made these expressions up themselves. Those of old who were able to compose literature were able to mold the myriad phenomena. They took the expressions of the ancients and entered them into brush and ink—it was like a pill of Spirit Cinnabar, which spots iron and turns it to gold.[55]

The verb *dian* (to dot, to spot) is employed in art criticism to refer to a painting technique, not unlike pointillism, that adds depth to the surface of the painting. Huang's apt use of the term here shows how latter-day poets can add depth to a prior work—the flat surface of "iron" is made to glisten like gold.[56] Indeed, for Huang this is the true art of poetry, and a true appreciation of this art depends on one's knowledge of literary history, specifically *textual* history. The reader must be able to see the particular nature of both the original text and the latter-day poet's use of it. Only then can he aspire to transform *wen*.

The importance of imitation is strongly felt in the late Northern Song; poets were more explicit than ever before in seeking models in prior greats and indeed in positing imitation as a necessary component of poetic composition. For example, the *Shiren yuxie* (Jade splinters of the poets), a Southern Song anthology of literary criticism, states:

The tomb inscription for Fan Zongshi [d. 821] says, "As far as poetic phrases, only the [very first] ancients necessarily obtained them from their own persons.... All those who follow then refer to these former lords and imitate them."[57] It is truly as this says.

[Sima Xiangru's] "Rhymeprose on Sir Fantasy" and the verse essay "The Great Man" completely imitate the "Distant Wandering" and the matter of Qu Yuan's mind.[58] It was not what Xiangru could spy into and understand himself, and thus the spirit and bearing differ.

[Tao] Yuanming's "The Return," the surpassing song of a thousand antiquities, has its ancestry in the intent of the "Rhymeprose on Returning to the Fields."[59] The poems of this category [of imitation] are numerous. For example, Han Yu's "Western Inscription on Pinghuai" completely displays the sentence technique of the *Classic of Documents*, and his poems "Cherishing Autumn" are completely in the style of the poetry of the *Wen xuan*.[60]

Tracing who imitated whom becomes a characteristic endeavor of Song literary criticism. For example, Hong Mai's (1123–1202) *Colophons of Rongzhai* contains numerous entries on the subject. Hong claims Su Shi imitates Wei Yingwu (737–?), Zhang Lei imitates Du Fu, and Huang imitates Xu Ling. Such inquiry was intended not to diminish the poet's craft but to trace out the paths poetry had taken, to seek out the kinds of sources that Huang refers to in his "Letter to Hong Jufu," and thereby to understand more completely the exact nature of the poem and its intent. In his "Commentary on Du Fu's Verse," Huang explicates the sources of thirty-five poems by Du Fu; this is precisely an exercise in finding out how Du Fu should be read, how he composed, and, by extension, how to use Du Fu's techniques.[61]

The complete and perfect assimilation of literary models was intended to allow one to write without being conscious of, and thereby hampered by, those rules. The question of authenticity was thus erased—what was other was now one's own. Still, at its root, this notion of art contains an inescapable contradiction. Next we will explore that contradiction and discuss the compromise Huang Tingjian struck.

THREE

The Illusion of Immediacy

Wang Zhifang, a follower of Huang Tingjian and a member of the Jiangxi school, recounts that Huang once said that "one should not pierce into the void and force composition—one should attend the scene and let it be born, then it will be naturally crafted."[1] Northern Song poets addressed the possibility that reference to prior texts and compositional models could interfere with the immediacy of poetic response in two ways. First, as we saw in the preceding chapter, the reference to prior texts, foregrounding the "learned" quality of the poem, could be seen as not being a gesture toward the outside, a reaching for something apart from the poet's own thoughts and feelings, if he had integrated the text's intent into his own. This called on a notion of intent that was both latent in the text and reformed according to the particular contingencies of contemporary readings of culture.

Second, compositional models could be assimilated so that, in following them, the poet was following a spontaneous intuition of how to write. In this response Northern Song poets combined two well-established notions of spontaneity through the poet's integration of himself with the object of contemplation and of compositional methods. The *Zhuangzi*, for example, contains numerous anecdotes, frequently cited in literary criticism, about artisans who have so perfectly mastered their craft that they exert no effort in performing their tasks. Nevertheless, in the late Northern Song, two things set the poet apart from the figures in the *Zhuangzi* and their evocations in such early texts of literary criticism as the *Wenxin diaolong*. First, the weight of texts and methods that he was supposed to integrate (writing now some five centuries after the appearance of such notions of spontaneity) had grown tremendously. Second, even as the poem was to appear effortless, the late Northern Song poet could achieve an identity only if his artfulness was perceptible as such.

In this chapter I examine how the paradoxical notion of "learned spontaneity" gave rise to an alternative response that aimed for an effect of spontaneity intended to draw attention to the art behind the illusion.

Spontaneity Through Assimilation

A parallel between poetic composition and artistic creation underscores Huang's notion of natural craft. In the following comment on a painting of bamboo by Dao Zhen (late eleventh c.), Huang begins by telling how the great painter Wu Daozi (?–792) surpassed his teacher. He then explains how an artist should employ his mind:

[Dao] Zhen has passed through Yuke's [Wen Tong, 1018–79] gate, and yet he has not entered his room. How is that? Wu Daozi surpassed his teacher by obtaining "it" from his mind, and therefore there was nothing that was not marvelous. Zhang [Xu, fl. 700–750] did not pursue any other skill and did not divide the employment of his intellect. Thus, he was able to enter the spirit [*ru yu shen*]. If the heart is able not to be entangled in outer things, then its heavenly conservation is complete; the myriad phenomena majestically come forth as from a single mirror. How can someone licking the ink, chewing on the brush, and squatting on the brick floor make art?[2] Thus I say that while Zhen wants to obtain the marvelous from the brush, he ought to obtain it from his heart.[3]

A famous poem by Su Shi contains a similar image of the object of art emerging from within:

> When Yuke painted bamboo
> He saw bamboo, not others.
> Was it that he alone did not see others?
> Oblivious, he left his body behind.
> His body was transformed into bamboo,
> Without limit putting forth pure freshness.
> This generation lacks a Zhuangzi,
> So who can understand this spirit?[4]

This concept of the artist completely integrating the object of contemplation into his self is akin to what Huang refers to as "entering the spirit." The term *shen* (spirit) has strong connotations of intuitive cognition, a mode of apprehension beyond reason and intellect; *shen* is the essence of the object, and by "entering the spirit" (*ru shen*), one makes the barrier between inner and outer disappear.⁵

"Entering the spirit" always points to something beyond technique. The process is sometimes referred to as *shen hui* ("joining in spirit"): "The excellence of painting and calligraphy should be sought through sympathetic identification [*shen hui*] and not through formal elements. Critics of painting can usually indicate faults of shape, composition, and coloring, but one seldom sees a man who understands its subtle ordering and profound beginning."⁶ The term *ru shen* is also used in discourses on connoisseurship to indicate both art objects of a "divine class" and an intuitive apprehension of that quality in the work of art.⁷ Here too we see the correlation between the essential quality of the object and its apprehension by the viewer.

The connection of the object, the apprehension of its essence, and the ability to translate that apprehension into moral action is implicit in one of the earliest appearances of *ru shen*, the "Xici zhuan" commentary to the *Classic of Changes*: "Investigate the principles of things with care and refinement until we enter into their spirit [*ru shen*], for then their application can be extended, and utilize that application and secure personal peace.... To investigate spirit to the utmost and to understand transformation is the height of virtue."⁸

In the late Northern Song conception of *ru shen*, the corollary to pre-reflective moral action is the spontaneous creation of art. One result of complete absorption is that the resulting artifact, be it a painting, a piece of calligraphy, or a poem, replicates the manifestation of the inner principle (*li*) of the object. It does not reproduce or represent the object; rather, it provides an ongoing embodiment of the object's inner logic—the poem, for example, unfolds itself in a manner that mirrors the unfolding of the object of contemplation.⁹ The artist's "mind" is thus in unison with both the *li* of the object and its manifestation as the object. Su Shi gives the following example from painting:

In the beginning of a bamboo's life, it is only an inch-long bud, and yet the joints and leaves are all in it. From cicada chrysalises and snake scales, it grows up, like a sword drawn out eighty feet, all because it was born with this [inherent pattern]. Today's painters make it joint by joint and add to it leaf by leaf. How can this be bamboo? Thus, in painting bamboo, one must first have a fully formed bamboo in one's breast. When one takes up the brush and gazes ardently and sees what one wants to paint, one rises hurriedly to follow it, grasping the brush forthwith to capture what was seen. It is like the rabbit's leaping up when the falcons swoop down; if there is any looseness [of concentration], then it gets away. Yuke taught me this, and [although] I could not achieve it, I understand the way it should be.[10]

By the late Northern Song the notion of *ru shen* incorporates more than the integration of self with the object of contemplation—the concept has been modified to accommodate a parallel integration of compositional models and prior texts. The poet is to "enter the spirit," but the "spirit" includes both the sense of the inner principle of the object *and* the ways in which others have responded in particular manifestations of *wen*. The opposite of this sense of the potentiality of the object, its inherent pattern, is a sense of it that is merely partial, which leads to an incomplete rendering of its spirit.

The image of absorbing *objects* (Yuke's bamboo) into one's "breast" finds a parallel in Huang's insistence that that the "breast" contains some "ten thousand *volumes*." Here that image represents the essential aspect of those texts, the intent of the ancients. For Huang this potentially confusing and chaotic scene is guaranteed order and clarity by the assimilation of all into the intent of the poet-artist, which both harmonizes and is in harmony with these elements.

Du Zheng (*jinshi* 1190) gives a detailed account of Huang on the subject of what should reside inside one's breast (*xiong zhong*) and its effect on one's endeavors:

Shangu said that Lianxi's [Zhou Dunyi, 1017–73] breast was elegant and unfettered like a glimmering wind, a clear moon after rainfall....

Shangu also said to those who were studying under him: "It is proper and fitting to constantly conserve this [spirit] in one's breast so as to benevolently nourish one's self." He also said, "In responding to matters and encountering phenomena, your breast must be without impediment or inertia. Then and only then can one be said to be 'elegant and unfettered.' If those who study with me arrive at this state, there will be nothing they cannot obtain."[11]

This state, once achieved, allows one to approach things and understand them without hesitation. The corollary to this in composition is that the writing of poetry is just as spontaneous.

This ideal is obviously hard pressed; the late Northern Song poet and artist confronted the necessity of reconciling these long-standing issues of inner versus outer, perception versus expression, learning versus spontaneity. To create a poetics that would reconcile these questions, to acknowledge the place of each opposition in traditions of both reading and writing *wen*, and, last but not least, to adapt this discourse as an argument for their manipulations of prior verse were the formidable tasks facing late Northern Song poets.

Northern Song poets were in the end unable to transcend traditional modes of reconciling "naturally formed" and "artfully formed" verse. Their argument for assimilating learning to effect spontaneous composition differs more in degree and focus than in nature from prior enunciations. What was different was their (and here I use Huang as the best example of the late Northern Song response) tactic of valorizing an *effect* of spontaneity that relied on the reader's apprehension of the craft involved. By shifting the focus to how the appearance of spontaneity had been achieved, poets could address at once the seemingly mutually exclusive values of art and spontaneity. Earlier critics urged poets to hide the traces of craft to make their writing appear natural, but the late Northern Song poets held that craft had to be perceived. In fact, at a crucial moment they abandoned even the attempt to downplay art in favor of the "natural" and gave artifice primacy.

Striking the Jade Gem Tone: An Effect of Spontaneity

Huang Tingjian often joins his contemporaries in condemning poets who follow rules too strictly:

Wang Guanfu's [Wang Fan, eleventh c.] verse has the bearing of the ancients. Although its breath and form completely transcend the vulgar, he has yet to strike the jade gem tone in an easy manner. On his left is the standard and the rule; on his right, the carpenter's square and compass. As for meaning, if in study one has yet to penetrate ten thousand volumes, then in looking on the compositions of the ancients, one will not be able to obtain their model fully. In reading, he [Wang] dusted off and inspected [the Classics], and obtained something; but in using them to set up [these] literary compositions, he did so as if he were merely toying with mountains and dragons and embroidery.[12]

The flaw in Wang's verse is that it shows the strain and effort of composition. The "gem tone" is struck in such a way as to make it seem at once contrived and haphazard. A concern for craft replaces a recognition of sense; only the latter gives the poem solidity and stability. Wang's poem is an ornament engendered by random strokes, blind choices of stock image. In writing poetry, one should effortlessly put into motion the integrated models of the tradition; no effort should be perceptible.[13]

But where, then, can one discern art? If intent is erased and effort is invisible, how is art (and thereby the work of the poet) perceived? If Northern Song poets were successful in erasing the mediation of prior texts by drawing on and intensifying the traditional prescription of perfect assimilation, they were still caught in the quandary: how to detach themselves from the union of self and other so as to appear different, distinct?

Perhaps more than any other Northern Song poet, Huang was engaged in constructing an identity through an art that called attention to itself. Still, as we saw above, he held to the notion that composition should appear effortless. In practice, Huang's poetics employs art to create an *effect* of spontaneity that withdraws enough for the thing itself to be presented without erasing the mark of craft, the mark of poetic identity. This is the problem with which Schiller grapples: "It is precisely this mode of expression in which the sign disappears completely in the thing signified, and in which language, while giving expression to a thought, yet leaves it exposed where otherwise it cannot be represented without simultaneously concealing it; and this it is we generally call a gifted style displaying genius."[14]

A better sense of what Huang seeks to accomplish in composing in this way can be gained from some poems with which he felt particularly satisfied. These poems are rather unlike the more famous poems in which he employs his intellect and erudition most emphatically and deliberately, seeming to dispense with the obligation to appear "spontaneous"—the well-known poems of recondite allusions and poetic borrowings. In the following poems, Huang strives to achieve a particular texture of effortlessness that partially masks the well-crafted and highly mediated nature of the poem. These poems illustrate one ideal for which Huang and other Northern Song poets strove; it is, however, only an effect, recognized too for its genesis in a craft that identified itself and its creator.

Begging for a Cat 乞貓

Autumn has come, and the rats are taking advantage of my cat's death.	秋來鼠輩欺貓死
They spy into the jars, overturn plates, and disturb my sleep.	窺甕翻盤攪夜眠
I heard your cat has brought forth several kittens,	聞道狸奴將數子
So I bought a fish and stuck it on a willow branch as a wedding gift for one who holds a cicada in its mouth.[15]	買魚穿柳聘銜蟬

4/ A Ming dynasty text by Wang Zhijian, the *Biao yi lu* (The record of announcements of extraordinary things; 9.73), tells that the Duke of Qionghua of the Latter Tang

The Illusion of Immediacy 77

Mei's second poem is a mock eulogy, and its parody of the convention finds a condensed parallel in Huang's oblique parody of the rhetoric of historical prose in his opening line. The poet marks off the continuum of time, but instead of the ascension or demise of a great ruler, he cites the death of the household cat, whose passing becomes the stuff the poem is made of. In fact, the cat's death is significant only insofar as it brings about the rats' mischief.

Like the abundant use of onomatopoeic words to describe the havoc of the rats and the self-reflective muttering "yi zhuo" (how silly, inept, clumsy) in Mei's first poem, his second poem is full of low diction and imagery—the graphic demise of the rat caught in the cat's jaws, the piss and gnawings of the rodents, and the parodic conclusion in which Mei's grief makes it difficult for him to go on eulogizing. Huang's poem also incorporates low diction and unusual locutions: from the plainly colloquial "I hear" of line 3 and its circumlocution "brought forth" (*jiang*) for "gave birth" to the use of the verb *pin*, which is usually reserved to denote inviting a bride to join one's household. Huang might also be playing with the *Classic of Changes*, literalizing the figurative "fishes" while borrowing the auspicious quality of the image. He makes them real enough to lure the cat into his household. Huang also plays on a metaphoric name for cats, "holding a cicada in its mouth" to anticipate what he hopes the cat will have in its mouth—his lure.

Although Mei's first poem is unabashedly comic, the second, for all its parodic elements, still allows the poet some authenticity of feeling. It is not as if the poet were absolutely feigning unhappiness; rather, he seems to catch himself being overly dramatic and indulges in an ironic self-perception. Huang's poem straddles these two in tone: like Mei's first poem, Huang's is clearly comic; like the second poem Huang's reveals a degree of self-irony.

The most impressive point of comparison is the extremely condensed treatment Huang gives the themes of both of Mei's longer poems. Huang's quatrain is no less well-crafted for it; in fact, this condensation reveals a high degree of artistry, evoking similar motifs, sentiments, and word play, while framing them in an even simpler, more refined form.[21]

Huang's poem calls attention to itself with its apparent artlessness, yet the poem works on the level of poetic logic, a logic that elides the coarseness of diction and flatness of narration. We can understand why others' appreciation of this poem derived largely from their recognition of how Huang had manipulated prior texts without losing the feeling of spontaneity behind the originals.

Another widely admired poem by Huang makes use of easy diction in a seemingly offhand way.

Climbing Kuai Gallery 登快閣

I, the bungler, finished up the official business 痴兒了却公家事
And wandered to and fro atop Kuai Gallery, close to the evening's clear sky. 快閣東西倚晚晴
The leaves of the trees fall on a thousand mountains, the sky looms large in the distance. 落木千山天遠大
4 The pure river a single path, the moon clear and brilliant. 澄山一道月分明
The purple strings already broken for the Fine Gentleman, 朱絃已爲佳人絕
For the moment I let the pupils of my eyes sweep across because of the fine wine. 青眼聊因美酒橫
I would finger a long flute on a boat ride home ten thousand *li*. 萬里歸船弄長笛
8 To this I make an oath with the gulls.[22] 此心吾與白鷗盟

This poem is often compared to the verse of Li Bo, in particular his "Long Song" (*Chang ge xing*). Huang similarly displays narrative ease, a graceful combination of colloquial and allusive diction, and the bravado of the poetic persona and introspection. What is of particular note in Huang's poem is the artful way he integrates allusions into the poem without attracting attention to them as such.

The brash and self-mocking term "*chi'er*" (foolish, stupid) in line 1 is an allusion to the "Biography of Fu Xian" in the *Jin shu*. Fu Xian (fl. 300) was a famous practitioner of "pure talk" (*qingtan*) in the Jin dynasty, who claimed that only dolts bothered with officialdom. Within that statement there is, however, as in much of "pure talk" discourse, a double reading; here, a tone of self-mockery. Huang plays with this allusion, diluting the perjorative sense and using the term literally in almost a self-congratulatory manner, "I'm foolish, but I got it done anyway." As Zhu Zeqing points out, this is only one of several possible readings.[23]

Zhu uses this poem as an example of ambiguity in Chinese verse; he finds four possible readings for the first couplet: (1) Huang is mocking his own ineptitude ("Stupid me, finally getting the business done"); (2) Huang is boasting of his transcendence of bureaucratic concerns by implicitly linking his capabilities to the expansive vista from the tower; (3) Huang is exhorting himself to leave official business behind ("Stupid! Stop doing official business!"); and (4) Huang is telling of his joy at being done with his duties. Each reading is possible, and this ambiguity prepares the reader for the ironic vision projected by the poet at the end of the poem.[24]

Line 2 begins by continuing the easy, informal tone of the first; placing the poet closer to the evening's clearing sky. This fusion of poet and locale marks the shift from the poet as pragmatic official to the poet as one who would, in Daoist fashion, merge with nature.

The next couplet (lines 3–4) is especially well crafted and owes a debt to Du Fu's lines, "Limitless, the descending leaves fall, *xiao-xiao*, Inexhaustible, the long river approaches, *gun-gun*."[25] The lines continue to free the poet from the confines of official duty and move him up to the gallery and into a constantly expanding scene. Huang's couplet is more conspicuously crafted than Du Fu's. Huang balances the scattered leaves falling on a thousand mountains against the single unified stretch of river, and both lines seem to end with a view toward the sky. However, in line 3 the view is up into the heavens; in line 4 it is down toward the reflection of the moon in the river. This play with reflection and perspective serves to complement the ambiguity of the poet's self-reference in line 1.

The next quatrain introduces a pair of juxtaposed allusions: the famous story of the friendship of Zhong Ziqi and Bo Ya in the *Lüshi chunqiu* and the story of Ruan Ji, who was able to roll his eyes up and hide the pupils. When he was pleased to see somebody, his eyes were centered, the pupils visible; when he disliked his company, he would roll up his eyes as a sign of scorn. If, as Huang says, the "strings are broken" (the one friend—the *zhi yin*—who could truly share his company and spirit is dead), then who is there for him to center his eyes for? Huang raises the question, but instead of a human being of deep moral and spiritual affinities, we find a token of solitary pleasure: the wine.

The poem closes by neatly drawing together images from the opening lines. The poet has sensed his isolation high up in the gallery and recasts the river as a way out. Whereas earlier the river was coupled with images of expansiveness and dissipation, here it is transformed into a possible conduit out of that emptiness and back to the company of his family and home. He even projects a vision of himself playing the flute on that boat journey home—this act is an outgrowth of his initial view from the tower, at once more specific and more unreal.

The poem ends with the poet's oath with the gulls, an image taken from the famous *Liezi* story of a young man who loved gulls and was able to frolic with them unnoticed every morning; but when he planned to attract them to show his father, the gulls suspected his intent and flew away.²⁶ The parable came to stand for an approach that is natural and uncalculated. Huang's use of it attempts to call forth the same ethos, but the poem's context questions the poet's ability to keep this oath. The poet is, after all, a "fool" in the sense of the *Jin shu* story. He is bound up in official matters and can only wish for the sentiment he calls forth; the image of him on the boat threatens to remain only a dream. The instability of the first couplet now comes back to haunt the vision set up by the poet in the last couplet and unbalance its flight. It is not certain if the poet's consciousness has truly evolved in the course of the poem, if the last line is a stalwart promise or a wistful projection of the poet's desire.

Huang's achievement here lies in his blending of various registers of diction; his offhand use of allusions masks a complexity at the core of the poem. The ironic message of the poem is not easily noticeable at first reading, since the poem moves so effortlessly and prosaically, and the very conventionality of the allusions lulls us into a sense that they are there simply to supply the required tropes. The recognition that comes when we read them as more than stock allusions (for example, when we recognize the wit behind the references to Zhong Ziqi, Bo Ya, and Ruan Ji), when we integrate them into the context of the poem, gives us a knowledge of an irony of which the poetic persona is ignorant. This poem is an example of the effect of effortlessness being put to specific use as a ploy, a diversion that adds a particular dimension to the poem.

One final example of a poem that hides a complex structure beneath simplicity is one of Huang's most famous poems, and one of which he was particularly proud.²⁷

Inscribed on the Painting of the Bamboo, 題竹石牧牛
Rock, and Herdboy

Zizhan [Su Shi] painted a cluster of bamboo and a bizarre rock. Boshi [Li Gonglin] added a slope in front with a herdboy riding an ox. It really struck my interest, and I playfully composed this.

   In the wilds a small craggy peak, 野次小崢嶸
   A secluded thicket of bamboo, stalks lean close against 幽篁相倚綠
      each other, green upon green.
   A young lad with a three-foot whip 阿童三尺箠
4 Drives an old, trembling ox. 御此老觳觫
   I really love that stone, 石吾甚愛之
   Don't let the ox sharpen his horns on it. 勿遣牛礪角
   Still, if the ox sharpens his horns, it's all right, 牛礪角尚可
8 But if the oxen fight, they'll destroy my bamboo.²⁸ 牛鬥殘我竹

Yoshikawa Kōjirō interprets this poem to be a mild chiding of Li Gonglin for meddling in Su Shi's painting; Chen Yongzheng sees political allegory signaled by the impending "fight." Ronald Egan, in an essay on Huang's poems on paintings, claims that "it is a private joke, and we are left out of it."[29] Certainly both the painting and the poem must share a point that has been lost to later readers. What we do know is that Su Shi and Li Gonglin made the painting as a diversion from the monotony of grading exams; perhaps Li added in the ox and herdboy to "threaten" Su's scene. Despite what has been lost, there is still a great deal to appreciate in this poem, and we may still derive some sense of why Huang loved it so.

The poem begins with a twist in perspective. As we saw in "Rising at Dawn in Linru," the binom *zhengrong* denotes a tall and precipitous peak. To precede the term with the diminutive *xiao* (small, tiny) creates an oxymoron and also a microcosmic model of a mountain. The weirdness of the stone painted by Su Shi is that its perspective is double.[30] The next line is again visually complex; the last three words, literally "mutually leaning green," evoke an intertwining of light and shadow, density of color. In this first couplet Huang establishes an eminently "painterly" scene.

The next couplet intrudes on this subtle image, not only with the young boy and the ox but also with its plain diction. The "trembling ox" comes from the *Mencius* (1A.7), where the speaker is moved to pity by the fright of an animal being led to the sacrificial block. Egan sees its appearance here as a touch of humor, and part of its humor derives from its inappropriateness. This seemingly arbitrary allusion may be a jibe at the examination compositions they were reading; elsewhere Huang criticizes those who employ allusions sloppily, "as if everything had some allegorical import."[31]

The placement of "stone" in the initial position in the next line emphasizes its importance; yet this importance is immediately dismissed two lines later, for the poet has anticipated another action after the horn sharpening—he sees the purpose behind the action.

The poem is playful, and much of that play comes from a set of linked expectations. The bamboo and stone are there first, both in the logic of the natural world and the fact of the composite painting. The ox and herdboy's appearance sets the poet's mind on a series of anticipated actions—the ox will sharpen its horns, and it will do so to fight another ox (not in the painting yet), and as a result they will trample the bamboo.

Each of these acts is immanent, but perhaps not. The wit of the poem is contingent on this projection of actions onto a static representation. Behind its seeming offhandedness, the poem is a play on the relation between painting and poetry, of paintings that represent presence and poems that may anticipate things as yet absent. This poem on a painting effectively comments on the powers and limits of both arts in a seemingly offhand manner.

The next poem raises the issue of natural craft to its highest point. While lauding the "naturalness" of the artist, Huang argues that such naturalness subdues Nature because of the very fact it is shaped by art; he inverts the hierarchy and places human creations above those of Nature.

Listening to [Li] Chongde Play the Zither 聽崇德君鼓琴

Moon bright, river still, in the midst of silence, 月明江靜寂寥中
Da Jia gathers her sleeves and strokes the lone paulownia. 大家斂袂撫孤桐
That ancient one already gone; the ancient music remains: 古人已矣古樂在
4 It seems like the remnant airs of the Odes and Elegies. 髣髴雅頌之遺風
A master hand is not easily come by; 妙手不易得
A good listener is truly difficult to find. 善聽良獨難
As rare as the *udumbara* flower, 猶如優曇華
8 They appear once in a generation. 時一出世間
We both forget the lute and our own thoughts; 兩忘琴意與己意
It is as though she were not playing, her ten fingers strumming. 洒似不著十指彈
The Zen mind is dumb; the Triple Abyss still. 禪心默默三淵靜
12 In the deep valley pure winds simply answer each other. 幽谷清風淡相應
Who says the sound of strings is not as fine as the sound of bamboo? 絲聲誰道不如竹
I've forgotten words and found true nature. 我已忘言得真性
She stops; beyond the window, the moon sinks into the river 罷琴窗外月沈江
16 The ten thousand pipes empty, the seven strings still.³² 萬籟俱空七絃定

This complex poem draws in a number of levels and styles of discourse within the long-established genre of *qin* (lute) poems. The first line sets the proper scenario for such a poem—under a bright moon, the poet contemplates the still night. Line 2 makes the first explicit allusion and introduces two of the key themes of the poem. "Da Jia" can be simply read as an honorific term of address: the *qin* player is Huang's maternal aunt Li Chongde, a famous calligrapher and the subject of several poems by Huang. But Da Jia was also the courtesy name (*hao*) of a musician and calligrapher of the Han dynasty named Ban Zhao, the sister of the famous historian Ban Gu.[33] Huang sees his aunt as the living embodiment of Da Jia, whose music lives on in Li Chongde.

But even as Li Chongde signals the presence of this paragon of womanly skill and art, she herself seems to be voided, emptied of self. This inversion of presence and absence is one of the key themes of the poem. The figurative density of this line continues with Huang's metonymic naming of the zither (the "lone paulownia"). Referring to the instrument by way of its constituent material is a commonplace, but in this poem Huang uses the trope as a condensed emblem of the central problematic of the poem: the relative values of human and natural music and, by extension, those of art and nature.

Line 4 is also crowded with wordplay that gestures toward both the natural world and the world of human cultural activity. The character *feng* (wind) does double duty—employed literally and for the fact that it refers to one of the three categories of poems in the *Classic of Poetry*, the other two being the "Odes" and "Elegies" that round off Huang's line. Li Chongde's music perpetuates these songs, but note that here Huang describes not the music itself but rather its effects; for Huang, this music reproduces the spiritual and moral effect the ancient songs were supposed to instill in their listener.

In lines 5–8, Huang combines several allusions to elaborate his meditation on art and nature, will and spontaneity. In line 5, Huang alludes to a line from Du Fu's "A Song for Liu Shaofu of Fengxian's New Landscape Painting on a Screen": "Painting masters are rare, but a master hand is impossible to come by."[34] Line 6 completes the parallel statement begun in line 5 and brings together the issues of artistic creation and reception—the production of art and the perpetuation of its intended effect (this harks back to Huang's lines on the effect of Li's music and the poems of the *Classic of Poetry*): the only thing rarer than a master *qin* player is someone who can "understand the tone."[35] Huang's lines paraphrase a couplet from the fifth of the "Nineteen Poems in the Ancient Style": "I do not pity [this] singer's bitterness; / I am only grieved that those who understand the tone are rare," but he alters the reference—finding a *zhi yin* now becomes as rare as the appearance of the mythical *udumbara* flower, which blooms only with the appearance of the Buddha.[36]

Another Buddhist allusion comes with the "Zen heart/mind" (*chan xin*), which is the revelation of Buddha nature that comes with complete detachment, a state brought about here by Li Chongde's music. But Huang quickly juxtaposes a reference to the Three Abysses of the *Zhuangzi*:

Just now I appeared to him as the Great Vastness Where Nothing Wins Out. He probably saw in me the workings of the Balanced Breaths. Where the swirling waves gather there is an abyss; where the still waters gather there is an abyss; where the running waters gather there is an abyss. The abyss has nine names and I have shown him three.[37]

Shi Rong (?–after 1201) notes that one commentary on the *Zhuangzi* takes "abyss" to refer to "still silence"; that is, in the midst of movement and sound there may be its utter absence.[38] By playing these allusions to Buddhist and Daoist texts off the initial citation of Confucian texts, Huang creates a specific discursive dynamic wherein the music of Li Chongde gives rise to its transcendence. By this period, references to Daoism, Confucianism, and Buddhism had lost much of their specificity, and images from these different philosophies were often used syncretically; one gets the sense, however, that here Huang is consciously manipulating these different discourses. He seems to set each up as an image that offers a timeless vision onto the universe, but he then subordinates them in turn to complement his particular vision of the artistry of the music. We begin to sense that all these philosophical discourses are being put into the service of an idea that transcends each one, a suspicion borne out with the next line.

"Who says the sound of strings is not as fine as bamboo?" comes from an anecdote about Meng Jia (mid-fourth c.):

[Huan Wen asked Meng Jia,] "When I'm listening to performers, stringed instruments don't sound as good as bamboo instruments, and bamboo instruments don't sound as good as flesh [i.e., the human voice]. Why should that be?" [Meng Jia] replied, "Because you're getting closer and closer with each one to what is natural."[39]

The citation of this allusion foregrounds the central question of naturalness. In Meng Jia's hierarchy, the closer one gets to the spontaneous sounds of the human voice unaided by instruments, the more wonderful the music. Huang challenges this assertion, claiming that the music of Li Chongde's zither has performed a miraculous feat—these "artificial" sounds have brought the myriad sounds of Nature under their spell, the mystic winds are stilled, and once she stops playing, the moon sinks.

The Illusion of Immediacy 85

For a moment, time is suspended, but once the music ends, the heavenly bodies move again. Art has subdued Nature.

Li Chongde's music has transported the poet to the state where words may be dispensed with, harking to the famous passage in *Zhuangzi*: "The fish trap exists because of the fish; once you've gotten the fish, you can forget the trap. The rabbit snare exists because of the rabbit; once you've gotten the rabbit, you can forget the snare. Words exist because of the meaning; once you've gotten the meaning, you can forget the words."[40] Huang here goes even further—the intent behind Li Chongde's music has never had to be verbalized; it has the power to immediately transcend language. This conjunction of forgetting words and understanding truth is found in the fifth of Tao Qian's "Drinking Wine" poems: "In the midst of this there is true meaning; / As I start to tell it, I forget the words."[41] But here again Huang modifies the allusion to suit his argument, replacing "meaning" (*yi*) with the Buddhist concept of "true nature" (*zhen xing*), the concept that at the core of every being is the basic nature of the universe: the Buddha nature.

But once again this discourse is broken off by another allusion to the *Zhuangzi*, one that confirms the power of Li Chongde's music:

Tzu-ch'i [Ziqi] said, "The Great Clod belches out breath and its name is wind. So long as it doesn't come forth, nothing happens. But when it does, then ten thousand hollows begin crying wildly...."

Tzu-yu [Ziyou] said, "By the piping of the earth, then, you mean simply [the sound of] these hollows, and by the piping of man [the sound of] flutes and whistles. But may I ask about the piping of Heaven?"

Tzu-ch'i said, "Blowing on the ten thousand things in a different way, so that each can be itself—all take what they want for themselves, but who does the sounding?"[42]

This passage, like the one from Meng Jia's biography, stresses the naturalness of earthly music. The greatest music is spontaneous and unfashioned. Li Chongde's music achieves this state ("It is as though she were not playing") by removing any trace of craft or intent, and the music so created dominates all other sounds. Her music, coming from the *most* artificial instrument, strings, transcends the state of its artifice. In the poem itself, the music is strangely absent; it is present only as function, and this enlarges the scope of Huang's critique to encompass all artistic endeavors, including, of course, poetry.

This fusion of Confucian, Daoist, and Buddhist allusion is a rhetorical construct from which Huang argues for a particular vision of art. Poetry, however mediated by language and craft, can achieve something *even greater* than perfect naturalness. Another set of mediations—not from philosophical discourse, but from poetry itself, texts that form an essential backdrop for Huang's poem—confirms this correlation of music and poetry.

The most famous piece on music in the poetic tradition is undoubtedly Bo Juyi's "Pipa xing" (Lute song).[43] This long narrative poem within a poem tells of the poet's encounter with a woman playing the *pipa*. On a still night, sending off a friend on a river journey, the poet hears the haunting melody of her playing; the men ask her to come to their boat and play for them. She proceeds to sing a tale of her life, which moves the poet to record it in his poem. Huang gestures toward that poem obliquely, but another of Bo Juyi's poems comments more precisely on the issues raised by Huang Tingjian.

Pine Sounds	松聲
The moonlight is good, good for solitary sitting;	月好好獨坐
there's a pair of pine trees in front of my roof.	雙松在前軒
From the southwest a faint breeze comes,	西南微風來
4 stealing in among the branches and leaves,	潛入枝葉間
making a sad and sighing sound,	蕭寥發爲聲
at midnight here in the bright moon's presence,	半夜明月前
like the rustle, rustle of rain on cold hills,	寒山颯颯雨
8 or the clear clean note of autumn lute strings.	秋琴泠泠絃
One hearing and the fierce heat is washed away,	一聞滌炎暑
a second hearing wipes out sorrow and gloom.	再聽破昏煩
I stay up all evening, never sleeping,	竟夕遂不寐
12 till mind and body are both wiped clean.	心體俱翛然
On the avenue to the south, horses and carriages pass;	南陌車馬動
from neighbors to the west, frequent songs and flutes—	西隣歌吹繁
Who'd suppose that here under the eaves,	誰知茲簷下
16 the sounds that fill my ears are in no way noisy.[44]	滿耳不爲喧

Huang inverts the "intent" of Bo Juyi's poem, borrowing all the effects this "natural music" supposedly possesses and attributing them to "artificial" music, in direct contrast to Bo's (and Meng Jia's) claim that human music is inferior to natural music and incapable of producing the same effects. Again, this defense of artifice is complemented by the allusiveness and clearly "artful" composition of Huang's verse, which forms its rhetorical argument from disparate textual elements.

Another text, one that predates Bo Juyi by more than five centuries, stands in the background of Huang's poem: Xi Kang's (223–62) "Qin fu" (Rhymeprose on the zither).[45] Huang was fond of Xi Kang's writings and exhorted all poets to memorize them. Xi Kang's rhymeprose contains many motifs used by Huang. Most important, in the preface to the rhymeprose, Xi Kang speaks of the art of the lute and its affective power:

> Now when the Lute is played, the sounds of the instruments made of metal and stone die out, and the breath blown into those made of a gourd or of bamboo ceases. Wang Pao [Wang Bao] breaks off his chant, Ti Ya [Di Ya] loses his gift of taste. But the God of the waters starts to dance in his deep vale, and the Immortal Wang Ch'iao [Wang Qiao] descends from the clouds. A phoenix pair begins to dance on the steps of the courtyard, and heavenly fairies, lightly floating down from on high, assemble there. As the Lute thus influences the harmony of Heaven and Earth, how much more then earthly beings that crowd about here below?[46]

Huang certainly borrows Xi Kang's rhetoric, but he adapts Xi Kang's text to address the question of how artifice can surpass Nature. This elevation of artifice over the natural emblematizes his own poetics of manipulation and artifice.

The intensely intertextual nature of Northern Song poetry, which demands that not only the sources of texts but also the manipulation of those sources be recognized, ironizes any naive claim to spontaneity. More than any other classical Chinese poet, Huang Tingjian embarked on a radical exploration of how to manipulate the voices of past poets. In this section I have outlined how Huang's poetics share in the general response of many late Northern Song poets to their particular situation in Chinese cultural history; in Part II, I examine in greater detail the particular methods Huang Tingjian employed that have given him his identity in classical Chinese literature.

PART II

Huang Tingjian's Theory and Practice

FOUR

Extending Verse

In Part I we noted Huang's particular responses to his position as a late Northern Song poet. Confronted with the mastery of the Tang over a huge area of the lyric tradition and the increasingly self-conscious intellectual and aesthetic concerns of his age, Huang and other Northern Song poets inscribed a decidedly "intertextual" dimension into their poetics, differentiating themselves from their predecessors and establishing a distinct mode of writing.[1] The bookish and philosophical nature of the Northern Song lyric can be understood as a departure from Tang poetics that does not necessarily exclude a concern for the traditional aesthetics of lyric verse. Indeed, as noted above, Huang sought to integrate the citation of prior texts, philosophic meditation, and aesthetic integrity.

Here I explore more fully both the theoretical notions and poetic practices Huang used to differentiate himself from other poets. One distinct way that he did so was to appropriate and manipulate traditional critical attitudes to suit, and even endorse, his program.

Difference and Transformation

The idea of transforming literature is well established in ancient Chinese literary criticism. The poet is told to attempt things never done before, so as to escape imitation. Lu Ji's (261–303) "Wen fu" (Rhymeprose on literature) states:

One takes in the literary works of a hundred generations where lacunae still remain;[2]	收百世之闕文
And collects the lingering echoes of a thousand years.	採千載之遺韻

> One dismisses the morning flowers that already have opened, 謝朝華於已披
> And causes the evening buds that have not yet stirred to reveal themselves.³ 啓夕秀於未振

Here Lu Ji rejects repetition and focuses on the potential of things left unsaid. For him, there are texts that are still immanent in the world. One could and should do something that the ancients had left undone, perceive something they had yet to speak about; further, one should bring out the untapped potential of the Classics.

In the early Tang, in describing the creation of *wen*, Yang Jiong (650–92) alters the image of following the ancients found in the *Analects*: "Tzu-chang [Zizhang] asked about the Way of the good people. The Master answered, 'He who does not tread in the tracks [of the ancients] cannot expect to find his way into the Inner Room.'"⁴ In his praise for Wang Bo (ca. 648–75), Yang writes: "[Wang] has the reputation of striking, mobilizing, and embracing the four seas, transforming and forming [*wen*] to fashion the style of his own school, treading on that which the prior sages had yet to recognize, and spying into what the former sages did not speak of."⁵

Like Lu Ji, Yang Jiong values developing those things left for the latter-day poet to discover, but there is an important distinction between discovery and invention. Rather than emphasizing the search for the unspoken, Wang Changling (690–756) stresses the manipulation of prior material:

> Imitate old writings, but don't follow their old ideas, or you will never advance far. In all cases *you must crisscross and zigzag, transform and appropriate the material in a hundred ways.* At the head of each section you must let your idea lead the way, then afterward return and gather up the original idea. [Italics added]⁶

This attention to appropriation and manipulation particularly interested Northern Song poets. Huang Tingjian writes: "In reading books, don't vainly use up several days. Get to the place where the ancients employed their minds, the heroic and marvelous part of the literary piece. Then you will be able to *twist old language into a thing of your own*" (italics added).⁷ Huang's statement is akin in spirit to Wang Changling's. Huang is not satisfied with ornamentally varying the surface of past poetry; he seizes the essential part of past verse and seeks to turn it into a thing of his own.

In his famous statement "Turn the old into the new, the vulgar into the refined," Huang underscores the transformative process: prior texts are changed; the deadened, commonplace diction of the past is transformed:

I am old and lazy now and haven't written verse for many years. I've already forgotten its forms and rules, but because [Yang] Mingshu is interested in this literature [*si wen*], I thought I would lift up the net and stretch out its ten thousand meshes. Surely one ought to make the vulgar into the elegant and the old into the new. ... These wondrous words of the Lord of Mei Shan shake and dazzle the whole age. Formerly I obtained these words from him and made much of them.[8]

The "Lord of Mei Shan" is Su Shi, whose statement is found in a colophon that reads in part, "In poetry it is necessary to have something by which to compose. In employing allusions, it is proper to take the old and make it new, and take the vulgar and make it elegant."[9] Huang's adaptation of Su Shi's statement calls for a radical reassessment of what was "old": How does one approach old texts? He also asks us to examine the precise character of the "new": How has the old been transformed, and what is significantly different in this new creation?

In the Northern Song, this imperative to transform intensifies; the highest praise is reserved for those who go the furthest toward exhausting transformability. Lü Benzhong (1084–1145) writes:

From ancient times when one speaks of the marvelousness of literary composition, of expanding and perfecting the mass of styles [*ti*] and bringing forth the strange without end, there is only one man—Dongpo [Su Shi]. In taking the transformation of the Airs and Odes [two of the classes of poetry in the *Classic of Poetry*] to the limit and exhausting the possible articulations [*ti*] of the tropes of *bi* and *xing*,[10] including all the masses of compositional [methods] and taking as one's basis new ideas, there is only Yuzhang [Huang Tingjian]. These two men should be eternally taken as models.[11]

The belief that Huang in particular creatively extended the classic texts of the tradition is also held by Xu Yin, who notes in his preface to the "Inner Collection" of Huang's poems: "The poems of Shangu Laoren of Our Dynasty bring to the ultimate the transformation of the '[Encountering] Sorrow' and the Odes."[12]

Nevertheless, even while experimenting with relatively radical modes of transforming *wen*, Huang Tingjian was always conscious of the need to legitimize those revisions according to the presumptions of lyric verse. Many of Huang's statements display a compelling and eminently self-conscious synthesis and revision of traditional notions in literary criticism and Northern Song ideas, showing the need both for the precedent of tradition and for a contemporary reinterpretation of it. Much of the rhetoric of his critical remarks balances these concerns with the traditional and the contemporary, paralleling the practice of poetic composition in the late Northern Song, which played off prior poetic materials and shaped them to its particular vision. One area in which this is especially evident is in Huang's correlation of *li* (principle) with orthodox literary composition.

In order for Huang to argue the necessity and, indeed, the inevitability of literary invention, particularly his brand of it, he adapted the traditional view that *li* is essential to the literary work. Without it, the piece, caught in its effort to depart from the mold of the Classics, lapses into meaninglessness. As early as the "Wen fu," we find mention of *li* as such: "*Li* supports its substance as a means to establish writing; / Patterning suspends its branches and ties together its multiplicity."[13] Again, the sixth-century critic Yan Zhitui (531–91) says, "Literary works should take perfectly bringing about *li* to be their heart and bosom."[14]

Huang uses *li* in a similar way in a letter to Wang Fan. First he compliments Wang for some recent compositions; then he chastises Wang for his use of "strange" (*qi*) diction. He quotes from the *Wenxin diaolong* to support his criticism that "if one is fond of creating weird language, one's literary compositions will suffer. One must take principle [*li*] as master. If the principle is obtained, then the expression will follow after it; the composition will naturally distinguish itself from the crowd of other works."[15] This condemnation of "strangeness" seems odd coming from a poet attacked for indulging in bizarre expressions. Huang's statement here is intended to show that he knew the dangers of choosing strange diction to give one's poems novelty, and thus he portrays himself as firmly aware of the necessity of adhering to inherent principle.

The urge to go beyond conventional literary forms, coupled with an awareness that those ventures had to be controlled, appears again in this statement by Huang's friend and fellow poet Zhang Lei:

Your *wen* can be called "strange"! Departing from the constant forms of diction, you exert yourself in circling around the unusual and teetering on the brink of the bizarre in the hope of leading men to read your works as if they were looking on what is recorded in the bird tracks of a myriad eons before us.[16] ... From what I know, those who are considered capable of making *wen* were hardly the same as those who were called capable of making the bizarre. Those whose writings are able to endure certainly did not take the bizarre as their master![17]

Even as Huang and Zhang caution against uncontrolled exercises in novelty, however, they convey a strong sense that the "constant forms" binding and giving order to literature had to be significantly modified. In a colophon praising Wang Anshi, Huang states: "The short poems of his latter years are elegant and beautiful, pure and surpassing; they slough off the common and ordinary, and cannot be apprehended according to ordinary principle."[18] Indeed, critics have commented that this appraisal applies as well to Huang Tingjian himself. Many of the comments discussed above concern generic transformations; critics often debated the flexibility of generic categories and forms. Huang broadened their application to refer to all manner of poetic revision.

Huang's more radical transformations of prior verse are most evident in his inventions wrought on allusions to past writings (examined closely in the next chapter). Here I first examine how Huang Tingjian addresses his Northern Song contemporaries and *their* revisions and extensions of pre-Song verse. His manipulations of these poems give a sense of the subtlety with which Huang read his fellow poets and how he inserted his presence into the contemporary literary scene.

On Su Shi's Poems Rhyming After Tao Qian	跋子瞻和陶詩
When Zizhan was banished to Lingnan,	子瞻謫嶺南
The Minister wished to kill him.	時宰欲殺之
Having his fill of Huizhou food,	飽喫惠州飯
4 Su meticulously followed the rhymes of Tao Qian's poems.	細和淵明詩
At Peng Marsh: a man of a thousand years;	彭澤千載人
At the Eastern Slope: a gentleman of one hundred generations.	東坡百世士
Although their backgrounds differ,	出處雖不同
8 In style and manner they do resemble one another.[19]	風味乃相似

5/ In Jiangzhou, where Tao served as commandant.
6/ In exile in Huangzhou, Su Shi adopted the name "Su of East Slope."

The main purpose of this poem is to praise Su Shi as a man and as a poet. Huang offers his highest compliment in the parallelism of lines 5 and 6, whose equation of Su and Tao seems to confirm the success of Su Shi's project to copy the rhymes of Tao Qian's poems. Still, beneath this message an undercurrent of manipulation disallows easy identifications.

Already in line 2 of the poem, we see traces of that mediation. Huang does not simply praise Su Shi; he borrows from another poet's praise of yet another poet to do so. The line is from Du Fu's poem on Li Bo, "No Recent News of Li Bo" 不見:近無李白消息:

It's long since I have seen Mr. Li;	不見李生久
His feigned madness is truly lamentable.	佯狂真可哀
The men of this generation all wish to kill him;	世人皆欲殺
4 My mind alone enjoys his talent.	吾意獨憐才
Quick-witted: a thousand poems.	敏捷詩千首
Floating and drifting in a cup of wine.	飄零酒一杯
To the Kuang Hills where he read books as a youth,	匡山讀書處
8 White-haired now, he may return.[20]	頭白好歸來

Huang's appropriation of Du Fu's phrase seems inappropriate. Du Fu's claims that the world would condemn Li Bo to death is sheer hyperbole and calculated to complement the tone of a poem praising a poet known for his hyperbole. After a brief tenure, Li was driven from a post in the Hanlin Academy in 744; the causes are not known, but the court's conservative literati were known to be disdainful of and discomfited by Li Bo's verse and manner. Du Fu refers to this attitude as the source of Li Bo's disfavor and not to a political intrigue in which Li Bo may have participated.[21]

In contrast, Su Shi's exile to Huizhou in Lingnan resulted from his strong and vocal opposition to Wang Anshi's reforms. The "minister" in Huang's poem is Zhang Dun (1035–1105), a staunch member of Wang Anshi's clique, an enemy of Su Shi's, and at the time governor of Lingnan. Huang's allusion thus copies Du Fu's hyperbolic tone, but Du Fu's tone of mock seriousness now becomes emphatically ironic.

Equally significant is that Huang's use of the line turns his poem praising Su Shi into one in which Huang himself is explicitly inscribed. The equation of Su and Tao Qian in lines 5 and 6 now becomes a backdrop against which two more important pairings are articulated—Du Fu praises Li Bo; I praise Su Shi by inventing on the words of Du Fu. To transfer praise bestowed on a famous figure of the past to a contemporary is hardly unusual; crucial here, however, is the way it makes Huang's identification with Du Fu stand alongside the ostensible topic of the poem, Su Shi's identification with Tao Qian.

Ren Yuan suggests that line 3 also alludes to a couplet by Du Fu: "If only in my diminishing years I could have my fill of food; / I would only wish that there be no business to attend to, and that we might long look at each other."[22] Again, Huang makes visible his ironic twisting of the original lines: whereas Du Fu wished for enough food, Su Shi has too much "foreign" food at his place of banishment; whereas Du Fu looks toward the peace of retirement, Su Shi can only "enjoy" the free time borne out of exile. Thus, while seeming to celebrate resemblance, Huang's poem ironically and subtly underscores the *difference* between former and latter poets, and this irony is articulated precisely in the manner in which these prior textual fragments are inserted into the new context of Huang's poem.

This reference to the state of exile evokes Su Shi's famous revisions of Tao Qian's "Five Poems on Returning to the Fields."[23] Both series speak of the hardships of rustic life, the need to work the earth and bring forth one's own sustenance. These poems evince Su Shi's conscious projection of his poetic persona on and against that of Tao Qian. By evoking this series, Huang further solidifies the identification of Su Shi with Tao Qian, but he also maintains the notion that these two poets are only approximately parallel, not identical. The sense that Su Shi is doing something with Tao Qian is always present.

Huang's likening of Su Shi to Tao Qian is further mediated in the closing lines, "Although their backgrounds differ, / In style and manner they do resemble one another." The couplet has many precedents, but it particularly brings to mind the last couplet of the second of Huang's "Two Poems in the Ancient Style Presented to Su Zizhan (Shi)": "Although the talents of the lesser and the greater differ, / In spirit and flavor they will always resemble each other."[24] In this couplet Huang humbly asserts that although he cannot claim equality with Su Shi, their basic spirit is the same. Huang's praise of Su Shi's literary skill and his manner as a man is genuine, but at the same time he never lets the reader forget that it is Huang Tingjian who is shaping this poem of praise—a poem praising Su Shi's emulation of Tao Qian has turned into an extended statement on Huang's position vis-à-vis these poets.

But this baring of mediation should not surprise us: Huang is, above all, praising Su Shi's transformation of Tao Qian's poetry. Su Shi's identity is not seen as fused with Tao Qian's (if so, how could he be visible?); rather, it is his use of Tao Qian's poems that is remarkable. What we have, then, is another pairing of Song poets with famous predecessors—Tao Qian and Su Shi, Du Fu and Huang Tingjian; yet what is remarked on is not equivalence, but difference. It is not so much that Su Shi and Huang resemble Tao and Du as that they become identified by their particular uses of them, uses that avoid repetition precisely because they emphasize invention and revision.

The next series also shows how Huang inscribes himself into the narration of another's experience in a poem written to the rhymes of Su Shi's "Guo Xi Paints the Autumn Mountains Level and Distant" 郭熙畫秋山平遠. Su Shi's poem reads:

The Jade Hall was closed during the daylight, I spent the spring at leisure.	玉堂晝掩春日間
In the midst of the hall there was a painting by Guo Xi of mountains in the springtime:	中有郭熙畫春山
Sounding pigeons and baby swallows beginning to rise from sleep,	鳴鳩乳燕初睡起
4 White waves, green peaks, are not of the mortal world.	白波青嶂非人間
Rich and abundant, on this short scroll there opens up a level and distant scene.	離離短幅開平遠
Vast and distant, the sparse groves convey the autumn evening.	漠漠疎林寄秋晚
It exactly resembles the time in Jiangnan when I was seeing off a traveler.	恰似江南送客時
8 In the midst of the stream I turned to gaze at the cloudy cliffs.	中流回頭望雲巘
At Yichuan the old man out of office has temple hair the color of frost.	伊川佚老鬢如霜
Now he reclines and looks at the autumn mountains, thinking back on Luoyang.	臥看秋山思洛陽
For him I make these lines of draft script to append to this painting:	爲君紙尾作行草
12 Bright and clear as the floating autumnal glimmerings off Mount Song and the Lo River.	炯如嵩洛浮秋光
I followed you in wandering, it seemed like a whole day;	我從公遊如一日
I didn't sense the green mountains casting their shadows on my yellow hair.	不覺青山暎黃髮
Paint for me the Dragon Gate of Eight Jointed Shoals,	爲畫龍門八節灘
16 Then I'll wait until I can buy a house in the mountain streams of Yichuan.²⁵	徒向伊川買泉石

Huang's poem is "Rhyming After Zizhan's 'Guo Xi Paints the Autumn Mountains Level and Distant'" 次韻子瞻郭熙畫秋山平遠:

At that time the traveler banished to Huangzhou had not yet been bestowed the jade token summoning his return.	黄州逐客未贈環
In Jiangnan and Jiangbei he saw his fill of mountains.	江南江北飽看山
In the Jade Hall he reclined before a painting by Guo Xi	玉堂臥對郭熙畫

4	And was inspired to think he was already within verdant groves.	發興已在青林間
	Guo Xi's academy paintings are only of desolate and distant scenes.	郭熙官畫但荒遠
	This short scroll, bent and curled, opens to a late autumn scene.	短紙曲折開秋晚
	Streaks of rain bright beyond the misty village by the river:	江村烟外雨腳明
8	By lines of returning geese, a surfeit of tiered mountains.	歸雁行邊餘疊嶬
	Somehow, because of this, he thought of golden oranges in the Dongting frost,	坐思黃柑洞庭霜
	And lamented that he could not follow the sun like those geese.	恨身不如雁隨陽
	Now Guo Xi is white haired, but he still has keen eyes:	熙今頭白有眼力
12	He can still handle a brush by the window's light.	尚能弄筆映窗光
	May his painting seize a scene of Jiangnan on a fine windy day.	畫取江南好風日
	To comfort this hair about to turn old in the mirror.	慰此將老鏡中髮
	It's just that Guo Xi is willing to paint only when the process is leisurely;	但熙肯畫寬作程
16	In ten and five days, a single river and one stone.[26]	十日五日一水石

As with most "rhyming after" poems, this one by Huang borrows the theme, structure, and much of the narrative and imagistic elements of its predecessor. Su Shi's poem begins by correlating real time with the time of the Guo Xi painting he views in the Jade Hall. The next couplet again matches what Su Shi perceives outside the painting with what he sees in it, but here the line between reality and representation is blurred. It is clear that Su Shi cannot perceive the sounds of the pigeons and swallows in the painting itself, but it is not clear whether he is, after correlating the spring scene in the painting with the spring scene outside the hall, noting the birds outside the hall or projecting the vision of the birds onto the imaginary landscape of the painting. Or he could be doing both at once. It is only at the end of line 4 that we have a clear designation that situates an image, albeit negatively and eminently abstractly—Su Shi tells us that the waves and peaks are "not of the mortal world."

In line 5, he continues to focus on the topic of Guo Xi's painting, but this time the specific painting has changed; Su is no longer gazing at Guo Xi's spring scene, but at an autumn landscape.[27] This sudden rupture in time sweeps away the spring scene without warning and complements the poet's meditation on the swift passing of time and his efforts to stall it. In contrast to the relatively detailed observation of elements in Guo Xi's spring scene, here we have only the vaguest of references to the contexts of the autumn painting—the scene depicted in the painting almost immediately recedes before the image it awakens from the shadows of Su Shi's memory.

As in the first quatrain, Su Shi correlates the scene in the autumn painting with his own world, but here it is with the world of the remembered past, not the viewed present. Significantly, Su first notes that the painting recalls not a spatial vision but a temporal one: "It exactly resembles the time...." Only after saying that does he reveal the image in the painting that prompts this memory—the cloudy cliffs. This memory, expressed in lines 8 and 9, replaces both the real scene of the present moment and the scene depicted in the painting. Line 10 recuperates the disjuncture of time sensed in line 6; the poet indicates that the present season is now autumn, and we are led to re-read the opening of the poem (the viewing of the spring painting during spring) as a distinctly distant memory. A more vivid memory has occurred to Su Shi—the memory of Wen Lugong.[28] Su Shi has artfully manipulated our sense of time by setting up a series of temporal "sites" that become stabilized only with the conjunction of memory and person, of dream and reality.

This is not a poem of art criticism per se; it includes only fragments of the conventional "poem on painting"; no mention is made of the art of the painting or its finer attributes, or, most important, the manner in which the painting reflects the character of the painter. Guo Xi simply does not appear in the poem at all. Rather, it is the power of fine paintings to recall past times and to make time static that is of importance to Su Shi, as they become a link between him and his absent friend. The poem ends with Su Shi asking his friend for a painting to compensate for their separation.

Su correlates the value of landscapes real and depicted directly with the emotions they evoke, but by the end of the poem it almost seems as if he declares that the painting is at best only a provisional compensation for the absence of the thing itself. Despite its ability to provide the illusion of transcending time, the poet realizes the illusory nature of the painting—he must be in the mountain streams of Yichuan and be with Wen. But the sad irony of his earnest insistence on fulfilling that dream is that he is still in exile and must resign himself to "mere" representations.

Huang's poem grapples with similar questions of representation. It opens by retracing Su Shi's situation and links it to the theme of landscape viewing: because Su was still in exile, he took in so much of the scenery of Huangzhou. He then speaks of Su Shi's viewing Guo Xi's spring painting and follows Su Shi's correlation of real scene and painting. But Huang does not even lightly touch on the actual painting; instead he projects a vision of what he imagines Su Shi felt at that moment. In this he has conspicuously expanded that section of Su Shi's poem in which Su imagines what Wen is thinking; this project becomes a major subtext for Huang's poem.

The blurring of the line between painting, the vision it evokes through association, and the "real" world of the viewer is particularly heightened in the Northern Song, but here Huang goes beyond remarking on the fusion of reality and imagination; he is both replacing Su Shi as the mediating point of view and directly evoking one of the primary tenets of Guo Xi's aesthetics.[29] In fact, one could say that imagination (Huang's projection of self into Su's mentality) takes precedence over reality, albeit only to succumb to reality at the end of the poem. With this double movement, Su Shi seems eclipsed.

Guo Xi felt that superior paintings would lure viewers to want to "dwell" midst their scenes: "Having no access to the landscapes, the lover of forest and stream, the friend of mist and haze, enjoys them only in his dreams. How delightful then to have a landscape painted by a skilled hand! Without leaving the room, at once, he finds himself among the streams and ravines."[30] By evoking Guo Xi's aesthetics, Huang is doing more than simply mentioning an aspect of the paintings; he is drawing forth the underlying premises of the works, the mind of the painter, and the calculated effect the painter wished to achieve. Again, as we saw in the previous chapter, the affective power of art is foremost in Huang's mind.

Line 6, which, like line 6 in Su Shi's poem, moves from the spring painting to the autumn painting without warning or preparation, describes the painting itself. Huang's choice of details from the painting are explicit indexes: Huang states that "because of" the misty village and the lines of returning geese in the painting Su Shi was led to think of his own village and wish that he, like the geese, could return. But there is nothing of this in Su Shi's poem. Su's poem operates on the basis of a private set of symbols that are visible to the reader only insofar as the logic of Su Shi's poem indicates their function. Huang had no recourse to these symbols or could only use them secondhand; instead he relies on a likely stock image, the misty village, and literary allusions, again showing the qualitative difference he is drawing between his poem and Su Shi's experience.

In his annotation on this poem, Ren Yuan notes that the *Shu shi* (History of calligraphy) by the celebrated Northern Song calligrapher Mi Fu (1051–1107) records a Tang copy of a couplet by Wang Wei: "I would offer you three hundred tangerines, but the frost not yet descended, I cannot obtain many," and that the Tang poet Wei Yingwu played on this: "As a postscript I want to inscribe three hundred tangerines. / At Dongting I will wait still longer for the groves to be filled with frost." The image of returning geese also is extremely common; the sentiment they evoke is found, for example, in Du Fu's "Climbing the Pagoda of the Temple of Compassion with Various Gentlemen": "You look at the geese following the sun, / And you too have the plan to return to the rice paddies and bridges."[31]

It is in drawing on these common allusions that Huang's attempt to approximate Su Shi's response shows the difference between the two poems. Huang cannot be Su Shi; he cannot adapt Su's psychological point of view any further than he has. Huang can rely only on shared poetic discourse and the aesthetics of landscape painting at the moment when Su's private and particular memories are at work in the original poem.

Huang then adopts an alternative strategy in "following" Su Shi. As in all "rhyming after" poems, the latter poet must inscribe himself in the second poem and make his creation primary, at least as primary (i.e., "original") as the convention allows. Huang breaks off from Su Shi and his poem and turns to the person most conspicuously absent from Su Shi's poem—Guo Xi. By focusing on his own "relationship" with Guo Xi (i.e., both his citation of Guo's aesthetics and the fictional address to Guo Xi), Huang is able to bypass Su Shi, having extracted what he could from the original poem: the theme of the effects of great painting and, in particular, the ability of art to stall the passing of time.

Huang again draws directly from Guo Xi's discussion in the *Linchuan gaozhi* about the relationship of painting and poetry:

It has been said by the ancients that poetry is a picture without form, and painting is a poem with form. Philosophers often discoursed on this topic and it has been my guiding principle. In my leisure hours, therefore, I often perused the poetry of the Tsin [Jin] and T'ang dynasties as well as the modern, and found that some of the beautiful lines give full expression to the inmost thoughts of men's souls, and describe vividly the scenery before men's eyes. Nevertheless,

Extending Verse

unless I dwell in peace and sit in leisure, with windows brightly cleaned, the desk dusted, incense burning, and ten thousand worries drowned and subdued, I am not able to get at the mood and meaning of beautiful lines, think excellent thoughts, and imagine the subtle feelings described in them.[32]

By choosing this last image, Huang has explicitly drawn the connection between himself and Guo Xi, between poetry and painting, even tighter, while cleverly using the allusion to Guo Xi's statement on the relationship of poetry to painting to comment in turn on his own poem on a poem about a painting. Huang then urges Guo Xi to make a painting of a scene of Jiangnan, Huang's home, that might serve him as Guo Xi's autumn painting served Su Shi. This will allow Huang to occupy a place alongside Su Shi, as a parallel poetic voice and as another viewer of painting.

Like Su Shi, Huang notes the approach of old age, but unlike Su, Huang again turns to the resources of the poetic tradition for precedents: Han Yu has the line "White hair suddenly fills the mirror," and Li Bo, "Don't you see in the bright mirrors of the Exalted Hall, a grieving for white hair, / In the morning like black silk, in the evening turning to snow?"[33] Huang closes his poem with yet another allusion; the line comes from the first quatrain of Du Fu's, "A Song Playfully Inscribed on Wang Zai's Landscape Painting":

> In ten days he paints one river;
> In five days he paints one stone.
> A real master won't allow himself to be hurried.
> Wang Zai was only then willing to leave behind true traces.[34]

Guo Xi's son also mentions his father's deliberateness: "Some years ago, I saw my father paint one or two pictures. Sometimes he put them away for ten and twenty days at a time, unfinished. As I think back on the matter, probably this was because he did not feel disposed to do them." Guo Xi himself cites these very lines of Du Fu to describe his method of painting.[35] With this accretion of allusions to both prior poems and biographical information on Guo Xi, we sense that unlike Su Shi's piece, which appears as a comparatively private and self-reflective poem, Huang's bares, and even revels in, its mediated nature. It is as if Huang were declaring his difference from Su Shi along these particular lines.

In this interesting moment, Huang seems to confront the poet he is following: at first he seeks to identify with Su Shi, to take on his point of view; then he gradually abandons this tactic and energetically attempts to take precedence over what preceded him. His area for ascendancy is precisely the space left open by Su Shi—a direct link with the painter Guo Xi.

This poem offers a particularly clear insight into the various levels of Huang's poetics of appropriation. His re-vision of Su Shi's poem evinces Huang's careful balance of lyricism and craft; he takes on the tone of Su Shi's poem but clears a space for his own voice, which emerges distinctly in its unique revision of Su Shi's poem in Huang's own particular discourse.

Continuing Du Fu

Although one can identify Huang's use of prior verse by tracing the source of an allusion or paraphrase (although this itself does not guarantee that Huang was making explicit use of that particular source), it is more difficult to trace his equally pervasive evocation of larger structures—individual poems or subgenres. The next poem is both a response to a specific poem and to a type of poem popular in the late Northern Song.

Honoring prior greats often took the form of poems inspired by gazing on their portraits; poems that took as their subject portraits of Du Fu were especially popular. In these poems latter-day poets often called forth their affinity to Du Fu; Huang, however, insisted on differentiating himself from Du Fu in the act of praising him. This becomes clear when we compare a poem by Huang Tingjian on Du Fu's portrait with one by Wang Anshi. First, Wang Anshi's poem: "On Du Fu's Portrait" 杜甫畫像.

As I gaze on Shaoling's poems,	吾觀少陵詩
I esteem them as equal to Primal Breath.	謂與元氣侔
His power can push open Heaven and revolve the Nine Lands;	力能排天斡九地
4 His valiant countenance and resolute expression cannot be sought.	壯顏毅色不可求
Vast and expansive, in the midst of the Eight Extremities,	浩蕩八極中
Living things, how can they not be dense and multifarious?	生物豈不稠
The ugly and beautiful, the great and tiny, a myriad differentiations.	醜妍巨細千萬殊
8 In the end, none could see by what means Du Fu carved and engraved them all.	竟莫見以何雕鎪
Alas! What a poor fate!	惜哉命之窮

Extending Verse

Turned back and overturned, not sought for proper service;	顛倒不見收
In the clothing of a commoner he grew old and was dismissed.	青衫老更斥
12 He walked half of China in hunger;	餓走半九州
His emaciated wife prostrate before him; his son falling dead behind him;	瘦妻僵前子仆後
Seizing and stealing, bandits and robbers, a dense forest of battle picks and lances.	攘攘盜賊森戈矛
Chanting and singing in such times,	吟哦當此時
16 Still he did not abandon his concern for the court.	不廢朝廷憂
He constantly wished that the Son of Heaven might become sagely,	常願天子聖
And that each of the great ministers might be as the Yi Governor or the Duke of Zhou.	大臣各伊周
He would rather suffer his own dwelling alone be destroyed, and that he freeze to death,	寧令吾廬獨破受凍死
20 Than the naked people of the four seas be cold in the soughing wind.	不忍四海赤子寒颼颼
In suffering difficulties, mourning and grieving for themselves only,	傷屯悼屈止一身
Alas, I am ashamed of the men of my time.	嗟時之人我所羞
Thus, seeing your image	所以見公像
24 I pay obeisance and tears gush forth.	再拜涕泗流
Even in antiquity those whose hearts could match yours were rare.	推公之心古亦少
I wish to raise you up from death and follow you in your wanderings.³⁶	願起公死從之遊

Huang's poem is "On Du Fu's Portrait at Wanhua Stream" 老杜浣花谿圖引.

The Completioner drifted into the City of the Brocade Bureau.	拾遺流落錦官城
His old friend was governor then, his eye pupils showed for Du.	故人作尹眼為青
To the west of Cyan Fowl School he built a thatched hut;	碧雞坊西結茅屋
4 In the deep pools of one hundred flowers he washed his cap strings.	百花潭水濯冠纓
His old clothes not yet mended, the new ones already rent;	故衣未補新衣綻
Vainly coiled in his breast, ten thousand volumes of books.	空蟠胸中書萬卷

Probing into the Way, he wished to cross before Fu Xi's era;	探道欲度羲皇前
8 In discoursing on his poetry, one never senses that the Airs of the States are distant.	論詩未覺國風遠
Shields and battle picks, high and precipitous, darkened all the world;	干戈崢嶸暗宇縣
At the Du Mound and Wei Bend there were no chickens or dogs.	杜陵韋曲無雞犬
His aged wife and offspring, all before his eyes;	老妻稚子具眼前
12 His younger brother and sister cut adrift; fallen away, unable to see each other.	弟妹飄零不相見
This lord, happy and easy, truly was a man of model nature.	此公樂易真可人
The old garden gaffers and the friends of rivulets were willing to be his neighbors.	園翁溪友肯卜鄰
When a neighbor had wine, he went whenever he was invited.	鄰家有酒邀皆去
16 Fish and fowl came and took him as an intimate,	得意魚鳥來相親
Boarding a wine boat on Wanhua Stream, I set my carriage horse to wander.	浣花酒船散車騎
By the wall in the wilds there is no master to look after its peach and plum;	野牆無主看桃李
His sons Zongwen and Zongwu preserve and support the household.	宗文守家宗武扶
20 In the descending sun a lame donkey rises bearing the drunken man,	落日蹇驢馱醉起
He yearns to hear the news to unfasten the saddle and take off the battle helmet;	願聞解鞍脫兜鍪
This old scholar has no use for the Marquis of Ten Thousand Households.	老儒不用千戶侯
24 At that time the Central Plains had not yet received news of peace.	中原未得平安報
In drunkenness he furrowed his brow over the myriad sorrows of the state.	醉裏攢眉萬國愁
On raw silk cloth, spread out on the wall, flecks of ink fell down.	生綃鋪牆粉墨落
All his life, loyal and patriotic, today his image is solitary and desolate.	平生忠義今寂寞
28 The son cries out but the father does not awake, the donkey loses its footing.	兒呼不蘇驢失腳
The man seems afraid that after waking there will be new things to write about.	猶恐醒來有新作

It constantly compels poets to pay obeisance to the portrait,	常使詩人拜畫圖
To boil the glue to mend the string: in all antiquity there have been none.³⁷	煎膠續絃千古無

1/ Du Fu's "Chun ye xi yu" (Enjoying the rain on a spring night; Du Fu, 798) relates his sojourn in this city. Located in Sichuan, the city took its name from the fact that it was the seat of the Bureau of Brocade. After the An Lushan rebellion, Du Fu served in the capacity of Left Completioner. See also Du Fu's poem "Bu ju" (Divination; Du Fu, 729).

2/ Du Fu's friend Yan Wu was an official in the Brocade City at that time.

3/ Du Fu's poem "Xi jiao" (The western suburb; Du Fu, 779) tells of his wanderings around that locale.

4/ This line combines Du Fu's location (Wanhua Stream) with an allusion to the "Yu fu" (Song of the fisherman) in the *Chuci* (*juan* 8, 110): "When the Canglang waters are clear I wash my hat-strings in them. / When the Canglang waters are muddy, I can wash my feet in them." Hawkes (91) explains: "This song is also found in the *Book of Mencius*. Tasselled hat-strings were a badge of official rank. The meaning is that you should seek official employment in good times, and retire gracefully when times are troubled."

5/ From the old *yuefu* ballad, "Yan ge xing": "My old clothes, who will mend them for me? / For new clothes, who will sew them?" (see Ding, *Quan Han Sanguo Jin Nanbeichao shi* 4.7b-8a).

6/ This refers to Du Fu's famous lines, "Reading books I break through ten thousand volumes, / And when the brush descends it is as if it were possessed of spirit" ("Twenty-two Rhymes Respectfully Presented to the Elder Councillor of the Left, Mr. Wei"; Du Fu, 73).

7/ Before the time of the legendary Fu Xi, men lived together in perfect harmony, acting virtuously with complete spontaneity.

8/ The "Airs of the States" are the *feng* poems of the *Classic of Poetry*.

9/ Du Fu has the line "You know that Heaven and Earth are full of shields and lances," in "Ye wen bili" (At night, listening to the Tartar pipes; Du Fu, 1941). Compare "Shields and battle picks still not settled. / My younger brother and sister, what has happened to each?" in "Qian xing" (On banishment; Du Fu, 750).

10/ Areas south of Chang'an where Du Fu once lived.

13/ From the *Liji* ("Miscellaneous Records," second section); the term *ke ren* refers to one who is worthy of emulation.

15/ "Every time the farmers invite me, I go; / When a neighbor asks me, I never tarry" ("Han shi" [Cold meals]; Du Fu, 806).

16/ This image draws from the famous and much-alluded-to parable in the *Liezi* (2.6a, section 2) of a young man who every morning went to the seashore to play with the gulls, who came to him naturally and without fear. This image is adapted in Li Bo's "Minggao ge song Cen Zhengjun" (A song of Mount Minggao, sending off Cen Zhengjun; Li Bo, 506). The final couplet reads, "The white gulls come flying, / They have long taken you as intimate."

18/ "It is not that the peach and plum I planted with my own hands have no master; / At the bottom of the wall in the wilds there still is a house" ("Jueju manxing jiu shou" [Casually inspired quatrains], first of nine; Du Fu, 788).

19/ Du Fu has two poems on these men who resided near Wanhua; see, e.g., "Zongwu shengri" (Poem on Zongwu's birthday; Du Fu, 1477).

20/ This describes the scene in the painting.

22/ A common way to refer to one who has no use for official title and responsibility.

The most striking difference between Wang Anshi's and Huang Tingjian's poems is the explicit presence or absence of the latter-day poet's voice. Wang takes care to make his presence felt—he is everywhere in the poem, calling out his appreciation of Du Fu. Indeed, in the last image, Wang assumes the full responsibility and power for reviving Du Fu; this particular allusion to the *Liji* even suggests that it is up to Wang to decide whom he should bring back to life.

In Huang's poem, however, Huang's presence is mostly felt in its absence. Only in line 17 does his voice whisper faintly—his image flickers briefly before us but then disappears, giving way to narrative fragments loosely yet consistently strung together. This hiding of poetic voice could be taken in two ways. If we take it as an act of modesty, we could say that Huang is conveying his admiration for Du Fu in the most honest and effective way possible: Huang is letting Du Fu speak for himself. But there is, as nearly always with Huang Tingjian, another way to read this modesty.

The last six lines form a rather horrific vision. The father refuses to wake from his drunken slumber, even as his son cries out. The poet would rather remain asleep, no longer wishing to witness the turmoil and sorrow of the world around him. For all the proliferating echoes of Du Fu, echoes that impress the reader in their sheer abundance and dominance of Huang's poem, we now have only a choked silence, and it is into this void that Huang steps. This theme of silence is foreshadowed in Huang's enigmatically brief appearance in line 17. Huang inserts himself into Du Fu's topos precisely to note that Du Fu is gone—there is no "host" to watch over the trees that Du Fu planted with his own hands. By implication, Huang is now heir to that function.

In the final quatrain, Huang again suggests that he might continue Du Fu's role. The image of fabricating glue to "mend the string" refers to a magical glue made of the horn of a unicorn and the beak of a phoenix. An ancient king was once given this glue as a gift to repair a bowstring. He then asked each of his chief ministers to try to break the string; when none could, it was taken as a sign that the state would remain unified. Most significantly, Du Fu has the lines, "The horn of the unicorn, the beak of the phoenix, none of this generation can discern their use."[38] In the late Tang, Du Mu (803–52) appropriated this image to refer to the lineage of poetic talent. In a poem praising Han Yu and Du Fu, he lamented that there was no one to continue their legacy: "There is no one who knows how to mix the glue to mend the string."[39] Huang plays with this last symbol in particular—the word translated as "mend" has the primary meaning of "to continue, to carry on." He would mend the string, re-form a continuity that has been lost, and make Du Fu's presence once again whole.

The image of the string made whole presumes, of course, that it has been broken, and this draws our attention to the even more famous breaking of another kind of string and to another kind of silence—the story of Bo Ya, who broke the strings of his lute after the death of his close friend Zhong Ziqi.[40] Bo Ya believed that since his friend was dead, there was no one in the world who could understand and appreciate his music. Bo Ya chose silence rather than play for a world that could not understand his music. The implication of the oblique allusion to this story in Huang Tingjian's poem might be that in the end Du Fu too chose silence; no one could understand his poetry and what it embodied (as is emphatically stated in Wang Anshi's poem). By mending these strings, the strings of Du Fu's "lute," Huang is saying, "Raise your song again, or I will raise it for you; you have someone who understands your verse."

Huang's poem makes a claim for the latter-day poet similar to that made in Wang's poem: both men both would cast themselves in the role of continuer of a lost voice, but Huang's claim is modestly muted (but nonetheless absolutely present) by the object of praise—Du Fu. Huang's poem shows a subtler grasp of the issue of poetic predecessors and a more conscious exposition of the problematic than Wang's poem. By "stringing together" these citations, and granting a particular poetic cohesion to them in the narrative logic of his poem, Huang has transformed the elements of the subgenre to make a comment on the relationship between emulation and composition, and the creation, citation, and perpetuation of poetry.

On Mortality and Poetic Talent

We may trace Huang's transformation of specific prior poems and more general references in another series, wherein Su Shi writes on a poem by Li Bo, and Huang Tingjian in turn writes on both Su Shi's and

Li Bo's poems. First, Li Bo's poem:

A Poem on Being Moved by Autumn at the Palace of Purple Extremity in Xunyang 潯陽紫極宮感秋作

From where do I hear the sound of autumn? 何處聞秋聲
Flapping, fluttering: bamboo by the north window. 翛翛北窗竹
Circling, dispersing: a mind for all antiquity. 迴薄萬古心
4 I try to seize them, but they do not fill one's cupped hands. 攬之不盈掬
Silently sitting, gazing on the horde of marvels. 靜坐觀衆妙
My feelings expansive, I stand alone in pleasurable seclusion. 浩然媚幽獨
White clouds come from the southern hills, 白雲南山來
8 And come to lodge beneath my eaves. 就我簷下宿
Lazily, I follow Scholar Tang's prediction, 嬾從唐生決
Too shy to inquire about Ji Zhu's divinations. 羞訪季主卜
My forty-nine years were full of mistakes, 四十九年非
12 Once they left they could not be made to return. 一往不可復
My mood in the wilderness gets increasingly easygoing, 野情轉蕭散
Life's way has its ups and downs. 世道有翻覆
Tao Qian returned; 陶令歸去來
16 The wine of the rustic household ought to be ready now.⁴¹ 田家酒應熟

3/ The term *huibo*, translated as "circling, dispersing," is used specifically to refer to the turnings of fate, the movement of time. For example, the *Su wen*, "Great Discourse on the Regulation of the Five Constancies," has the lines, "The Great Void unimaginably empty, / The Five Movements circle and disperse in it." Pan Yue's (247–300) "Qiu fu xing" (Rhymeprose on autumn; *WX* 13.192) has the lines, "The four seasons are sudden in their alternation; / The myriad phenomena scatter as the seasons circle and disperse."

10/ The "Biography of Cai Ze" in the *Shiji* (79.2418) tells that Scholar Tang (Tang Ju) predicted that Cai would live to be forty-three. Cai, a wealthy but ignorant man, left off studying and devoted himself to enjoying his time on earth. Ji Zhu is also noted in the *Shiji* (127.3216) as a diviner who made predictions in the eastern market of Chang'an.

11/ The *Huainanzi* ("Yuan dao xun") says, "Qu Boyu went into his fiftieth year and recognized the mistakes of his forty-ninth year."

Su Shi's poem is "Matching Li Bo" 和李太白.

Preface: Li Bo has a poem entitled "A Poem on Being Moved by Autumn at the Palace of the Purple Extremity at Xunyang." What was once the Palace of Purple Extremity is today the Daoist Monastery of Heavenly Blessing. The Gentleman of the Way Hu Dongwei presented me with a stone-cut rubbing of the poem; most likely it was cut by his teacher Zhuo Qi. Mr. Zhuo possessed the Daoist art of Regulating Purity. The stone passed through the hands of others, today it has been lost.

Extending Verse

Li Bo's poem goes: "My forty-nine years were full of mistakes, Once they left they could not be made to return...." I am now also forty-nine, and am moved by these lines. Therefore I have followed the rhymes of Li Bo's poem.

One name for Jade Fungus is Grass of the Jade Fields. Hu Dongwei planted some about seven or eight years ago, saying, "In a few more years they will be able to be eaten." Perhaps he left them behind for me, and thus I record this account of them along with this poem.

I lodge in the empty, silent hall;	寄臥虛寂堂
The moon's radiance drenches the sparse bamboo.	月明浸疏竹
Cool and breezy, it washes clean my mind.	泠然洗我心
4 I wish to drink, but cannot cup the waters.	欲飲不可掬
In the flowing radiance I give out a long sigh.	流光發永歎
From former times it has not been that I have been alone;	自昔非余獨
But at forty-nine,	行年四十九
8 I've returned here, lodging by the north window.	還此北牕宿
I think fondly of the man of the Dao, Mr. Zhuo,	緬懷卓道人
White-headed, he lived as a physician and an augurer of the universe.	白首寓醫卜
The Banished Transcendent must certainly be far away!	謫仙固遠矣
12 This gentleman also is hard to bring back.	此士亦難復
Life's way is like a chessboard;	世道如奕棋
Change and transformation do not yield to being covered.	變化不容覆
Only should the Jade Fungus grow old;	惟應玉芝老
16 I'll wait for the peaches of immortality to ripen.⁴²	待得蟠桃熟

preface/ "Jade Fungus" refers to a fungus that was thought to give long life; its properties are recorded in the *Shi Zhou ji* (Record of the Ten Islets).

3/ The term "cool and breezy" appears in the *Zhuangzi*: "Lieh Tzu [Liezi] could ride the wind and go soaring around with cool and breezy skill, but after fifteen days he came back to earth" (trans. Watson, *Chuang Tzu*, 32). The commentary on the Buddhist Canon, the *Yiqiejing yiyi* provides another reading for the term: "'Cool and breezy' carries the meaning of sudden enlightenment." Here Su Shi is playing with the fusion of Daoist and Buddhist usages.

6/ Compare Tao Qian (p. 11), "Ting yun" (Lingering clouds), lines 29–30: "How could it be that there have been no others? / Yet I remember you the most fervently."

12/ Su Shi is playing on two of the meanings of the character *fu*: "to cover," "to defeat." Wang Wen'gao cites a tale about the Jian'an poet Wang Can. Wang came upon a man playing go with a "fixed" set. Wang played him and defeated him. The man didn't believe that Wang could have beaten him, so he covered the chessboard with a handkerchief and insisted that Wang play him again on another board. Here Su Shi says that change and transformation are not easily concealed (covered over), or defeated. Su Shi may also be drawing on Du Fu's fourth "Autumn Meditation": "They say that Chang'an is like a chessboard: / In a hundred years the matters of the world have yet to surpass this sorrow. / All the mansions of royal retainers and princes have new lords: / Those in civil and military caps and garb differ from old times" ("Qiu xing," Du Fu, 1489).

16/ A "flat peach." As the fruit of immortality, it is associated with the goddess Xi Wang Mu. It lends its name to a festival in honor of the deity.

Huang Tingjian's response is "Following Su Shi's Rhyming After Li Bo's 'A Poem on Being Moved by Autumn at the Palace of Purple Extremity in Xunyang,' Cherishing Li Bo and Su Shi" 次韻子瞻和李太白潯陽紫極宮感秋詩韻懷太白子瞻.

I cannot see the Two Banished Transcendents;	不見兩謫仙
For a long time I think fondly of sheltering myself under the tall bamboo.	長懷倚脩竹
Pacing around the Palace of Purple Extremity,	行邀紫極宮
4 Bright pearls fill cupped hands.	明珠得盈掬
All their lives others wished to kill them,	平生人欲殺
Glorious and great, they received a unique fate.	耿介受命獨
If those who are gone can be brought back to life;	往者如可作
8 I would come holding a blanket and lodge together with these two.	抱被來同宿
The Pillar of Mount Di examines the collapsing billows;	砥柱閱頹波
If one has no doubts, then why divine?	不疑更何卜
One need only gaze on the autumn of grasses and trees,	但觀草木秋
12 Their leaves fall, but their roots naturally restore them.	葉落根自復
I have been in discomfort these twenty years;	我病二十年
Long has the Great Dipper been unconcealed.	大斗久不覆
I rely on it to pour a cup for Messrs. Su and Li;	因之酌蘇李
16 The crabs are fat; the festival wine fully brewed.⁴³	蟹肥社酒熟

4/ Ren Yuan (*Shi, nei* 17.2a) suggests this refers to Du Fu's lines, "With what fills my grasp, why is it necessary to have the pearls of the Watchet Sea? / What has entered my bosom has its roots in the Jade of Mount Kun." Du Fu has in his grasp a letter from a friend; he is saying that it is more precious than pearls, and comes from something more wondrous. The poem is "Mu qiu Wang Pei Daozhou shouzha . . ." (The letter written by Wang Pei in late autumn from Daozhou is so fine that it makes me forget about eating; I bestow this poem respectfully on the censor Mr. Su; Du Fu, 2016).

6/ The term "glorious and great" comes from the poem "Encountering Sorrow," lines 30–31: "Glorious and great were those two, Yao and Shun, / Because they kept their feet on the right path" (trans. Hawkes, 24.) Huang couples that allusion to an allusion to the *Zhuangzi*: "Of those that receive life from the Earth, the pine and cypress alone are the best—they stay as green as ever in winter or summer. Of those that receive life from Heaven, Yao and Shun alone are best—they stand at the head of the ten thousand things" (*NHZJ* 2.32a–b; trans. Watson, *Chuang Tzu*, 69).

9/ Mount Di is a famous symbol of permanence and steadfastness amid turmoil and change; cf. Liu Yuxi (772–842), "The world agitates like collapsing waves, / My heart is like the Pillar of Mount Di."

10/ This may refer to the "Divination" poem of the *Chuci*, which tells of Qu Yuan's visit to the diviner Zheng Zhanyin. He asks what amounts to a set of rhetorical questions:

> Is it better to risk one's life by speaking truthfully and without concealment,
> Or to save one's skin by following the whims of the wealthy and highly-placed?
> Is it better to preserve one's integrity by means of lofty detachment,
> Or to wait on a king's mistress with flattery, fawning, and strained, smirking laughter?

Zheng replies,

> My lord, for one with your mind and with resolution such as yours,
> The tortoise shell and the divining stalks are really unable to help.

(Trans. Hawkes, 89–90.) The motif had a more recent poetic expression for Huang in Wang Wei's "Song you ren gui shan ge" (A song seeing off a friend returning to the mountains), first of two: "I vow to take leave of office to follow you: / How is this something Zhanyin could divine?" (Wang Wei, *Wang Youcheng ji* 1.4b) The *Zuozhuan* (Duke Huan, eleventh year) also has the lines, "Use a diviner to decide uncertainties; if one is not uncertain why divine?"

12/ This plays on the *Laozi* (16.1; trans. Lau, *Lao Tzu*, 72):

> I do my utmost to attain emptiness;
> I hold firmly to stillness.
> The myriad creatures all rise together
> And I watch their return.
> The teeming creatures
> All return to their separate roots.
> Returning to one's roots is known as stillness.
> This is what is meant by returning to one's destiny.
> Returning to one's destiny is known as the constant.
> Knowledge of the constant is known as discernment.
> Woe to him who wilfully innovates
> While ignorant of the constant.

13/ Ren Yuan (*Shi, nei* 17.2b–3a) notes that Huang wrote his "Fa yuan wen" (Piece on setting forth my intent) in which he vowed abstinence from wine and meat about twenty years before composing this poem.

14/ The "Record of Astrology" in the *Sui shu* tells that if the Northern Dipper's stars are hidden, there will be a good harvest of grain; if they are not, then the crop will not be bountiful. Ren Yuan (*Shi, nei* 17.3a) says that Huang is in effect saying that if his large wine dipper is covered over, he is paying attention to drinking and guaranteeing a good grain harvest; if the dipper is not covered, then he is not paying attention to drinking. Kurata Junnosuke (214) says simply that if the dipper is uncovered, then the poet is not paying attention to keeping it spruced up and clean for use; if he leaves it uncovered, then he is not thinking of drinking.

Su Shi has turned Li Bo's poem into a specifically Daoist vehicle, blending the occasion (receiving both the stone-cut print of Li Bo's poem and the herbal plant from Hu Dongwei) with the circumstances surrounding his relationship with the donor (a Daoist Master) and the place (a Daoist monastery). Su Shi takes both gifts (the print of Li Bo's poem and the plants left behind) and combines them in his poem.

Su Shi's failed attempt to cup the lunar rays and mists refers obliquely to another poem of Li Bo's, "A Parting Bequest for the Collator Shuyun at the Xie Tiao Lodge in Xuanzhou," and its famous image of futility and fatalism: "Drawing out a knife to cut the waters, the waters flow even more swiftly. / Raising a wine cup to dispel sorrow, sorrow only becomes more sorrowful."[44]

Su's third quatrain begins by addressing the carver of the stone print, Mr. Zhuo, who is paired with Li Bo. Su Shi brings out their metaphysical affinities by using the name taken by Li Bo, the "Banished Transcendent" (a Daoist transcendent banished to the mortal world after committing a celestial crime), to name them both. But the irony of this reference is that Li Bo is no longer on the earth; neither is Zhuo. The stage is cleared; Su Shi remains alone. He cannot bring these men back from the flow of time, any more than he can cup the rays of the moon, any more than Li Bo could relive his forty-ninth year to correct his mistakes. But where Li, on realizing this, returns to enjoy the rustic life and imbibe the village wine (suggested in the evocation of Tao Qian in both Li Bo's and Su Shi's poems), Su Shi tries a Daoist alternative—ingesting life-prolonging drugs and herbs.[45]

The fact that Su Shi has "inherited" two things is important, for these two objects complement each other. The poet hopes that the plant (and the peaches of immortality) will help prolong his life, if not grant him immortality. But this hope is undercut by the loss of the only concrete image of permanence: the stone on which Li Bo's poem was carved. This stone, which would hold the words of Li Bo safe against the workings of time, has inexplicably disappeared, slipped through the hands of men.

Huang's poem takes up these meditations on permanence and transitoriness. In Huang's version, the poet *is* able to grasp something, but it is neither the shadows cast by a bamboo nor the rays of the moon. He holds "bright pearls," which, through a prior poetic usage in Du Fu, represent the *poems* left behind by Li Bo and Su Shi—the embodiments of the men who are absent.

Here Huang's argument becomes most acute: he points out the truth that Li Bo and Su Shi seek to question or evade—time cannot be stalled or denied by those things to which Li and Su cling. The image of Mount Di symbolizes the only constancy there is—the understanding that all things rise and collapse—a constancy referred to later in line 12's allusion to the *Laozi*. But the image of collapsing billows recalls a line in Li Bo's "Ancient Airs," no. 1: "Yang [Xiong] and Ma [Sima Xiangru] aroused the collapsing billows."[46] Huang thus incorporates images of the collapse and the resurrection of poetic talent and twists the words of *Laozi* to fit this vision. The "pearls" alone can effect what Su Shi's medicinal herbs cannot. Huang has effectively made poetry the only means of thwarting time.

His final quatrain plays on the vain attempts to grasp something present in the first quatrains of all three poems. As noted, the dipper has a double reading; it is both a literal instrument and the name of a constellation. Huang cannot use the constellation to pour his libation to Li and Su, for it is a dipper in name only.[47] This illusion sets the stage for Huang's ultimate debunking of Su Shi's belief in Daoist transcendence. He caps his poem with a wonderfully skeptical response to Su Shi's closing image. Su Shi waits for the peaches of immortality to ripen, for the magical fungus to be ready for consumption. He leaves the poem in the posture of a Daoist adept waiting for the arts of immortality to fulfill their promise. Huang, on the other hand, shifts the reference to the fruit of immortality from the transcendent to the everyday. The peaches have been brewed into wine for the festival and are to be consumed along with fatty crabs.[48] The magic of the peaches has been stripped away; now they are only indications of a quaint belief and are, if nothing else, eminently *material*. As with the names of constellations, simply calling the peaches "immortal" will not make them so.

We can better understand this closure if we understand how Huang ultimately draws on a poem that is in the background of all three poems.

Nineteen Poems in the Ancient Style, no. 13

I sped my carriage to the Upper East Gate;	驅車上東門
In the distance I gazed at the tombs north of the walls.	遙望郭北墓
In white poplars, how desolately the winds blow.	白楊何蕭蕭
4 Pines and cypresses border the wide road.	松柏夾廣路
Below there are those long dead;	下有陳死人
Secluded and dim, passing the eternal dusk.	杳杳即長暮
Sinking in sleep beneath the Yellow Spring;	潛寐黃泉下
8 In a thousand years, never waking.	千載永不寤
Rippling like waves, the Yin and Yang elements alternate;	浩浩陰陽移
But man's allotment of years is like the morning dew.	年命如朝露
Life is sudden, but a sojourn;	人生忽如寄

12 Longevity lacks the stability of metal and stone.	壽無金石固
For a myriad years one man has sent another man off to these tombs.	萬歲更相迭
Even sages and wise men, none can escape.	聖賢莫能度
Imbibing drugs, seeking to become a transcendent,	服食求神仙
16 Many have been misled by these potions.	多爲藥所誤
Better to drink fine wine;	不如飲美酒
And clothe oneself in fine white silks.⁴⁹	被服紈與素

    1/ The northernmost of the three eastern gates outside Luoyang.
    2/ A cemetery on Mount Beimang, north of Luoyang, the burial ground of many Eastern Han figures.
    3–4/ The poplar, pine, and cypress were planted beside graves.

Jean-Pierre Diény notes that this poem follows the structure of a rhetorical demonstration.[50] We find a similar structure in Huang's poem. Huang turns away from Su Shi's brief indulgence in Daoist notions of immortality and back to the carpe diem spirit of the *original* poem—Li Bo's. But Huang does not repeat Li Bo; instead he fuses both Li's and Su's poems in his own and draws out the ancient precedent for both poems.

The poems analyzed above reveal the attention Huang paid to writing within the literary world of the Northern Song. In these poems, he displays his ability to address his contemporaries wittily and to rise to the challenge of answering them within the poetic discourse of the time—he shows he can transform and extend contemporary and ancient poetry and construct a signature from and on the words of others. Next we will look at how Huang used the atoms of poetic language—words themselves and allusions to prior discourses—in like fashion to make a place for himself within the tradition.

FIVE

Words and the Shaping Will

In the preceding chapters, I examine Huang Tingjian's appropriation and extension of critical and poetic discourse to suit his poetic project. By borrowing the rhetoric of traditional poetics and its aesthetics, Huang validated his untraditional revisions of poetic material; by appropriating conventional forms and specific poems, he explored ways to manipulate and extend those enunciations to distinguish himself from other poets. In this chapter and the next, I examine Huang's investigation of the power of the poetic word and some of his characteristic stances toward language, for it is here that the theoretical underpinnings of Huang's transformations are best revealed. Huang argues against the weighty dust of readings that deaden language, against *chen yan*, words that have lost their power to evoke meaningful responses, and seeks to reinvigorate language through many methods. In particular I examine how Huang sought in his poetics to approximate the workings of Spirit Cinnabar.[1]

Huang's poetic language is characterized by a constant doubling of reference, at once focused on prior articulations and aimed at twisting words to imbue the poem with semantic values often at odds with their original significances. Huang both traces the etymologies of words to use primary and recondite meanings and ironizes conventional readings. By pointing up the gap between prior readings and his own constructions, Huang identifies himself as both revisionist and poet.

Instead of believing in the possibility of *creating* poetic language, Huang invents the spectacle of poet after poet grasping and manipulating the words of others to speak his mind. Huang Tingjian never lets language rest, never accepts the notion that the word is anchored absolutely by either its original or its accreted meanings. By freeing the word from any absolute and unchanging origin (in his claim that not even the great poets *originated* poetic language), Huang frees it for appropriation. Nevertheless, this liberation gives rise to vertigo, for now words are open to a wide range of articulations—they may be made to say a number of things, with no chance of appealing to an authorizing and stabilizing "nature."

Late Northern Song poetry often openly questions the nature of language, as in this poem by Su Shi on viewing the stars:

Traveling at Night, Observing the Stars	夜行觀星
The heaven is high, the night vapors sternly chill.	天高夜氣嚴
The arrayed constellations, dense and clustered, take their positions.	列宿森就位
The rays of the greater stars shoot out to one another;	大星光相射
4 The smaller stars are as tumultuous as spume.	小星鬧若沸
Heaven and Man do not interfere with one another.	天人不相干
Alas, in what are they rooted?	嗟彼本何事
Common men strain to point out and choose—	世俗強指摘
8 One by one they set up names:	一一立名字
The Southern Winnowing Basket and the Northern Dipper.	南箕與北斗
Now these are household tools fashioned by man;	乃是家人器
How can the heavens also have them?	天亦豈有之
12 Is it not that men call them what they will?	無乃遂自謂
Closely observed, does one really know what they are like?	迫觀知何如
Imagined from afar, perchance there is a resemblance.	遠想偶有似
So vast, it cannot be comprehended,	流流不可曉
16 It brings me to sigh long and deep.[2]	使我長歎喟

In borrowing his conceit from poem no. 203 of the *Classic of Poetry*,[3] Su Shi turns its whimsical notion into a sustained speculation on the relationship between metaphoric naming and the realm of knowledge and on naming as an act of will. This focus on the human will to name and thereby apprehend the natural world is signaled in Su's substitution of "man" for "Earth" in the conventional dichotomy Heaven and Earth.

Here the central problem is the nature of knowledge—How does one come to know things? "In what are they rooted?" The answer "language" only raises the question "What are words rooted in?" and its concomitant "What effect does our will to name have on the nature of our knowledge of ourselves and of Nature?" These questions inform my

Words and the Shaping Will

discussion of Huang's poems in this chapter, for they both legitimize Huang's play with language and destabilize the game being played.[4]

The Trap of Convention

One text that illustrates these issues is Huang's long poem "Elaborating on the *Erya*." Huang edited this poem out of his collected works himself, and it has largely been ignored by both Chinese and Western critics.[5] It has, however, been the subject of a number of Japanese studies, many of which Arai Ken catalogues and assesses in his article on the poem.[6]

Arai, Ōno Shusaku, and Ogawa Tamaki all focus on the last quatrain, finding in it an image of Huang's "transcendence" of self, of his projection of self onto the natural world.[7] I see the poem in exactly the opposite manner—for me, it betrays a deep skepticism and wariness regarding poetic language, which is connected to the impossibility of transcending self. Rather than escaping into Nature, the poem seems to illustrate the way in which we mark nature with our desire to name, classify, and allegorize—to see ourselves projected on nature, and to see nature only through our tropic activities. Most important, it shows the strength with which words and representations are anchored in conventional modes of interpretation. The poem may be read as a serious extension of some of the concerns noted in Su Shi's poem, and as such, it helps illuminate a central characteristic of Huang's poetry and poetics.

"Elaborating on the *Erya*" is a long, complex "mosaic" (an image employed by all three Japanese critics) of allusions. To obtain a full sense of its nature, one must read the poem with all its allusions, in its entirety.

Elaborating on the Erya 演雅

The silkworm, making its cocoon, winds it around itself;	桑蠶作繭自纏裹
Spiders weave webs, artful at intercepting their prey.	蛛蝥結網工遮邐
When swallows have no homes, they begin building hastily.	燕無居舍經始忙
Butterflies are enticed to destruction by the glimmerings of the wind.	蝶爲風光勾引破
An old crane takes a stone in its mouth and stops up the water to take a drink.	老鸛銜石宿水飲
Tiny bees hurry to congregate and gather the levy of nectar.	稺蜂趁衙供密課

	The magpie transmits auspicious words; how can he find leisure?	鵲傳吉語安得閑
8	Roosters press the morning's rise; daring not to lie down.	雞催晨興不敢臥
	Its vital energy surpassing a thousand *li*, a fly will attach itself to a swift horse.	氣陵千里蠅附驥
	Spending its entire life in vain, an ant revolves on a millstone.	枉過一生蟻族磨
	Even as the lice hear the bath boiling, they drink blood;	蝨聞湯沸尚血食
12	Sparrows, happy when palaces are constructed, congratulate each other.	雀喜宮成自相賀
	In the clearing morn the happy mayfly shakes its wings.	晴天振羽樂蜉蝣
	In a hollow cave a wasp prays for offspring to make into its own.	空穴祝兒成螺蠃
	The dung beetle rolls shit into balls and looks down on rose storax.	蛣蜣轉丸賤蘇合
16	A flying moth alights on a candle, willingly accepting its demise.	飛蛾赴燭甘死禍
	When there are spoiled plums by the well, it means that the grubs are terribly fat.	井邊蠹李蠐苦肥
	Drinking dew from the tips of branches, the cicada is constantly hungry.	枝頭飲露蟬常餓
	Moles hide in cracks in walls and record the speech of men.	天螻伏隙錄人語
20	The Archer holds sand in its mouth, waiting for shadows to pass.	射工含沙須影過
	When the Xungu pecks on the roof, it is setting ominous and bizarre things in motion.	訓狐啄屋真行怪
	When a long-legged spider reports pleasure, it greatly multiplies good fortune.	蟢蛸報喜太多可
	The cormorant stealthily spies on the fish and frogs taking their repose.	盧鷀密伺魚蝦便
	The white egret cannot withstand the taint of dusty earth.	白鷺不禁塵土涴
24	When did crickets ever know about weaving?	絡緯何嘗省機織
	The Grain Spreader doesn't have to be diligent at planting or sowing.	布穀未應勤種播
	The flying squirrel, mastering the Five Skills, laughs at the pigeons' clumsiness.	五枝鼯鼠笑鳩拙
28	The hundred-footed centipede pities the turtle's lameness.	百足馬蚿憐鼈跛
	In the embryo of an old oyster, the pearl is a thief.	老蚌胎中珠是賊

Words and the Shaping Will

How vast the sky for a gnat in a wine jar! 醯雞甕裏天幾大
The mantis stops in the wheels' ruts angrily stretching 螳蜋當轍恃長臂
  out its arms;
32 The bright Night Walker boasts of its shining flame. 熠燿宵行矜照火
The Gourd Raiser is yet able to order wine. 提壺猶能勸沽酒
The Golden Mouth only knows to covet its feed. 黃口只知貪飯顆
People don't question the loquacious shrike; 伯勞饒舌世不問
36 But once a parrot starts to speak they shut it up. 鸚鵡纔言便關鏁
In spring the frogs and in summer the cicadas get even 春蛙夏蜩更嘈雜
  more clamorous.
But earthworms and bookworms, how indistinct they 土吲壁蟫何碎瑣
  are!
The waters of the plains of Jiangnan are bluer than the 江南野水碧於天
  sky.
40 In their midst an old familiar gull at leisure seems just 中有白鷗閑似我
  like me.[8]

1/ Compare Bo Juyi, "The silkworm winds its cocoon around itself," in his poem "Jiangzhou fu Zhongzhou zhi Jiangling yilai zhouzhong shi shedi wushi yun" (Going from Jiangzhou to Zhongzhou, I arrived by boat at Jianglu and showed my younger brother these fifty rhymes; Bo, 374). By beginning this long poem with a citation of Bo Juyi, Huang draws a link to Bo Juyi's series (see below).

2/ Ren Yuan (*Shi, nei* 1.7b) claims this alludes to a story from the *Lüshi chunqiu* ("Tang zhu gang"), which says that "a spider making its web leads men to imitate it." Arai Ken (*Kō Teiken*, 55) says it alludes to the *Lunheng* ("Xing mai pian") of Wang Chong (27–ca. 91), which draws an analogy between the web of a spider and the strategies of man.

3/ For "begin building," see *Classic of Poetry*, no. 242: "He planned and commenced the Divine Tower, he planned it and built it; the people worked at it, in less than a day they achieved it" (trans. Karlgren, *Book of Odes*, 197).

4/ Compare Du Fu, "When shadows touch the cyan waters, the depths of the pools are enticing," from "Feng yu kan zhouqian luohua xi wei xinju" (In the wind and rain I look on the falling flowers before my boat and playfully make these new verses; Du Fu, 2050). Also, Bo Juyi, "Enticing the spring winds, emotions without limit," in "Yangliu zhi ci" (Lyric on the willow branch; Bo, 849).

5/ Ren Yuan (*Shi, nei* 8a) cites passages from both the *Bowu zhi* and the *Ben cao* that portray this water bird gathering stones to surround its eggs and warm them. If the weather grows hot, it adds cool water to the enclosure. It also gathers water to make mud for its nest.

7/ Magpies are thought to be auspicious birds.

8/ Roosters are sometimes referred to as "commanding the morn" (*si chen*).

9/ From the *Hou Han shu* 80.3: "The fly cannot wing it past ten paces, but if it attaches itself to a swift horse it can make a thousand *li* in a day."

10/ From the *Jin shu* ("Tianwen zhi"), which has a parable of an ant on a millstone trying vainly to move in the direction opposite to that of the millstone.

11–12/ From the *Huainanzi* ("Shuo lin xun"): "When a bath is prepared, the lice console each other; when a tall building is set up, the swallows congratulate each other." The term "drinking blood" originally referred to the offering of ritual sacrifices to the gods. Both Arai (*Kō Teiken*, 55) and Kurata (44) say that the term here connotes defiance in the face of death.

13/ The mayfly is born in the morning and dies that evening.

14/ The *Fayan* (Model words) tells of the wasp that seized a silkworm larva and took it into its nest in a hollow log. It then prayed for seven days; the larva was transformed, and the wasp claimed it for its own offspring.

15/ In his annotation to the *Zhuangzi* ("Qi wu"), the Jin dynasty commentator Guo Xiang says that "the intelligence of the dung beetle resides in its ability to roll shit into balls, and those who laugh at the dung beetle prize rose storax" (rose storax is a gum derived from the *Liquidambar orientalis* tree).

17/ From *Mencius* 3B.10: "K'uang Chang [Kuang Zhang] said, 'Is Ch'en Chung-tzu [Chen Zhongzi] not truly a man of scruples? When he was in Wu Ling, he went without food for three days and as a result could neither hear with his ears nor see with his eyes. By the well was a plum tree, more than half of whose plums were worm-eaten. He crept up, took one and ate it. Only after three mouthfuls was he able to hear with his ears and see with his eyes'" (trans. Lau, *Mencius*, 115).

19/ The notes of Recluse Tao (Tao yinju) to the *Ben cao* claim that moles often were found in the walls of prisons. Prisoners would give the animals scraps of food. These animals, possessing a special spiritual ability, could understand human speech.

20/ Many sources have accounts of the Archer (*she gong*). It is variously a turtle-like creature, a toad, or an evil spirit (poem no. 199 in the *Classic of Poetry* calls it a *yu*). It lurks by the banks of rivers and ponds. It takes sand into its mouth, and when the shadow of a passing traveler falls on it, it spits the sand at the person, killing him. A paradox in this legend makes it all the more magical—according to the *Shuowen jiezi*, the Archer has no eyes and only senses the footsteps of the traveler with its sharp ears.

21/ The *Xunhu* is a bird of ill omen. Compare Han Yu's poem "Shooting the Xunhu," which tells of the bird casting its black shadow on the poet's roof.

23/ Arai (*Kō Teiken*, 56) and Kurata (44) gloss *ci* and *bian* together as "waiting for its chance."

26/ The name for crickets literally means "reeling in a woof" and refers to the sound of their chirping. The Grain Spreader is the cuckoo. Qian Zhongshu (*Tanyi lu*, 6) notes that the play on words of these two lines is found first in the poem no. 203, "The Great East," of the *Classic of Poetry*, which closes with sixteen lines that play on names (see note 47 to Chapter 4), and was used as well by Su Shi in "Traveling at Night, Observing the Stars."

27/ The Five Skills mastered by the flying squirrel are flying, alighting on branches, swimming, burrowing, and walking.

28/ This line alludes to the "Qiu shui" chapter of the *Zhuangzi*:

The K'uei [Kui] envies the millipede, the millipede envies the snake, the snake envies the wind, the wind envies the eye, and the eye envies the mind.

The K'uei said to the millipede, "I have this one leg that I hop along on, though I make little progress. Now how in the world do you manage to work all those ten thousand legs of yours?"

The millipede said, "You don't understand. Haven't you ever watched a man spit? He just gives a hawk and out it comes, some drops as big as pearls, some as fine as mist, raining down in a jumble of countless particles. Now all I do is put in motion the heavenly mechanism in me—I'm not aware of how the thing works." (*NHZJ* 6.21b–22a; trans. Watson, *Chuang Tzu*, 183)

30/ From the "Tianzifang" chapter of the *Zhuangzi*: "Confucius said to Yan Hui, 'My understanding of the Way, how does it not resemble the gnats in a wine jar? If it were not that the Master opened my jar lid, I would certainly not know the great completeness of Heaven and Earth'" (*NHZJ* 7.35a).

31/ "Renjian shi" chapter of the *Zhuangzi*: "Don't you know about the praying mantis that waved its arms angrily in front of an approaching carriage, unaware that they were incapable of stopping it? Such was the high opinion it had of its talents" (*NHZJ* 2.21a; trans. Watson, *Chuang Tzu*, 62).

32/ Another name for a glowworm. Compare poem no. 156 in the *Classic of Poetry*: "Brilliant is the glow worm—it is not to be feared, it is to be loved." Karlgren notes, "It might look frightening, reminiscent of the will-o-the-wisp, which is an emanation from the blood of killed men; but it is only a harmless creature, symbolic of peace and rest at home" (see Karlgren, *Book of Odes*, 102).

34/ Ren Yuan (*Shi, nei* 9a) cites the story from the *Kongzi jiayu*: "Confucius saw a group of netted birds, all of them small yellow-beaked swallows. He said, 'The larger swallows are good at taking warning and are thus hard to capture; little swallows covet their food and thus are easy to trap.'"

35/ Arai Ken (*Kō Teiken*, 57) cites the "Discourse on Inauspicious Birds" by Cao Zhi, which claims that the shrike bears bad news.

36/ For the allusion to the parrot, Arai (*Kō Teiken*, 57) refers to the "Jiaoliao fu" (Rhymeprose on the tailor bird) by Zhang Hua (232–300). The *Wen xuan*'s note to the *fu* says, "[The parrot's] nature is contentious, and it is able to speak. People shut it up in engraved cages" (*WX* 13.201).

It is difficult to make sense of this poem. Attempts to read it as an allegory fail because there is no unified allegorical subtext; the poem is rather a series of illustrations of separate points, couched in more or less independent parallel couplets.[9] The poem uses the rhetoric of allusion and allegory, yet the result is a confusing catalog of seemingly unrelated observations.

Huang's poem draws on two texts: first, the *Erya* dictionary, which contains entries on animals, insects, and birds that include related parables and beliefs.[10] Huang's poem presents its birds, insects, and animals in roughly the same order as they appear in the *Erya*. Second, Huang's poem has a precedent in Bo Juyi's "Twelve Pieces on Birds and Insects."[11] In his preface to this series, Bo outlines his reasons for composing it:

Many of the parables of the *Zhuangzi* and the *Liezi*, and the similes and allegories of the *Classic of Poetry* borrow insects and birds to be "fish traps" and "rabbit snares."[12] Thus the Six Meanings of the *Classic of Poetry* begin with the poems "*Guan-guan* cry the ospreys" and "Now the magpie has a nest," and the explication of the Way [the *Zhuangzi*] puts a discussion of the *kun*, the *peng*, the cicada, and the *yan* first.[13] These are examples of this type.

Once, when I was living in retirement, roused up by a sudden inspiration, I dashed off twelve pieces to "record wonders" and "speak my mind."[14] Now each one of these pieces might bring about a smile, but they also have something to warn the reader against misconceptions of feeble old age and cranky obstinacy.

Bo Juyi's series was written not only to amuse and instruct but also to explore the use of natural phenomena as tropes in poetry. Their use of natural phenomena as symbols provides a useful way to approach Huang's poem.

Any attempt to find a unified meaning in "Elaborating on the *Erya*" will most likely follow the modern Japanese commentators by focusing on the final image. As noted above, these critics take this image to be a sign of transcendence, an image wherein Huang projects himself onto and into Nature. But what if Huang is signaling not transcendence but rather entrapment? What if we do not ignore the dense textuality of what precedes the final image, but look at this long catalog of animals and birds as documenting our ardent desire to impose our will on the natural world? Natural things cease to simply be; they are now appropriated as illustrations for our purposes and are understood primarily through metaphoric displacements (as Su Shi says, through artifacts). The length and breadth of the catalogue evinces the range and energy of our will to make Nature signify; there seems to be no escaping. The perception of things is mediated by layers of accreted readings, interpretations, and conventionalized usages. Things are not simply themselves but allegorical indexes of human behavior.

All commentators regard the final image as an echo of Du Fu's famous closing couplet:

| Wind-tossed, fluttering—what is my likeness? | 飄飄何所似 |
| Between Heaven and Earth, a single gull of the sands.[15] | 天地一沙鷗 |

This is certainly Huang's source, but how does it relate to what precedes it? If we read the catalogue as preparation for the final image, there is a strong case for reading this final image as a consciously crafted negation of Du Fu's couplet.

Du Fu's analogy is original, striking, evocative. It answers his poem's embedded question: What is Du Fu like? In Huang's poem, the image is exactly reversed. The poet is not compared to the bird; rather, the bird is compared to the poet. The couplet is not a question "What am I like?" It is an assertion that inverts the logic of the simile to make the statement "A gull is like me." This inversion follows the direction of all similes in the poem—natural beings are like human beings, or follow our imaginative projection of our being, in this or that respect. Furthermore, the terms of the comparison are even more specific: the bird is compared to the poet at leisure. But how are we to evaluate that comparison? How "leisurely" has Huang been? The preceding thirty-eight lines may even be taken as evidence of his lack of leisure and his dogged explanation of a mass of natural phenomena in terms of the human mind as evidence of his intent to find meaning, and, specifically, meaning endowed only by its common reference to humans.[16]

Another aspect of Huang's play on Du Fu shows his line's absolute difference from Du Fu's: no one after Du Fu can use that image, or any semblance of it, without evoking Du Fu's analogy. Any comparison of poet and gull automatically recalls Du Fu's line and leads the reader to interpret the passage in terms of this strong poem (perhaps this is why Huang calls the gull "old and familiar"). This underscores one of the central themes of Huang's poem and his poetic theory in general: phenomena are apprehended and understood through the mediation of prior poetic articulations.

All poetic material shows the marks of another; as Huang has said, one cannot "transcend" this condition. His "Elaborating on the *Erya*" is best understood, I think, as an allegory of this condition and Huang's response to it. The final image is indeed the key to the allegory, but it also exhibits the twin of allegory: irony. Although one could argue that the poem is a vision of the universal nature of things, the cosmic correspondences among all phenomena, it is crucial to remember that the unquestionable center of all these reflections is humankind. Humans are no longer seen as being of the same order as other natural beings, able to "learn" lessons from the natural world; rather, the natural world is now a reflection of humanity's shaping vision and achieves significance only through a tradition of naming it and reading it, rather than through any essential ontological link. The following section discusses a number of poems that appear to confirm this reading; poems that reiterate the problem of poetic language, human will, and conventional poetic modes of apprehending phenomena.

Huang Tingjian's Poems on Objects

According to Ōno Shūsaku, Huang's "Elaborating on the *Erya*" is representative of his stance toward objects. Ōno argues that many of Huang's poems on painting exhibit a similar fusion of self with the object of contemplation. Yet, as with the treatment of transcendence embedded in the *Erya* poem, I believe that a number of Huang's poems show the poet's consciousness of his separation from the natural world. Huang's poems on objects (*yongwu*) are justly famous for their display of poetic technique, but other important issues are raised in Huang's attempts to describe objects via poetry. Many of these poems reflect Huang's conception of how poets appropriate natural objects as poetic symbols and the effect of such appropriations on our understanding of the world.

Two key characteristics of the *yongwu* subgenre are that the object of the poem is rarely mentioned directly (the title of the poem names the object, but within the poem itself the object is indirectly suggested through various witty tropes), and this indirect naming is most often conveyed via allusion.[17] What is most interesting in Huang's use of allusion in his *yongwu* poems is how he often turns the subgenre's own conventions against it. Huang's *yongwu* illustrate a verse technique that readily accommodates his use of indirection and allusion and attests to his exploitation of the interpretive conventions of the subgenre.

Wang Chongdao Sent Me Fifty Stems of "Water Transcendent Blossoms"; Our Minds Shared an Appreciation of Them, and Thus I Made This Poem on the Object	王充道送水仙花五十枝欣然會心爲之作詠
Skimming over the waves, the transcendent with Raising Dust slippers.	凌波仙子生塵襪
Atop the waters, nimble and shapely, pacing on the dim moon.	水上輕盈步微月
Who is it who has summoned this bowel-breaking soul,	是誰招此斷腸魂
4 Planted to become a cold flower, lodging utmost sorrow?	種作寒花寄愁絕
Harboring its scent, its body immaculate, ready to topple a citadel;	含香體素欲傾城
The mountain flower is her younger brother, the plum her elder brother.	山礬是弟梅是兄
Sitting across from it, I truly become aroused by its blossoms.	坐對真成被花惱

8 Then, coming out of the garden gate, I laugh at once: 出門一笑大江橫
   the Great Jiang River lies horizontal.¹⁸

This poem conspicuously plays off a quatrain by Du Fu:

On the Riverbank I Pace Alone Searching for Blossoms, 江畔獨步尋花
first of seven

Aroused no end by the flowers on the river, 江上被花惱不徹
No place to tell of this mad turmoil, 無處告訴只顛狂
I went to look for my neighbor to the south, my 走覓南鄰愛酒伴
   companion in loving wine.
He was out drinking for ten days; I found only an 經旬出飲獨空牀
   empty bed.¹⁹

Huang uses more from Du Fu's poem than just its first line; he draws forth the general tone of the entire poem. The beauty of the flowers arouses both poets, but both poems contain an emptying out. In Du Fu's poem it is caused by the ironic frustration of his second search (the first being the search for the blossoms). It is precisely because his neighbor is as fond of drinking as Du Fu that the poet seeks him as an appreciative audience for his recitation of his flower-inspired "madness," but it is also because of their shared love of wine that Du Fu finds only an empty bed—his friend is out drinking just as Du Fu was out searching for blossoms. Du Fu is faced with the realization of his double frustration. He has experienced something that he wishes to share, but the one with whom he would share it is gone.

Huang's poem contains a similar disruption of scene, but although both poems end with an irony, here it brings relief rather than disappointment. The poet emerges from an almost claustrophobic scrutiny of the flowers, whose appearance and scent overwhelm him. The broad expanse of water provides a striking constrast to the minute focus of the poem; the effect of this constrast shocks the poet out of his obsession with the object of his intent, and his quest to represent it in the elaborate language of poetic indirection. This last moment recalls another of Du Fu's poems. Chen Changfang points to the similar structure of Du Fu's "Bound Chickens":²⁰

Poem on the Bound Chickens 縛雞行

The serving maid bound the chickens for sale at the 小奴縛雞向市賣
   market;
The fowl were annoyed by the rope, they struggled as if 雞被縛急相喧爭
   they were in battle.

My family dislikes the fact that the chickens eat the insects;	家中厭雞食蟲蟻
4 Don't they know that once the chickens are sold, they will be cooked?	不知雞賣還遭烹
Why should men favor either the chickens or the insects?	蟲雞於人何厚薄
I yelled at the servant to untie the ropes:	吾叱奴人解其縛
"There is no end to the dispute between chickens and insects!"	雞蟲得失無了時
8 I fix my eye on the cold river and lean against the mountain gallery.²¹	注目寒江倚山閣

Chen notes the sudden change in focus and tone in the final couplets of both pieces, a similar shift of focus that provides a release from the concerns of the poem.

Du Fu's poem is quasi-allegorical, its moral rises to the surface with the declaration of the poet in lines 5 and 6. Huang's poem is an allegory of a different sort. Du Fu, realizing the ceaseless and eternal conflict between things, steps outside the immediate scene and switches his gaze to the expanse of the river and the surrounding landscape; Huang seems to realize he has been involved in a quest to appropriate the natural object as a poetic vehicle, a quest that has "bewitched" him even more than the flowers. Du Fu seeks to liberate himself from the lesson he sees in the dispute of the creatures; Huang becomes aware of his own involvement in constructing the dilemma from which he finally withdraws. Huang's poem thus borrows the rhetorical strategies and poetic language of Du Fu's poem and transforms them into a comment on the act of writing poetry.

As with "Elaborating on the *Erya*," this poem speaks of the manner in which natural objects are appropriated as objects of poets' intents. Although this poem cannot compare in terms of density of allusion with "Elaborating on the *Erya*," one might say that it is not the flowers that have vexed the poet; rather, his effort to describe them has frustrated him, and in his quest for the adequate trope, he is partially identified as the "summoner" of line 3, who ironically has burdened the transcendent blossoms with mortality and metaphor in order to lodge his intent.

The irony of this destructive metaphorization is heightened by the fact that the first couplet derives from a couplet from Cao Zhi's famous "Luo shen fu" (Rhymeprose on the Luo River goddess): "Skimming over the waves, she lightly paces; her gauze slippers raise up dust."²² The poem thus announces itself as a poem about transcendence in direct and indirect ways; yet it proceeds in exactly the opposite direction—

Words and the Shaping Will

toward mortality. The irony is that the flowers are, of course, only natural—their names, bestowed on them by human beings, give a false immortality.²³

The following poem again observes the human projection of mentality on natural objects:

Following the Rhymes of "Appreciating Plums"	次韻賞梅
How does she know that Song Yu is at the neighboring wall?	安知宋玉在鄰牆
Smiling she stands, the clear spring sky shines on the powdered surface, glimmering.	笑立春晴照粉光
Tranquil and quiet, she seems able to know my thoughts.	淡薄似能知我意
4 Secluded, refined, never fragrant for the sake of men.	幽閑元不爲人芳
A faint wind brushes over and gives life to chaste thoughts.	微風拂掠生凉思
A light rain, a slight drizzle, washes her dusky countenance.	小雨廉纖洗暗妝
I only fear that the rain-soaked blossoms will be tossed on the dusty earth,	只恐濃葩委塵土
8 And then who can blend the fragrance to bring back a soul?²⁴	誰令解合反魂香

4/ "Secluded, refined" is a standard term for modest, virginal women.

Huang first charts the poet's awareness of the distinct otherness of the object. He plays on Song Yu's "Rhymeprose on Master Dengtu's Fondness of Debauchery,"²⁵ which tells of a beautiful girl in a neighboring household who once climbed on the garden wall, an act that seemed to the poet to signal her desire for him. Huang first personifies the plum blossoms as the girl and then scoffs at the idea that the flower has any awareness of men. She stands beyond their will, glistening in the spring sky. This is not to say that the flower is insentient; indeed, the flower recognizes the thoughts of the poet, but she refuses to exist for his or any man's benefit.

The next quatrain begins with the poet observing the effect of a light rain on the blossoms and fearing that the rain might knock the blossoms off the branch to fall on the "dusty earth," a term used to denote the mortal world. Huang closes with an allusion to a drug noted in the *Bowu zhi* as capable of resurrecting those dead less than three days. The question is "Who can blend the fragrance to bring back a soul?" This rhetorical question correlates precisely with the query of line 3 of "Wang

Chongdao Sent Me Fifty Stems." Again, the poet is inscribed in the response. He would break the natural cycle of birth and death and restore the fallen blossom to life, but only for his purposes and even after noting that the flower has no desire to be the object of human will.

The poet is put in precisely the role he scoffs at in line 1—a naive Song Yu wishing to attribute his desires to the other, who nonetheless resists this projection of intent. Behind this conventional *yongwu* poem there is an implicit exploration of the philosophical ramifications of the tropic activities at the basis of the subgenre. The manner in which poets describe objects is linked to the human desire to act on nature.

Yongwu poems are supposed to be witty displays of a poet's mastery of indirection and embellishment, observation and invention. These poems reveal Huang fulfilling these requirements while expanding them to probe the presumptions of poetic language. He adapts the subgenre as a vehicle for a philosophical inquiry on the use of the natural object as poetic trope. We view here Huang's interest in how poetic language mediates the perception of the object and in how poets transform the natural world to convey their intent. This has an immediate impact on notions of knowledge and language, for if objects are perceived only through the mediation of language, then that mediation can *de*nature the natural world. Metaphoric transformation *dis*places natural objects, emptying them of materiality. *Yongwu* poems come out of a strong allegorical tradition; Huang's *yongwu* are remarkable meta-allegories that reflect back on their own creation.

The moment that mediation intercedes between subject and object, it gravitates toward greater and greater density and opacity; the object itself may be obliterated, perceivable only as a trope, a token of something else. This state is most extreme in the case of *yongwu* poems that rely on allegory and allusion, but by closely examining others of Huang's poems we can see the wider extensions of this critique.

Old Words and New Contexts

Much of Huang's energy is devoted to detaching words from the sediment of conventional readings so as to reinvigorate them. This often entails using those readings against themselves: the reader is caught in the trap of conventional expectations as Huang reverses direction, ironizes the enunciation, or switches the poem's frame of reference and thereby distorts the perception of the line.

As we have seen, traditional poetics argued against the notion that

Words and the Shaping Will 131

words are locked into one meaning, an argument against the polarity of predetermination. For example, in the *Wenxin diaolong*, Liu Xie notes:

> The *Erhya* was compiled by the disciples of Confucius, and is the lapel and sash of the *Poetry* and *History*.... [It is] the prime source of philological elucidation. ... Those who understand the new by inference from the old are savants in the art of writing.
>
> The meaning of a character changes with the passing of time, as new senses are adopted and old ones are discarded.[26]

Liu Xie here proposes that the meaning of a word is largely determined by use—contingent on the historical use of the word to signify different things. Liu's statement is largely a rhetorical move to allow an account of linguistic change and a rationale for literary invention. But an interesting part of that rhetoric is his adaptation of a famous line from the *Analects*: "He who by reanimating the Old can gain knowledge of the New is fit to be a teacher."[27]

Several later critics adapted Liu Xie's axiom to the field of poetic language. In their hands Liu's observation on the "natural" evolution of language became an endorsement of the willed transformation of poetic material. In this section I focus on Huang's attempts to slough off the effects of the mediation of conventional readings. He counters their power to deaden the vitality of the poetic word with an experiment in expanding the signifying power of the word by placing it in different contexts. As Yokoyama Iseo notes, Huang did not create a new language; rather, he took an established form (verse) and expanded the potential of poetic language by radically altering the contexts into which words were placed.[28]

Huang's transformations of language began at the smallest unit—the word. One technique he learned from Du Fu's verse was the trick of making the "verse eye" (the third character in a five-character line or the fifth in a seven-character line) signify in a number of ways, to call attention to itself and complicate the reading of the line.[29] For example, consider Huang's couplet:

Chang-e leads the Blue Lass by the hand; 姮娥携青女
With a single laugh they brighten the myriad roof 一笑粲萬瓦
  tiles.[30]

(Chang-e is the famous immortal beauty residing on the moon; the Blue Lass is a goddess who brings the frost and snow when she flies over the world in autumn and winter.) The "verse eye" of the couplet is the third character of the second line, *can*. The primary meaning of the word is "bright," and it is specifically linked to the brightness of white teeth; hence it has acquired secondary readings of "fresh" and "laughing." Huang plays on all these readings at once. The goddesses' laughter is sparkling and brilliant, but it is no longer only a synecdoche for the dazzling beauty of the goddesses; it also describes the elements they represent: the moon and its light, and the icy snow. Huang extends the use of the word even further—it functions not only as a retroactive modifier for the goddesses but also as a transitive verb—"to brighten." Again, because of the specific semantic properties of the word, the moonlight and snow both "brighten" and "freshen" the roof tiles. This impediment to an immediate reading of the line causes the reader to linger and to notice the condensation of several meanings and their attendant images in a small space.

Huang expands this technique to entire poems. He has often been criticized for the unconventional structures of his verses—rapid shifts of tone and context, and disruptions in narrative logic.[31] As with his use of the "verse eye," these shifts often impede the smooth reading of the poem and lead to a more complex reading. The following exemplifies Huang's technique of rapid shifts of context.

A Poem Sent to Huang Jifu 寄黃幾復

I live north of the ocean, you live south of the ocean.	我居北海君南海
I regret that it's not possible to use a goose to carry a letter.	寄雁傳書謝不能
Peach and plum in the spring wind: a cup of wine.	桃李春風一杯酒
River and lake in the night rain: ten years before this lamp.	江湖夜雨十年燈
To prop up your house there are but four bare walls;	持家但有四立壁
To cure illness one doesn't need three broken arms.	治病不蘄三折肱
I imagine you reading books, your hair already white.	想得讀書頭已白
On the other side of the stream, gibbons wail amid the vines of the swamps.[32]	隔溪猿哭瘴溪藤

Yokoyama remarks on the "gaps" between conceptual frames, gaps that require a "leap" of reasoning. The first couplet is a good example of this technique at work.

The poem opens with an allusion to the *Spring and Autumn Annals* (the fourth year of Duke Xi): "You, milord, reside to the north of the ocean, and I to the south. [This distance between us] is what neither wind nor horse nor oxen can reach over." Chen Yongzheng says that Huang is only borrowing a rhetorical formula.[33] But this formula had, by Huang's time, become a commonplace. Although the contexts certainly differ,

Huang is clearly borrowing the phrase to draw on the *next* sentence, which argues the tremendous distance between the states and the futility of attempting to wage a campaign across it.³⁴ By rejecting simply a commonplace formulaic borrowing, we can see how Huang is bypassing the phrase's worn-out allusion and exploiting its original context.

The latter part of the allusion then feeds into line 2 of Huang's poem, which draws on another commonplace image: the messenger bird. Critics have praised the second couplet of the poem for reinvigorating stock imagery; here Huang performs a similar act of regenerating commonplace images by combining them in a specific context. The theme of the futility of attempting to communicate via the messenger bird derives greater poetic logic from the use of the allusion to the *Spring and Autumn Annals* and vice versa.

The poet then speaks of his friendship with the addressee of the poem. As in the first couplet, Huang here follows a pattern of opening and closing possibilities—time and distance recede, only to return and erase the illusion of presence. The cup of wine becomes a faded memory recalled alone in the glow of the lamplight long ago shared with his friend.

The second quatrain follows the same pattern as the first. It opens with an allusion to the *Shiji* biography of Sima Xiangru (*juan* 117). After Sima seduced and married the daughter of a host of his, the couple lived in abject poverty, with nothing but "four bare walls."³⁵ The next line calls forth a common adage derived from the *Zuozhuan* (Duke Ding, thirteenth year): before any physician can master his craft he has to have sufficient experience—three broken arms. Here Huang denies that one need suffer hardship to succeed.

This assertion complements the first line of the couplet. Sima Xiangru's father-in-law later relented and took back his daughter and son-in-law; Sima became a famous and accomplished poet. But the logic of the couplet seems slightly skewed. First Huang implies that Huang Jifu will rise above his impoverished condition; then he claims that his hardship is of no use. In other words, Huang Jifu should not accept the popular consolation that poverty breeds loftier verse. The couplet ends up as a sigh of lament rather than an encouragement, and this lament is amplified in the remainder of the poem.

Huang cannot see Huang Jifu; nor has he heard from him. So he projects this vision of his friend, a vision that has not a little of himself in it. He then closes with an image of the miasmal marshes of the south.³⁶ The two quatrains thus follow a similar pattern—first an allusion, then a second allusion that radically modifies the first, and finally an emotional response to the overall theme. By recognizing the similarly complex and ironic use of allusion in the two quatrains, we can better grasp the logic behind the construction of the poem.

Some attribute the difficulty of poems such as this one to Huang's penchant for allusions. But I believe that the difficulty often stems from reading the allusions in a conventional manner, the kind of reading that is second nature to readers well versed in the commonplace allusions of classical poetry. If one ignores the manner in which Huang plays the contexts of the allusions off their conventional reading, one easily misses the logic of his juxtapositions. The "leap" required to bridge the seemingly missing logic stalls the automatic reading of the images and prompts an exploration of the other significances of the words and images. This de-automatization of reading is similar to the effects of Huang's verse eyes. The context and form of Huang's poems guide us against the expected readings to their significance.

Irony

It is clear by now that a chief characteristic of Huang's verse may be partially attributed to a desire to exploit the polysemic nature of language. Just as Huang is interested in stalling the conventional reading of his verse by placing familiar poetic tokens in unusual contexts, he practices an active ironizing of poetic language, the poetic voice, and even the act of reading. He startles the reader's expectations and complicates and enriches the reading of the poem.

The next poem has an uncharacteristic lack of allusion; yet even without source texts to ironize, Huang complicates the subgenre of temple poems by playing on poetic perspective.

On the "Room of Rising Mountain Mists Rippling" of Falling Star Temple, third of four	題落星寺嵐漪軒
The monk of the Falling Star Temple built a small room, deeply secluded.	落星開士深結屋
The Old Man of Dragon Gallery came here to compose his verse.	龍閣老翁來賦詩
A light rain conceals the mountain; the traveler sits there a long time.	小雨藏山客坐久
4 The Yangtze River connects with the heavens, a sail slowly arrives.	長江接天帆到遲
We sit in meditation in pure fragrance, separated from the world.	宴寢清香與世隔

Words and the Shaping Will

The paintings and scrolls are surpassingly marvelous, but no one else knows.	畫圖妙絕無人知
In the beehive each latticed window opens of its own accord.	蜂房各自開戶牖
8 Everywhere the monks brew tea, lighting the brazier with a single vine branch.³⁷	處處煮茶藤一枝

As in many temple poems, this piece speaks of the parallel worlds of the visiting poet and the monks of the temple. During a brief visit, the poet is struck by the isolation and serenity of the place and in them sees his own desire for such peace and the topos that offers it. The first couplet follows this theme in sense and form; the monk's construction of the chamber is immediately paralleled by the arrival of the poet.³⁸

The second half of the first quatrain introduces nature, yet the images are strangely vacant. They appear, but, as with many temple poems, the mind behind the viewing eye is detached from the scene. A light rain conceals the mountain, and the traveler sits for a long time before the landscape; yet even though the two facts are juxtaposed, no specific relation is established between them. The poet seems uninterested in penetrating the rain; rather, he appears satisfied with the vague knowledge that the mountain exists somewhere behind it. In the next line, the Yangtse fuses with the horizon; but this commonplace illusion of unity, like the illusion of the disappearing mountain of the previous line, has no relation to its neighboring image—the slowly moving sail. Again, we do not know why the poet's eye has chosen this object. The point shared by the poet and the boat is their detachment, stillness that coincides with that of Nature.

The opening couplet of the next quatrain underscores this detachment from the world, this lack of involvement in the relationship between what is viewed and what seems to be there. As in the first couplet of the first quatrain, Huang connects the life of the monks and a token of that life with affinities to the outer world. And, once again, the token is aesthetic; this time, it is specifically visual objects: the paintings.

This focus on the visual draws together the imagery of lines 3 and 4 and sets the stage for the closing couplet—one of Huang's most famous. The temple was built against a rocky mountain; the metaphor of the beehive is original and unique. But, as in lines 3 and 4, Huang fuses two images of a different register in the same line. The metaphoricity of the beehive image dissolves into the literal; by a kind of implied synecdoche, the windows both partake of the metaphor that precedes it and move into the real.

But this is not his final move, for Huang then animates those windows, which seem to "open of their own accord." This complex rhetorical process takes us from the metaphorical to the metonymic to the literal, and then to what seems to be a projection of animate sentience on the same object. This complexity shows Huang's mastery of exploiting the power of poetic language in very condensed form and his talent for making words function simultaneously in a number of ways. But it is in the final line that Huang masterfully ironizes all these visions.

The image of the daily life of the monks that closes the poem is a deceptively simple line. Even though we move out of the complexity and richness of the penultimate line, the final line says more than "now they are making tea." Huang carefully underscores the natural ease of the place and its inhabitants—things happen spontaneously and harmoniously; each monk sets about brewing his tea at the same time. Yet the poem ends on a note of quiet regret, for it is clear that even though the quatrain begins with the poet meditating with the monks, he has now left that existence. He could invent the image of the beehive only by viewing the temple from outside; he could know that each window was open only from a perspective at some remove from the temple. He surmises that the windows opened for a purpose, but he can deduce that purpose only from the recollection of a life he no longer shares: the final line is a projection of his imagination informed by his distance from the actual scene. Where in line 5 he joined the monks in their separation from the mortal world, he is now a part of that world. Mo Lifeng notes that not a single line in the poem adheres strictly to prosodic rules, and thus evinces Huang's use of *aolü* (unregulated tonal patterns). As Michael Duke remarks, "Huang's deliberate unconventionality consisted in the creation of what was later called an *aoti* (unregulated style), a deliberate rejection of conventional diction and sentiment, and a passionate search for novelty and strangeness." In this poem we see a fine example of how Huang's poetics use prosodic and imagistic invention to subtly create a subtext; here it is one of alienation and estrangement from the harmonious scene of a temple poem.[39]

The next poem illustrates Huang's penchant for subtly problematizing the premise of a poem in its final lines.

Following the Rhymes of Senior Secretary Gai Leading Senior Secretary Guo to Retire from Office	次韻蓋郎中率郭郎中休官
Your earthly form has completely turned over the thousand transformations,	世態已更千變盡

Words and the Shaping Will

But your mind's fount has not received a single speck of dusty intrusion.	心源不受一塵侵
On a bright day in verdant spring, you have no official business;	青春白日無公事
4 The purple swallow and yellow oriole both have fine tones.	紫燕黃鸝俱好音
You entrust it to your children to observe the days of fullest summer and the winter sacrifice;	付與兒孫知伏臘
While you listen to instruction from fish and birds, and follow their example, pursuing flight and sinking in depths.	聽教魚鳥逐飛沈
Beneath the wine shop at Huanggong, you once knew the flavor of wine;	黃公爐下曾知味
8 Certainly because of this you "retreated into Zen," entering the Shaolin temple.[40]	定是逃禪入少林

This is a poem of high compliment, praising the virtue of recluses wise enough to leave behind the dusty world of illusion and embrace Zen. The parallel couplets are simple and plain, tracing out the oppositions between the world the men have left and the one they have joined.

They have endured much, "exhausted" a thousand fluctuations of fate, yet they have never let a single speck of dust stain their virtue. Their retirement has made it possible for them to enjoy the music of the birds and the clear spring day, and given them the chance to turn their duties over to their children and grandchildren while they watch the seasons pass and follow with their minds the free movements of the fish and birds. This last image is derived from the *Nanshi*: "I am not so far removed from the fish and birds. Fish and birds fly and float, serving their own intents and natures. My advancing and retreating are constantly under my control."[41]

To this point the poem follows the tradition of praise for a rustic recluse—the diction is plain (the only tropes, the conventional "thousand transformations" and "dusty intrusion," are so commonplace as to elide figurativeness), the parallelism neat and uncomplicated. Huang's one bit of syntactic play, inverting the subject-verb order in line 6 (fish and birds fly and sink) is copied from the *Nanshi*. Huang has set the reader up for an ending that summarizes the wisdom the retired official has gained. But we find something more complicated.

The Huanggong wine shop was the site of the drinking bouts of the famous Seven Sages of the Bamboo Grove of the Jin dynasty. The group included Ruan Ji, Xi Kang, and others who set themselves off from the court, drank, composed, sang, and played their lutes. Later Ruan Ji passed through this spot and mourned the deaths of his friends. The topos thus resounds with the ethos of the man of virtue who would rather retire or even die than serve a corrupt court. Pan Boying feels that Gai and Guo realize the transitoriness of life's pleasures because they have passed through the same spot and drank as the Seven Sages did. Reclusion is not enough; Zen is the answer.[42]

Nevertheless, the juxtaposition of the last two lines creates a double image, evolving from the term "retreat into Zen." The primary meaning of the graph *tao* is "escape," and glosses on the term *tao chan* insist that it means to escape *from* Zen, not *into* it. "To get drunk and rebel against this teaching is called 'escaping from Zen.'"[43] Du Fu's poem "The Song of the Eight Immortals in the Midst of Drinking" has the line "Honoring an embroidered Buddha, Su Qin is an avowed vegetarian; / But being drunk, he is often fond of escaping from Zen."[44]

Huang's poem has usually been interpreted as alluding to the Buddhist master Bodhidharma's entering the Shaolin temple after passing through the same spot. As Gai and Guo lead each other out of office and into retirement, so the spirit of Bodhidharma leads them to study Zen. But the primary meaning of *tao chan* stubbornly asserts itself; the pun on the word *tao* as meaning "escape" in contrast to the term *ru* (to enter) is more than a play on words. Its bifurcation of meaning unbalances an otherwise placid poem. The poem would persuade us to accept the alternative meaning of *tao chan* and read it with *ru Shaolin* "enter Shaolin temple," but the drunken Seven Sages' revels and Du Fu's line present a counter, albeit muted and secondary, image. Perhaps all this is sleight of hand, and the poem only lightly entertains this proposed reading. But it is precisely this kind of subtle balancing act that Huang often exploits to imbue his verse with irony and wit.

Huang uses irony to stretch the semantic boundaries of a word, especially in terms of its prior poetic uses and readings. He also expands on irony to reflect on another major concern noted in this chapter—the human desire to control oneself and one's world. Again, in opposition to the assertion that Huang successfully transcends self, we see a deeply skeptical stance regarding such a notion.

An example of Huang's ironic spin on these questions is a piece in which he gently berates a friend for aspirations to asceticism.

Playfully Responding to Chen Yuanyu　　　　　　　　　　　　戲答陳元輿
From what I had heard all my life about Mr. Chen of　　　平生所聞陳汀州
　Dingzhou,

Words and the Shaping Will 139

Locusts wouldn't enter his territory, and every year's crop was abundant and rich.	蝗不入境年屢豐
At the East Gate, when he was presented with his commission, we began our acquaintance.	東門拜書始識面
4 Fortunately our hair had yet to turn into that of old men.	鬢髮幸未成老翁
We officials ate of the same dishes, and soon had our fill of fish and meats.	官饗同盤厭腥膩
Tea cups shattered our sleep, the autumn hall was empty.	茶甌破睡秋堂空
You told yourself that you would no longer dream of moth eyebrows,	自言不復娥眉夢
8 Withered and bland, you would rather be like lesser men.	枯淡頗與小人同
I'm only afraid that when you see the welcome-home smile, a floriate branch will redden.	但憂迎笑花枝紅
Outside the evening window, a cool rain strikes the slanting wind.	夜窗冷雨打斜風
For autumn clothes the aloe wood is exchanged in the basket used for scenting.	秋衣沉水換薰籠
12 Behind the silver screen you turn and turn again.	銀屏宛轉復宛轉
The roots of your intent are as difficult to eradicate as shallot root.⁴⁵	意根難拔如薤本

    2/ The "Biography of Lu Gong" in the *Hou Han shu* (55.4a–11a) relates that Lu Gong ruled by humaneness and virtue rather than by corporal punishment. Bad things naturally stayed away from his land.
    4/ Compare Cao Pi, "Yu Wu Zhi shu" (Letter to Wu Zhi; *WX* 42.591–92): "Goals and intents, when will they again be as in the old days? Already we have turned into old men, it's only that our hair has yet to turn white."
    7/ "Moth eyebrows" is a common metaphor for beautiful women.
    8/ This is a difficult term to translate in this context. It means "withered," "barren," "hollowed out," and is applied to vegetation. Here it refers to spiritual detachment, a sense derived from the *Zhuangzi*: "Can you really make the body like a withered tree and the mind like dead ashes?" (trans. Watson, *Chuang Tzu*, 36)
    12/ Compare Zhang Ji, "Yuanzhuan xing" (To the tune of "Tossing and Turning"; *Quan Tang shi*, 4289): "Tossing and turning, again tossing and turning, memories, memories, still not yet ended."

Chen vows to lead a simple life in the future—no more chasing after women, no more indulgence of vulgar appetites. Huang responds skeptically to Chen's pronouncement and provides an imaginative projection that illustrates the reasons for his skepticism. It is all well and good for Chen to vow abstinence quietly to himself and to his friend, but once Chen returns home, Huang sees him trapped by his desires—in a comic borrowing of erotic euphemism, Huang points to the "reddened branch" unconsciously reacting to the woman's smile of welcome.

The final quatrain echoes late Tang seven-character quatrains: lush, sensual imagery complemented by discrete narrative details. But then the last line of the poem switches to the rhetoric of Zen parable: "roots of intent" refers to the Six Roots of man's physical and mental being—the eyes, ears, nose, tongue, body, and the mind. These are the sources through which we perceive illusions; Huang rebukes Chen's assumption that he can simply deny himself without understanding the depth of his desires. Just as their indulgence in food and drink made it impossible for the men to sleep, so here Huang suspects that Chen is still vulnerable to his sexual appetite and that it will keep Chen trapped in fulfilling his immediate desires.

This is, of course, a playful poem, a gentle chiding of a friend, but the theme of self-delusion, particularly of overestimation of one's control and power, recurs in Huang's poetry with various degrees of seriousness. Huang's poetry is known for the role played by dreams and half-dreams, and I believe that this emphasis stems from his interest in the workings of the mind, specifically, in the problem of will that informs all the poems analyzed in this chapter.

In one poem, Huang writes of a noble man who has decided to retire from officialdom and lead the life of a rustic recluse. Huang details the man's situation—both his moral stature and his poverty.

Rhyming After Zizhan, Sent to Wang Xuanyi of Mount Omei	次韻子瞻寄眉山王宣義
Your children don't have enough to fill their bellies, and yet they still diligently study;	兒無飽飯尚勤書
Your wife has no lined trousers; but she still wears a short jacket.	婦無複褌且著襦
The earthen jar of the village may be filtered and drunk from; the rivulets may be fished.	社甕叮漉溪可魚
4 You inquire if the chicken is fat or skinny.	更問黃雞肥與瘦
Drunk in the forest, you encounter men chopping trees;	林間醉著人伐木
Yet in your dream you think you are in office, hearing the shouts of yamen runners and clerks.⁴⁶	猶夢官下聞追呼

All the attributes of the recluse slip away with the last line—even drunk on the village brew, the recluse's unconsciousness betrays him.

This kind of involuntary response, which belies the rootedness of that aspect of self one would escape from, is found again in "Rhyming After

Words and the Shaping Will

Huang Binlao, Wandering in the Evening by the Pond by the Pavilion," second of two 次韻黃斌老晚游池亭.

In the east garden, isolated and lovely, one may disperse one's sorrows.	岑寂東園可散愁
Confused, in turmoil, my dreaming spirit goes wandering.	膠膠擾擾夢神遊
Ten thousand mouth pipes of bitter bamboo—pennons and flags curled.	萬竿苦竹旌旗卷
A single crying frog, a drumbeat heralding autumn.[47]	一部鳴蛙鼓吹秋

Here again that rootedness of what one would evade is manifested in the metaphors that the poet employs. The natural world—this place that offers solace and peace—is unconsciously metaphorized into synecdoches of worldly flags and drums, symbols of turmoil and stress.

Even monks who have achieved detachment should be wary of slipping back into worldly ways. The following is a poem on a famous painting by Huang's friend Li Gonglin.[48]

On Boshi's Painting of a Monk Gazing at a Fish	題伯時畫觀魚僧
A single net traversing the waves will make the marketplace smell of fish.	橫波一綱腥城市
At dusk the river is empty, the smoky waters cold.	日暮江空煙水寒
Though his mind is already dead to the myriad matters,	當時萬事心已死
Still he fears the fish will look on him with the gaze of former times.[49]	猶恐魚作故時看

The story comes from the *Chuandenglu*, which tells of a monk of Xuansha, surnamed Xie, who was extremely fond of angling as a youth. At age 30, he suddenly became enlightened. He leaped off his fishing boat, shaved his head, and obtained *dharma* at Mount Xuefeng. But Li Gonglin's painting and Huang's poem tell us that he fears the lure of his past affections. One way to read the last line is that the monk worries that the temptation will be too great; another interpretation could be that he fears that the fish will recognize him as an angler at heart, and with their recognition his detachment will be shattered.[50] In either case the poem has strong affinities to the theme we have been speaking of—the issue of self-awareness and the limits of will. In either case, the monk has, somewhere in his mind, a consciousness of the incompleteness of his transformation.

Our tenuous grasp over our actions, the ironic tension between self and self-perception, is also the informing subtext of the next poem. Huang tells of a gallery that he has built and of a gathering of friends.

The basic theme of the poem is ostensibly the enjoyment the men take at the gallery, the rustic pleasure of the monks who live nearby, and the eternal, cyclic patterns of the universe. Huang urges his friends and himself not to worry about mortality, but to seize the day for all that it is worth. Nevertheless, an unmistakable undercurrent of uncertainty is present in the poem, even as Huang raises another goblet of wine.

The Gallery of Pine Winds at Wuchang 武昌松風閣

I built a gallery against the mountain to look on the level river. 依山築閣見平川
As the night wanes, the Winnowing Basket and the Dipper stick into the beams of the building, 夜闌箕斗插屋椽
I came to name it, the name is appropriate to my intent. 我來名之意適然
4 The old pines, the grand *wu* trees, hundreds of years old, 老松魁梧數百年
What the hatchet spared today juts into the heavens. 斧斤所赦今參天
The wind cries on the fifty strings of Queen Wa. 風鳴媧皇五十絃
Since it cleanses the ears, the Stream of the Bodhisattva is unnecessary. 洗耳不須菩薩泉
8 How felicitous that you gentlemen, very fond of worthies, 嘉二三子甚好賢
Exhausted your meager resources to buy wine and let all get drunk here on this mat. 力貧買酒醉此筵
At night the rain cried in the outer hallways, suspended there until dawn. 夜雨鳴廊到曉縣
Looking at each other, we did not return home, but reclined on a monk's blanket. 相看不歸臥僧氈
12 The stream was parched and its rocks dry, now there is again gushing water. 泉枯石燥復潺湲
The mountain stream glimmers, making itself alluring for us. 山川光輝爲我妍
The rustic monk was starving, unable to eat thick porridge, 野僧旱飢不能饘
Yet at dawn one sees steam and smoke by the cold streams. 曉見寒溪有炊烟
16 The Man of the Way of East Slope has already sunk into the Yellow Spring; 東坡道人已沉泉
When will Mr. Zhang be before my eyes? 張侯何時到眼前
At Angling Terrace, startling billows—there one may sleep during the day. 鈎臺驚濤可晝眠
At the Pavilion of Contentment one sees the seal script calligraphy—flood dragons entangled. 怡亭看篆蛟龍纏
20 How can one slough off these bodily shackles? 安得此身脫拘攣

| Let a boat carry these friends to linger long in pleasure.[51] | 舟載諸友長周旋 |

6/ Consort of the legendary Fu Xi, who gave her a lute with fifty strings.
7/ The name of a stream near the gallery.

The poem constructs two different stances. On the one hand, we have the symbols of replenishment—with last night's rain the streams are full again, the monk who went hungry now cooks fish by the riverside. But there are also symbols of exhaustion. This second facet to the poem is implied negatively in lines 4 and 5. The stalwart trees have been there an eternity, yet this longevity is purely conditional and arbitrary—these are trees that happened to be "spared by the hatchet." They may have been spared, ironically enough, from being material for Huang's gallery; their very existence is contingent on an unexplained reprieve that allows them to fulfill another destiny—to provide shade and make a special sound.

Huang goes on to speak about the tones of the wind passing through the trees: this supernatural music makes the stream that flows by his gallery unnecessary—the revelers' "ears" are purified by the wind on these strings.[52] But even these images of replenishment and purification seem unstable. The poet marvels at the fact that things can change overnight, without being bidden to, and yet that very changeability can work in either direction. Even as he observes the signs of the monk by the river, by a strange transfer of association he thinks back on another spiritually enlightened man—his lost friend Su Shi. His place is not by the rivulet where he often visited Huang, but by the Yellow Spring, the land of the dead; the poem was written in 1102, one year after Su Shi's death.

In the next line, Huang wonders when he will see Zhang Lei. In the juxtaposition of these two lines, we may see Huang's anxiety at being separated from another dear friend: Huang wishes to see Zhang Lei *now*. Huang knows this is impossible—Zhang Lei had just been banished to Huangzhou—and the urgency of Huang's desire is understandable in light of his loss of Su Shi, and in the context of this poem on the instability of things.

The rhetorical question opening the final couplet finds an implicit answer in the poet's final line. Since we cannot escape mortality, let's enjoy life while we can. But this bravado is unconvincing—had Huang set up an explicit confrontation with mortality and then defeated it with a strong statement of carpe diem, the last line might be more convincing. But he has instead shown his vulnerability to skepticism by evading his anxieties. The poem moves smoothly—there are no severe disjunctures of logic or imagery—but this effortlessness cannot gloss over the undercurrent of contingency, which lets men starve or feast, live or die. The seeming distance between the monk who last night nearly died of thirst and Huang and his companions who drank wine sets up a false sense of difference. Huang's poem evinces the intelligence behind the effort to elide this condition, an intelligence that senses its own blindness and constructs the poem to reflect that blindness.

Crumbled Texts and Necessity

Ultimately, these questions regarding the nature of language (particularly the manner in which poetic language is constructed and read) and our attempts to exercise our will to know the world and ourselves lead to a questioning of the very status of texts. Huang ironizes his own will to read despite his recognition of the tenuous status of texts and the limits of knowledge derived from them.

Two other late Northern Song poets also address the issue of permanence and texts.

First, Su Shi writes:

In the twelfth month of this year I came to Huzhou on official business. I thoroughly examined [the Hall's calligraphy] and sighed [in appreciation]. Xinlao [Sun Jue] requested that I write an account. Someone said to me, "All phenomena must return to annihilation. And relying on external forms to be durable is particularly hopeless of success. Though it may have the sturdiness of stone and metal, in a moment it turns to ruin. As for an honorable reputation and writings, though they pass to later generations, the only difference is that they last longer. Now to entrust [one's writing's] to [one's reputation] gives long survival. Conversely, to seek aid from that which speedily comes to ruin—this is a misconception of men of old. But Xinlao still builds a deep-eaved, large building to preserve [words on stone and metal]. Drawing the implication, is it not almost [equivalent to saying] that he does not understand fate?" I consider that one who understands fate must complete his tasks as a man, and only afterward will reason be satisfied and he be without regret.53

Second, a poem by Wang Anshi:

Studying Historical Texts	讀史
Since antiquity, accomplishing a reputation has been a bitter and toilsome thing.	自古功名亦苦辛
Engagement and detachment, in the end, to whom do we intend to ascribe it?	行藏終欲付何人

Words and the Shaping Will

These times are murky and indiscernible; there are errors and untruths;	當時黯黮猶承誤
4 For later generations this confusion and fragmentation will be even more chaotic.	末俗紛紜更亂真
Only dregs will be transmitted to them, not quintessential beauty.	糟粕所傳非粹美
What is difficult to convey by means of the brush is the spirit.	丹青難寫是精神
How can these trifling texts completely record the intents of the lofty worthies?	區區豈盡高賢意
8 But one can only preserve the dust on the pages of a myriad autumns.54	獨守千秋紙上塵

Both Su Shi and Wang sense the tenuous nature of our attempt to preserve things. Su Shi cites the eternal truth that all things disintegrate, but he maintains that one cannot relinquish the task to preserve culture (*wen*) merely because it is ultimately futile. Without texts, and other cultural indexes, civilization is impossible. Wang approaches the subject from a different angle. He does not question the permanence of things; rather, he is skeptical about the reality that is being conveyed. All history, he says, is at best incommensurate with reality and at worst a lie. Writing simply cannot convey the human spirit. Wang's nightmare vision is a perpetuation of lies and half-truths instead of proper precepts for virtuous conduct and proper modes of governing the state. And yet he too resigns himself to the necessity of even these inadequate tools.

Huang expresses a similar sentiment but in a particularly lyrical manner.

Lingering in the Wind and Rain by the Pond for Three Days	池口風雨留三日
Alone in the city for three days, wind blowing the rain.	孤城三日風吹雨
The households of petty merchants have only vegetables to eat,	小市人家只菜蔬
The river distant, mountains stretch out, a pair of purple water fowl.	水遠山長雙屬玉
4 The body at ease, but the mind bitter: one white egret.	身閑心苦一春鉏
An old gaffer comes from next door to draw in the nets,	翁從旁舍來收網
I face the abyss of the waters, but I do not covet the fish.	我適臨淵不羨魚
Within the time of a nod of the head, everything becomes traces,	俯仰之間已陳迹

8 At dusk I return to the window to finish studying the crumbled books.[55] 暮窗歸了讀殘書

The poem begins by immediately moving from an observation of natural phenomena to the effect on the human world: the heavy rains have damaged and impoverished the people. From this dismal scene, Huang shifts his gaze back to nature. The water birds fly freely over the mountains and across the waters. This image is complicated by the image of the egret, who seems as leisurely as those birds, but whose mind is occupied with finding food.[56] This image is a corollary to the first couplet—a passive, "natural" scene is followed by one of stress and want.

The next couplet presents another contrasting pair; this time the order is inverted. The poet's neighbor, intent on catching fish, comes to draw in his nets, whereas Huang remains detached. This scene is an allusion to the "Shuo lin" chapter in the *Huainanzi*: "Leaning over the river and coveting fish is not as good as returning home and weaving a net."[57] Huang rejects both: he neither covets his neighbor's catch nor constructs his own net. We find out shortly what he will return home to do.

Huang returns home, but this seems foolish and ill-advised compared to the practicality of his neighbor. Huang is anxious over the fact that things become mere traces in an instant. This alludes to Wang Xizhi's (303–79) "Preface to the *Lanting Collection*": "What we had just enjoyed turned to mere traces in the nod of a head."[58]

The tendency of things not to be as they seem (i.e., the egret) is complicated by their fragility. We are always vulnerable to the fluctuations of nature (as in the first couplet). The Lanting preface argues for a continuity across time granted by what it is introducing—the collected poems: "Though times and happenings alter and differ, may men in what moves them be brought together. They who regard us from the future will also be touched by these writings."[59] Huang is lured back home to read such writings, yet he transposes the image of effacement and disappearance from the things noted in the preface ("what we had just enjoyed turned to mere traces") to the texts that the preface asserts will be permanent.

"Crumbled books" refers both to texts that are incomplete or faulty, as in Wang's poem, and to texts that have actually decayed. Even in recognizing that the books are faulty, Huang cannot give up his desire to read them. His attachment to even these crumbled texts is stronger than the lure of nature; the will to know supersedes and belies the tokens of detachment.

Huang's poem may be seen as a lyric counterpart to Wang Anshi's more rhetorically discursive poem, but the act of returning to read seems sudden and strangely inspired. We might now reread the image of the egret—in his hidden anxiety perhaps Huang is closer to the egret than he imagines. The final irony is, of course, that the very poem that Huang composes to convey these ironies is itself vulnerable to decay and incompleteness.

Here we have traced Huang's attempts to reinvigorate the words of prior texts by recontextualizing them, by exploiting the gaps between former readings and the readings engendered by Huang's new constructs. Besides a clear sense of reading words against the backdrop of earlier poetic manifestations, we see Huang's grasp of how poetic composition can foster new readings. Finally, the irony present in so many ways in Huang's verse can largely be attributed to his stance on the poet's will to poeticize language and appropriate natural objects as poetic vehicles and to his sense that such control ultimately is problematic—we return once again to Huang's pronouncement, one that never ceases to implicate Huang Tingjian as well: "Even [Tao] Yuanming and Shaoling [Du Fu] were unable to achieve mastery using limited talent to pursue inexhaustible meaning."[60]

SIX

Allusion: Writing and Reading

In Chapter 5 I began an investigation of how Huang Tingjian plays on the reading of allusion. Here I extend that analysis and probe more deeply into the issue of textual citation and, specifically, Huang Tingjian's key theoretical remarks on poetic revision. Attention to the poetics of allusion is not new in Chinese literary history: two especially allusive poets who come to mind are Luo Binwang (ca. 640–84) and Li Shangyin (813?–58). Their poems often contain so many allusions that a reading without a firm knowledge of preceding literature yields little sense. Luo drew from the rhetoric of parallel prose and employed allusion to construct specific, discursive arguments. Li Shangyin borrowed the ornate figuration of Six Dynasties rhetoric, often employing allusion to construct a vague mood or ambience or to make a particularly subtle and evocative point. Late Northern Song poets, especially Wang Anshi, Su Shi, and Huang Tingjian, further developed these and other methods in such ways as to create a new role for allusion.[1]

Late Northern Song poets often integrate allusion into the argumentative logic of their poems, but their arguments tend to be less reducible to prose paraphrase than Luo Binwang's. One often gets the sense in reading Luo that he uses allusion merely to distinguish his verse and imbue it with a sense of seriousness and moral authority. It usually fails as poetry, and the ideas expressed might have made rather common prose.[2] In contrast to this type of allusiveness, the better Northern Song poets frame allusion in a complex rhetorical construct that more often sets up paradoxical positions without a finite logical closure.

Li Shangyin too is famous for creating an ineffable and indefinite ambience through allusion, but many of the major Northern Song *shi* poets,

Allusion: Writing and Reading

while admiring and even adapting Li Shangyin's technique, doubted the intellectual and moral content of his verse and the value of the ideas he so carefully and craftily conveyed. They also reacted against the poetry produced by Li's latter-day admirers, particularly by the Xikun poets' often vacuous imitations of Li's atmospheric poetics.[3]

The main characteristic of the late Northern Song poets' use of allusion was their serious consideration of the most positive aspects of Luo and Li—the ethical and philosophical applications of Luo and the complex poetics of Li—in their deliberations on integrating allusion into their poetry as part of their reassessment of past culture. Indeed, in the late Northern Song, the source of an allusion becomes identified as a structural unit of a poem: "In their method of constructing parallel lines, [Wang Anshi and Su Shi] exhausted all the possible transformations of that technique. One cannot surpass their marvelous way of using the allusion [*shi*], the meaning [*yi*], and the source of the allusion [*chu chu*] together."[4]

A brief look at Du Fu and Li Shangyin, two major influences on Huang's technique, will help in distinguishing Huang's use of allusion from prior uses. Huang's high regard for Du Fu's use of allusion and his keen interest in understanding this craft are evident in his study of Du Fu's use of allusion, which traces the sources of some thirty-five Du Fu pieces.[5] For Huang, Du Fu's mastery in this area came from his ability to employ allusions so that they became the key to the poem. This is not to say that allusions are simply puzzle pieces that, once in place, are locked into a single function. Rather, and I believe this is what Li Shangyin shares with Du Fu, allusion provides the dynamic force within the poem; fused with the imagery of the poem, allusions constantly generate varied nuances and richer ways to read the poem.

Huang's praise of one of his contemporaries acknowledges this art: "Gao Zimian [He; fl. 1086] takes Du Zimei [Fu] as his standard in composing poetry. He employs an allusion as a general leads troops and places a single word as a key to a strategic pass."[6] This description of allusion as a "key" echoes the *Wenxin diaolong*: "The function [of allusions] may be compared to that of a linchpin of a wheel which, though only an inch in length, controls the whole wheel, or to the bolt of a gate which, though only a foot in length, controls the gate."[7] Although Huang borrows Liu Xie's analogy, as we shall see, Du Fu, Li Shangyin, and Huang use allusion to construct a more complex structure, one that cannot be simply "unlocked."[8]

The following example from Du Fu's works illustrates this use of allusion:

Poems on Ancient Sites, fifth of five 　　　　　詠懷古跡

The great name of Zhuge is suspended over the universe; 　諸葛大名垂宇宙

The image that remains of the revered minister is awesome in its purity and loftiness. 　宗臣遺像肅清高

The empire fractured into thirds, hampering his strategies; 　三分割據紆籌策

4　In an eternity of cloudy skies, a single feather. 　萬古雲霄一羽毛

Among his brethren he might view Yi and Lü; 　伯仲之間見伊呂

Had his control been established, he would have surpassed Xiao and Cao. 　指揮若定失蕭曹

But the movement of fate decreed that the Han's fortunes would be hard to restore, 　運移漢祚終難復

8　His ambition blighted, his body annihilated, his martial service futile labor.⁹ 　志決身殲軍務勞

Du Fu's admiration for Zhuge Liang (181–234) is well known. Here Du is inspired to write after viewing Zhuge's portrait in the Wuhou temple at Kuizhou. The poem begins by making an absolute and unsurpassable statement: Zhuge Liang's name covers the entire universe, the infinite realms of both time and space. From that sweeping statement, the movement to the specificity of line 2 seems anticlimactic. Indeed, this reductive movement is continued by an explicitly mournful line: Du Fu leads us from the expansive and abstract praise of the first line (Zhuge's all-pervasive name) to the literal image of the second line (the portrait on which Du Fu gazes) to the bleak historical reality of Zhuge Liang's life: a life of heartbreaking disappointments. His greatness dream was to reunify the shattered empire and restore the Han dynasty, but the sad fact was that the name Han had become merely an empty token. The greatness of Liu Bang (256–195 B.C.), founder of the Han, had no corresponding reality in Liu Bei (162–223), the man whom Zhuge Liang sought to make emperor of all China.

Line 4 is ambiguous: the single feather floating about the skies of all antiquity may be a symbol of transcendence, perhaps associated with the "purity and loftiness" of line 2. But the image also has an aspect of frailty and comes close to the conventional "tumbleweed" image of late Han poetry—a symbol of the vicissitudes of fate and our helplessness before them. (This sentiment reappears in line 7.)

The second quatrain follows much the same pattern as the first: it begins with Du Fu's praise of Zhuge Liang as equal to Yi Yin and Lü

Shang, legendary heroes who aided in the establishment of the Shang (1766–1122 B.C.) and Zhou (1122–249 B.C.) dynasties, respectively. But the next line dilutes this praise—had his plans been successful, Zhuge would have surpassed the *mortals* Xiao He and Cao Shen, who helped Liu Bang found the Han. But Fate had a different intent, and his life's efforts were in vain.

The key motif throughout the poem is the tension between worthy ambition, which may gain one respect and admiration, and accomplishment, which attests to the real value of one's ambitions. Du Fu's great admiration for Zhuge Liang is evidenced by his ranking Zhuge alongside the legendary worthies who helped establish the most ancient of China's empires. But that praise, while of the highest order, seems undercut by Du Fu's recognition of Zhuge's absolute failure; Du Fu's kind shifting of the responsibility to Fate does not diminish the harshness of the reality. The final line is explicit and brutal in its recitation of Zhuge Liang's defeat, the catalogue of topics and predicates is terse, emphatic, and fatalistic.

Du Fu's use of allusion here centers on the legendary and historical figures called forth as standards for measuring Zhuge Liang. The pairs are of a different nature. The first pair is obviously grander and more unreal. Du Fu has not been shy about granting Zhuge Liang the most lofty praise. But in reality Zhuge could not even match the real historical ministers who did set up the first Han emperor. This dichotomy is, as noted above, the central motif of the poem. Du Fu integrates these allusions into the poem in such a way that, on first reading, they seem unproblematic, simply grand points of comparison. But as the reader reaches the end of the poem and senses the grim paradox of Zhuge's fame and his fortune, these allusions, because of the context, offer another, more profound comment on that theme and enrich the poem's significance.

Li Shangyin is famous for creating rich textures through his use of allusion; both he and Du Fu are particularly praised for using allusion to create a sense "beyond words."[10] Yokoyama Iseo notes that Li Shangyin built off the allusive techniques of the Six Dynasties.[11] Whereas, however, in the Six Dynasties the use of allusion tends to be limited to a comment on the relationship between past and present events (the allusion draws out the complementariness or contrast between the alluded-to situation and the present one), Li Shangyin expanded allusion by investigating the language of the figure, by exploring the ways in which allusion could signify. In Yokoyama's words, Li's poems of allusion became almost "symbolist" vehicles in their evocativeness and suggestiveness. Therefore, although some of Du Fu's and Li Shangyin's allusive techniques may be similar, the nature of the thing "beyond words" is vastly different. Li's most famous poem is known precisely for such evocativeness:

The Patterned Lute   錦瑟

Mere chance that the patterned lute has fifty strings.   錦瑟無端五十絃
String and fret, one by one, recall the blossoming years.   一絃一柱思華年
Chuang-tzu dreams at sunrise that a butterfly has lost its way,   莊生曉夢迷蝴蝶
4   Wang-ti bequeathed his spring passion to the nightjar.   望帝春心託杜鵑
The moon is full on the vast sea, a tear on the pearl.   滄海月明珠有淚
On Blue Mountain the sun warms, a smoke issues from the jade.   藍田日暖玉生煙
Did it wait, this mood, to mature in hindsight?   此情可待成追憶
8   In a trance from the beginning, then as now.¹²   只是當時已惘然

A. C. Graham, whose translation I have used, explains the first line as an allusion to the story that the legendary Fu Xi ordered the White Lady to play the fifty-stringed lute; because the music was too sorrowful, he then forbade her to play. When she refused to stop, he broke the lute in half. Line 3 refers to the famous anecdote that Zhuangzi once dreamed he was a butterfly and found that he did not know if he was a butterfly dreaming he was Zhuangzi or Zhuangzi dreaming he was a butterfly.[13]

Wangdi, ruler of Shu, sent Bie Ling to deal with the floods and then seduced his wife; later he became ashamed of his actions and, thinking Bie a better man, abdicated in his favor. When Wangdi left, a nighthawk began to call, and when Wangdi died, his soul turned into that bird. The next line refers to the belief that when the moon is full the oyster has pearls and when the moon is dark the oyster is empty. This joins with the belief that beyond the South Sea are mermaids whose weeping eyes can exude pearls. This convergence of allusive reference further complicates the image.

The "jade" of line 6 refers to the story of a king who caused the death of a young woman named Purple Jade. On seeing her spirit, he asked, "How can it be that you are alive?" She replied, "Once young Han Zhong came to seek me in marriage, and Your Majesty would not allow it; I lost my good name and atoned for it by my death." Her mother came to embrace her, but Purple Jade dissolved into smoke. Li is here referring to Dai Shulun's (732–89) remark that the scene presented by

Allusion: Writing and Reading 153

a poet is like smoke that issues from fine jade when the sun is warm on Blue Mountain—it can be seen from a distance but not from close by.[14]

This poem has puzzled readers since its appearance; it lends itself to a number of interpretations.[15] This multiplicity of possibilities emanates from Li's use of allusions to form the entire poem. Most important, he has integrated allusion into a particularly involved rhetorical and imagistic frame. The terse, telegraphic style remains constant, but the images share a vague, ephemeral nature that counterbalances that cryptic and fragmented quality. This in turn is complemented by the confusion engendered when the sources of the individual allusions are played against one another. The general themes of dissolution, transitoriness, and the problem of memory and presence are nuanced by this integrated structure—particularly notable is how much we can sense Li Shangyin drawing on modes of reading allusion to effect this text. He artfully manipulates and frustrates the reader's expectations of stability and closure.

Debate about the meaning of this poem becomes particularly intense in the late Northern Song. Huang Tingjian himself supposedly said that he "had no idea what [the poem] meant."[16] Although this perhaps apocryphal anecdote may be intended only to poke fun at a poet who himself was accused of writing unintelligibly allusive poems, the point is that what impressed late Northern Song poets in this poem was its evocative craft and what put them off was its lack of discernible meaning. Huang's allusive poems too are often disparaged for these qualities. But many of Huang's seemingly unintelligible poems are quite approachable if one understands how they are constructed according to Huang's particular sense of poetry and poetics, how he uses allusive structures similar to those of Du Fu and Li Shangyin to forestall an automatic reading of the poem, to force the reader to rethink and reassess each image, allusion, word. Therefore, before moving to a consideration of his poems of allusion, let us consider his theory of allusion and its relation to prior critical treatments of the topic.

Allusions: The Question of Source

There was no clear critical consensus on allusion prior to the Song. In general, allusion occupies an ambivalent position in traditional Chinese poetics. The term sixth-century critics use to denote allusion is *yong shi*, which refers specifically to the citation of historical events. The term *lei* is used to refer to what Vincent Shih terms "textual reference," that is, extra-historical materials.[17] Later, *yong shi* comes to include the citation of prior poetic enunciations, material previously considered part of *lei*, and *yong dian* and *dian gu* are used to refer to allusions to the Classics.[18]

Traditionally, the use of allusion is considered proper to prose writing; its use in lyric poetry is thought either superfluous or inappropriate. A oft-quoted example of this criticism comes from the Preface to the *Shipin*:

> When composing a document of state policy, it is necessary to draw broadly on the past; or when composing a memorial in praise of someone's virtue, it is fitting to run through the catalogue of ancient heroes. But when one expresses one's feelings in poetry or song, then of what value is the use of allusion? "My thoughts of you are like flowing waters"—this is precisely writing what one sees before one's eyes.[19] "In the lofty tower, there is plenty of sorrowful wind."[20] This too is only what he envisions directly. "In the clear morn I ascend Longshou" has no prior source.[21] "A bright moon shines on the piled-up snow," how could this have come from the Classics or the histories?[22] When I look over the surpassing phrases past and present, the majority are not allusions; all instead come from direct description.[23]

Here Zhong Rong makes clear his belief that allusion is anti-lyrical, a mediation that favors the show of erudition over the direct expression of emotion. It becomes a sign of poetic weakness and an impoverished imagination. (As noted in Part I, this same critique is applied very strenuously centuries later to Huang Tingjian and late Northern Song poets in general.)

Allusion was to be used judiciously, if at all, with a firm respect for the source of the allusion. In no case was one to detach the allusion from the context that gave it significance. This prescription is directly related to the purpose behind the use of allusion. Liu Xie cites instances of the sages using allusions in their writings and goes on to give examples from the realm of historical composition: "When Ts'ui [Cui Yin; ?-92], Pan [Ban Gu], Chang [Zhang Heng], and Ts'ai [Cai Yong] began to select passages from the Classics and histories, spreading their flowers and fruits far and wide, and established their reputations through writing, they became models who were imitated by later scholars."[24]

In contrast to the orthodox use of allusion, Liu then gives examples of those who not only plagiarize inferior sources but also are ignorant of the origins of their allusions:

> In speaking of Master Chang, Emperor Wu of Wei [Cao Cao; 155-220] said that his work was poor; for Chang was superficial in his scholarship and limited in his literary experience, and his only speciality was plagiarizing the insignifi-

cant writings of Ts'ui and Tu. Not everything he wrote could be inquired into too closely, for if it were, he could not have identified its original source.[25]

In the late Northern Song, knowing one's sources and the proper way to read texts was considered evidence of deep and wide learning. As we saw above, Huang Tingjian was one of the staunchest proponents of this view and attacked poets for precisely the same thing that Cao Cao did.

The general ambivalence toward allusion thus stemmed from a dual concern for perpetuating the words and ethos of the Classics by alluding to them and for preserving the basic nature of lyric poetry—the direct expression of emotion. A concomitant fear was the misuse of allusion by those who disregarded the original meaning and import of the citation and thereby distorted the very thing their work was supposed to perpetuate. The convergence of these concerns is implied in these pronouncements from the *Wenxin diaolong*:

When a writer's allusions to past events are appropriate to the situation in question, it is as if he himself has created them. But if the facts alluded to are out of harmony with the context, their use will always be a blemish.

To be able to use the words of others as if they were one's own creation is to have perfect understanding of the past.[26]

If the later writer understands the source of the allusion perfectly, then it does not block his expression; rather, it seems so natural to him and so apt that the allusion may be identified as his own expression. The values of authentic lyric expression and faithfulness to the source of allusion show up clearly here. In being faithful to the source, one could apply allusion by making a statement either of equivalence (the present repeats the past) or of difference. In both cases the original meaning of the allusion remained fixed, invariable. Those who put primary value on their own voice and infringed on that fixity of meaning risked accusations of distorting the tone of the original enunciation. Yet how else was one to identify one's particular *use* of the allusion?

This dilemma developed from the history of allusion. Allusion first appeared in the rhetorical strategies of historical writings, where precedent took the shape of allusion and where the cyclical and corresponding nature of human and cosmic action was central. Things of a like nature confirmed patterns of experience; one learned to emulate or to abhor various models of behavior. The origin of an allusion framed it in its proper context; to disrupt that context bordered on invalidating an entire ethical and epistemological system.

When allusion as a rhetorical device was transposed into the realm of poetry, it brought with it the prescription regarding the sanctity of the origin, and that prescription precluded any radical invention on the allusion, any manipulation that would allow the later poet to call it his own. In the late Northern Song, however, poets grew more interested in challenging traditional assumptions of how allusion could be used in poetry, and Huang Tingjian was foremost in arguing for very particular modes of "creating" poetry out of the past.

Changing the Bone

Huang is famous for proposing two ways of treating prior enunciations: a poet could borrow the general import of a poem but change its mode of expression (*huangu*, "change the bone"), or he could borrow the general expression or even repeat the same word of the intertext but alter its meaning (*duotai*, "seize the embryo"). I focus on these phrases and their antecedents in the Conclusion. Here I concentrate on how these modes offer different means of appropriating prior verse.

The Zen monk Huihong (1071–1128) recorded these utterances by Huang in his *Lengzhai yehua*:

[The meaning of] poetry is inexhaustible, and yet human abilities are limited. Even [Tao] Yuanming and Shaoling [Du Fu] were unable to achieve mastery using limited talent to pursue inexhaustible meaning. Not changing the meaning of a prior poet but creating language [by reformulating past phrases] that matches his [original] phrase [*zao qi yu*] is called "the method of changing the bone." To penetratingly imitate the meaning of the prior poet and yet further nuance it is called "seizing the embryo."[27]

The former is clearly the more conservative mode; one does not take issue with the meaning being expressed; rather, one seeks to improve the formal constructions of the prior poet by changing how that sentiment or thought is expressed. (The phrase *zao qi yu* is difficult to translate. It probably means to create language that matches ["reaches"] that of the original, but the poetics of the Southern Song contains a strong sense of creating new language specifically by modifying prior phrases.) The second mode is more radical; the link between word and meaning is broken. The area of invention is not on the surface of the work but within its very semiotic and semantic structure.

Many critics propose a reading that takes the two phrases as one: the general sense, then, is to take the basic idea but change the wording. This interpretation appears as early as the Southern Song. But this does

Allusion: Writing and Reading

not account for the second facet of Huang's use of prior verse, in which he makes the same words mean something different. I will argue that the phrases designate separate methods: seizing the embryo involves a radical appropriation of the original significance of an enunciation set in the rigidity of conventional readings in order to both foreground the original intent and engender new meanings.[28]

Some examples of the more conservative technique of revising and incorporating prior verse will highlight Huang's more radical manipulations of allusion. Critics have traditionally used Huang's poem "Sleeping Ducks" as an example of his success in "changing the bone" to improve a prior poet's work:

Sleeping Ducks 睡鴨

The pheasant vainly loves its shining reflection;	山雞照影空自愛
The lone phoenix dances before the mirror, but doesn't make a pair.	孤鸞舞鏡不作雙
Of all below heaven that truly forms an everlasting union:	天下真成長會合
Two wild ducks nestling close to each other, asleep by the autumn river.[29]	兩鳬相倚睡秋江

Ren Yuan notes that line 1 alludes to an account from the *Bowu zhi* about the pheasant's vanity: it spends all day looking at the reflection of its beautiful plumage in the water. Line 2 comes from the *Yiyuan*. A king obtained a songbird that would not sing. Someone then placed a mirror before it, and, thinking that its reflection was its mate, the bird cried out mournfully.

Line 3 is taken verbatim from Xu Ling's "Yuanyang fu" (Rhymeprose on the mandarin duck).[30] This reference calls attention to the fact that Huang's entire poem imitates Xu Ling's quatrain:

The pheasant glimmering in the water, how could it reach its mate?	山雞映水那相得
A lone songbird's reflected shadow doesn't form a pair.	孤鸞照鏡不成雙
Of all below heaven that truly forms an everlasting union,	天下真成長會合
Nothing surpasses a pair of mandarin ducks, wings side by side.	無勝比翼兩鴛鴦

In his commentary on "Sleeping Ducks," Ren Yuan says that Huang felt that Xu Ling's verse was deep in meaning but weak in expression, and therefore he decided to improve it.[31] The last line differs most markedly from Xu Ling's, and critics have singled it out as the strongest and most successful revision. One modern reader, Tiang Seng-yong, disagrees:

> In Hsü's [Xu's] original line, the symbol for happy love is the mandarin ducks; in Huang's, the same idea is represented by two wild ducks which are larger in size than the mandarin ducks. It seems to me that the image of "wild ducks" has destroyed the delicate feeling about love created by mandarin ducks in Hsü's line. Although Huang had added "autumn river" in the concluding line to serve as a setting, and suggest the season at the same time, he also seemed to imply that the lovers should help each other in coping with the unforeseen hardships that are symbolized by the cold autumn water in which they "lean against each other and sleep" together; the image "wild ducks" fails to impart the sense of beauty and delicate love that is so adequately present in the "mandarin ducks." ... Poems written in this manner should therefore be considered as failures.[32]

Tiang notices two important and complementary changes in Xu Ling's line. The ducks (mallards) are indeed larger and less delicate than mandarin ducks, and the autumn river adds an element of hardship to the poem. But autumn symbolizes more than bad weather: it is the season of separation and death. The replacement of the delicate birds with the wild ducks complements the increased severity of the line and makes the entire scenario harsher. Although the imagery of Huang's poem may be harsher, its rhetoric is much more subtle than that of Xu Ling's. Huang replaces the straightforward assertion of Xu Ling's line, which forms a continuous rhetorical statement with the preceding line (i.e., opening topic and closing reply), with an answer that is only implied. This disjuncture foregrounds the imagistic nature of the last line, which in turn overturns the similarly imagistic first couplet.

Both Xu Ling's quatrain and Huang's poem make similar use of allusion: the allusions are relatively inconspicuous, and the poems could be understood without referring to the origins of the allusions. What carries the poems is the rhetoric of value embedded in the allusions and conveyed by the images themselves—the ethos of deep and mutual love contrasted with self-love and superficial beauty. Huang's substitution of wild ducks for the more courtly, proper, and conventional "mandarin ducks" is calculated, I believe, to amplify this argument and make it more logically consistent. Huang's final line then does two seemingly contrary things at once: it makes the poem more subtle and more forceful.

The next poem exemplifies Huang's use of allusion that is neither "changing the bone" nor "seizing the embryo." In this piece Huang displays his technique of mixing complementary allusions from disparate sources and levels of discourse, and, as Yokoyama Iseo points out, these are in turn fused with a deeply personal message.[33]

Allusion: Writing and Reading

Rhyming After Uncle Gongze 次韻公擇舅

After last night's dream the yellow millet is still only half-cooked.	昨夢黃粱半熟
No sooner having stood to speak, receiving a pair of pale jade disks.	立談白璧一雙
A startled deer needs the grasses of the wilds;	驚鹿要須野草
A crying gull's basic yearning is for the autumn river.³⁴	鳴鷗本願秋江

Line 1 refers to a well-known Tang parable about the illusory nature of fortune, the "Zhenzhong ji" (Story upon a pillow). A poor traveler falls asleep at an inn just as the innkeeper begins to cook millet and dreams that he follows the entire course of a life of success and failure. When he awakes, he finds that the millet has not finished cooking. Line 2 comes from the *Shiji* biography of Wu Qing.³⁵ When Wu was presented to King Xiao of Zhao, the king took an immediate liking to him, bestowing tokens of high rank and esteem before Wu had even stood to speak. Here again the allusion bespeaks the capricious nature of fortune.³⁶

Huang is clearly using these two commonplace allusions from different types of discourse (*xiaoshuo* "anecdotes" and *shi* "history") to complement each other; in the second couplet of the poem Huang again uses commonplaces, but they are more identifiable as general poetic allusions. The first couplet outlines the vicissitudes of fortune; the second argues from another direction for detachment. Why bother with the contingencies of officialdom? In your anger and sadness, you should imitate the animals of the wilds and withdraw to the proper environment. These last two lines have definite echoes of *gushi* (ancient-style) imagery and carry the poem from general observations about fate to more directly personal urgings. Specifically, line 3 evokes poem no. 161 of the *Classic of Poetry*, which parallels the ease and pleasure the deer find with each other with the companionship and enjoyment the poet shares with his friend. Huang draws that sentiment out by presenting its mirror image, underscoring his sadness at being separated from the addressee of the poem, his uncle Li Chang (1027–90).³⁷

Both these poems are fine examples of the "orthodox" use of allusion. Although the tone of "Rhyming After Uncle Gongze," which argues detachment from official life, belies the dramatic praise inherent in the Wu Qing allusion, by Huang's time the allusion had lost much of that primary seriousness; it is hardly an example of twisting an allusion away from its source. Again, the poems satisfy the traditional criterion: allusions here augment, rather than detract from, the expression of emotion.

One last example of Huang's more conventional use of allusion displays his talent for integrating allusion into the logic of the poem and is particularly notable for the manner in which Huang combines allusions into a sustained narrative.

Song on Listening to Song Zongru Play the Ruan Lute 聽宋宗儒摘阮歌

   Your ancestor, Master Song Qi, was minister at the Hanlin Academy. 翰林尚書宋公子

   His cultured talent and free style today still exist. 文采風流今尚爾

   You might suspect that Qi Yu was your former incarnation. 自疑耆域是前身

4 From within a satchel you draw out a pellet and raise men from the dead. 囊中探丸起人死

   Your countenance is like the withered branches of a thousand-year-old pine. 貌如千歲枯松枝

   Drunk, down and out with nowhere to stop and rest. 落魄酒中無定止

   Obtaining a million in cash, you give it all over to the wineshop, 得錢百萬送酒家

8 Smiling all the while, you don't care how much of it is left today. 一笑不問今餘幾

   With your hand you stroke the lute and send off the wild geese in flight; 手揮琵琶送飛鴻

   The hurried strings cause a din in drunken ears, startling the guests. 促絃聒醉驚客起

   Cicadas hurry on their weaving: moonlight surrounds the autumn sky; 寒蟲催織月籠秋

12 A lone goose calling the flock, the sky strikes the waters. 獨雁叫羣天拍水

   From the Chu state the banished minister was cast off for ten years; 楚國覊臣放十年

   The beauty of the Han palace was betrothed a thousand *li* away. 漢宮佳人嫁千里

   Deep in the inner chambers words of affection and anger. 深閨洞房語恩怨

16 The purple swallow and yellow oriole harmonize their tones in the peach and plum trees. 紫燕黃鸝韻桃李

   The Madman of Chu sings his song, startling the people of the marketplace. 楚狂行歌驚市人

   The Old Fisherman brings his boat over to the young reeds. 漁父拏舟在葭葦

   I ask you, this hollow piece of wood adorned with vermilion strings, 問君枯木著朱繩

20 How can it speak the matters that reside in men's thoughts? 何能道人意中事

Allusion: Writing and Reading

You say that this object has been handed down through several different families,	君言此物傳數姓
Atop the dusky jade oval inlaid cross-patterns.	玄璧庚庚有橫理
You closed your door and studied this art for three months from an imperial musician,	閉門三月傳國工
24 I now see before me the real Ruan Zhongrong.	身今親見阮仲容
I have a small hillock in Jiangnan,	我有江南一丘壑
How can I get drunk there with you,	安得與君醉其中
And bend my elbow to make a pillow and listen to you perform "Airs of the Pine"?[38]	曲肱聽君寫松風

title/ The Ruan Lute is similar to the *pipa*; it is named after its reputed inventor, the noted Jin dynasty musician and poet Ruan Xian (234–305), who appears in line 24.

1/ Song Qi (998–1061) helped compose the *Xin Tang shu*, the revised official history of the Tang dynasty. He is also known for his *Song Jingwen gong biji*, a discussion of historical precedents and anecdotes.

3/ Qi Yu was a monk from India reputed to have great healing powers.

6/ Compare Li Bo, "In my youth, not able to obtain my intent, / Drunk, down and out, nowhere to peacefully live" ("Zeng cong di nan ping tai shou," first of two, first couplet; Li Bo, 748).

7/ An allusion to a story from Xiao Tong's (501–31) "Biography of Tao Yuanming" (Xiao, 2.7b–8b): Tao once received a huge sum of money and spent it all on wine.

11/ With the approach of autumn the cicadas begin to sound; their chirping sounds like the shuttles of looms.

13/ A reference to Qu Yuan, who drowned himself in grief over being cut off from the benevolence of the king.

14/ The famous story of Wang Qiang, who was sent to marry a barbarian king in 33 B.C. (see *Han shu* 94B.7b–11a).

17/ For the famous story of the Madman of Chu, see *Analects* 18.5.

18/ The "Old Fisherman" is both the name of a section of the *Zhuangzi* (NHZJ 10.5a) and the name of a poem from the *Chuci*. Here it probably refers to the latter, picking up the Qu Yuan theme of line 13. After Qu Yuan was banished, he "wandered along the river's banks or walked at the marsh's edge, singing as he went, his expression was dejected and his features emaciated" (trans. Hawkes, 90). Here he met the fisherman.

23/ A common image signifying ardent and concentrated study.

The poem begins with an obvious echo of the opening of another famous poem praising a great artist: Du Fu's "Poem on Painting" 丹青引:

My general is the descendant of the Martial Emperor,	將軍魏武之子孫
But now you are a poor commoner.	於今爲庶爲清門
The former hero put the contending lords under his will; that is all over now.	英雄割據雖已矣
But his cultured talent and free style today yet abide.[39]	文采風流今尚存

By immediately calling forth Du Fu, Huang declares the allusiveness of his poem. He makes no pretense that his poem will be a simple and direct tribute; rather, his poem suggests that the best way to pay tribute to Song is to echo a hallowed poem. As soon as Huang evokes Du Fu's poem, however, he leaves it and takes on other modalities.

The second couplet gives Song Zongru another ancestor, but Huang invents this one. Huang declares Song kin to the Indian monk Qi Yu, famous for his medical skills. This image adumbrates the major theme of the poem—the magical powers of Song's music. The "pellet" pulled out of a satchel may well be a play on the image of Song's plectrum.

Before embarking on a long catalogue of allusions and common poetic images, Huang inserts two more motifs. The "withered pine," a stock image connoting the moral fortitude and endurance of a good man, complements the august image of Song with which Huang begins the poem. But Huang immediately follows it with another image: the downcast, drunken musician. Just as Du Fu juxtaposes the heroic lineage of his addressee and his former circumstances against his current fallen state, Huang describes Song's reduced circumstances. This image also draws forth another figure: the famous Jin dynasty poet and musician Ruan Xian, reputed inventor of the lute Song Zongru is playing, one of the famous Seven Worthies of the Bamboo Grove, and a byword for drunkenness (some accounts say that he died of drink).

This combination of moral seriousness, esoteric magic, and drunken melancholy is followed by a long segment dealing with various kinds of art. The next five couplets (lines 9–18) pair up allusions and poetic commonplaces, each with strong emotional resonances. Huang combines these with various kinds of "music"—the sounds of nature, murmured phrases from the imperial boudoir, the songs of recluses. Only in line 20, at the end of this catalogue, does Huang give us a way to identify a common ground—these images form a composite portrait of the "matters that reside in men's thoughts." The seemingly disparate allusions and images now become freely associated fragments emanating from the listener's mind, startled out of its drunken stupor and set on a wild, imaginative journey filled by the images evoked by the music.

The last quatrain (lines 24–27) returns to themes set up in the opening section of the poem: Song has, through careful study, assimilated the art of his teacher so well that he becomes his re-embodiment. In a sense, Huang offers this poem as a consolation to his addressee. Song's fortunes may have fallen, but by his art he may effect a kind of self-revival. Just as Qi Yu was able to resurrect the dead, Song Zongru wakes up the drunken guests with the power and beauty of his music. But beyond that, Huang implies that Song's talent endows him with immortality—at once he is both the descendant of a great house and the heir to an artistic legacy. The images of resurrection and revival, of continuing a tradition, are neatly linked here. Huang's narrative subtly transforms the topos from a fragmented public scene to a unified and intensely personal vision with deep cultural and aesthetic implications.

This poem displays Huang's ability to draw on stock imagery and combine it in a uniquely different context. The allusions and images are well-known commonplaces, but Huang combines them within a dramatic narrative structure that imbues them with a different identity. They come to serve as examples of something specifically evoked under the spell of the music Huang has set out to praise. The root meanings of these allusions have, nonetheless, remained the same.

Seizing the Embryo

The strict value placed on keeping the original intent (*yi*) of the allusion is gradually modified in the late Northern Song; at least one critic argues the opposite point of view and directs writers to alter the allusion's application so as to avoid the commonplace:

Once I looked at a vulgar text that read, "In composing literature and employing allusion, one must use a new meaning." For example, if you are discoursing on the topic of friendship, and you employ [an allusion to] Guan [Zhong] and Bao [Shuya], this certainly would be nothing new! In the past Zhuo Wangsun said, "What others abandon, I seize; what others seize, I give; thus I have been able to achieve wealth." This idea perfectly accords with what the common book said. They both bespeak the proper method scholars should follow.[40]

This passage reminds one of Su Shi's famous grain analogy, but Xu Ji (1028–1103) adds a new element. Su argued that charges of plagiarism were nonsensical since words could not be owned anymore than grain could be "owned" by anyone except the God of Agriculture (I return to this argument in the Conclusion). Xu agrees with Su about the legitimacy of allusion but goes on to argue that in employing allusions, one should change the meaning.

By the Southern Song, the notion of an aesthetic imperative to alter the meaning of poetic sources was established by one of Huang Tingjian's strongest advocates, Yang Wanli (1127–1206). Others had noted that in employing allusion one could either adopt the original meaning of the allusion or negate it, the latter being the more artful use.[41] Yang suggests that neither replicating nor simply reversing the allusion is the supreme allusive art: "When poets use the words of the ancients and at the same time do not employ their meaning, it is the most marvelous method of allusion."[42]

Huang admired Gao He (Zimian), a fellow poet whose name is listed in the "Register of the Jiangxi School" by Lü Benzhong (1084–1145),[43] for Gao's use of allusion (see above). Huang wrote a series of ten poems matching Gao's rhymes; these poems contain Huang's more distinctive use of allusions and common poetic images. These next two poems may serve as examples of this series.

Ten Poems Rhyming After Gao Zimian, third of ten 次韻高子勉十首

To the south of Mount Xian: the Well of Travelers;	峴南羇旅井
Above Baling: the Pavilion of Returning from the Hunt.	灞上獵歸亭
The sun revolves to where they distribute fish at the market.	日曉分魚市
4 The wind returns to the sandbars where geese descend.	風回落雁汀
I grasp the brush on behalf of the poet;	筆由詩客把
And listen to the flute for the sake of my old friend.	笛爲故人聽
I only fear that when the Su Dan crane	但恐蘇耽鶴
8 Returns, it will be named Ding.[44]	歸時或姓丁

The first couplet plays off allusions to the locus of Huang's poem. The first line echoes Du Fu's poem on visiting the site of Wang Can's home, "This must be the same place as Wang Can's abode, / A well remains before Mount Xian."[45] Line 2 alludes to the biography of the military commander Li Guang in the *Han shu* (54.1a). He resided in Lantian and hunted in its southern hills; after hunting, he would drink and then return to his pavilion. Conspicuously absent in Huang's borrowing is any consideration of the reason this activity is mentioned in Li Guang's biography in the first place. The story has it that once after drinking, Li was stopped by a watchman, who said that even generals could not freely wander about the watch station. When Li Guang later went on a military campaign, he requested that the watchman be assigned to his troops. He then had the man killed. This incident is usually cited as an example of Li Guang's pride and his ferocious temper. This allusion was well-known, and Huang's partial use of it immediately strikes one as strange and arbitrary.

The next couplet is strange in another way: the syntax is difficult, the actions and movements seemingly unrelated. Time passes, marked by the movement of the sun and the wind; and the poet notices correlated actions in the world of men and animals. The tone of the first quatrain is subdued; even the echoes called forth by the allusions are now muted,

Allusion: Writing and Reading

the *huai gu* feeling of line 1 and the drunken ghost of Li Guang give way to these quiet, slow-moving images. The topos, which gave rise to the recollections conveyed by the allusions, now takes precedent over those echoes.

The next couplet brings us to the subject of the poem: Huang's friend Gao He. The impetus for Huang's response is double—the rhymes sent by Gao and the music Huang hears. The reference to the flute alludes to a story in the *Jin shu* (49.1374) about Xiang Xiu (ca. 221–ca. 300), a member of the Seven Worthies of the Bamboo Grove. He once passed the former households of his friends Xi Kang and Lu An (d. 262). Someone was playing a flute and its beautiful tones made Xiang think back on the days he had spent with Xi and Lu. He sighed sorrowfully and then composed the "Rhymeprose on Former Times."[46] Although this is a vivid image in Huang's poem, it is not clear whether the line is literal or figurative. Does he really hear music and think back on Gao, and then think on a correlative in the preface to the rhymeprose? Or is it the abstract statement "One listens to music because of its power to evoke memories of dear friends"?

The echoes of the latter reading carry over to the next, and final, couplet. Another friend has been recalled in the course of the poem—Su Shi. Huang's final couplet is at once amusing and bittersweet. He plays off two legends of men being transformed into immortal cranes. The *Shenxian zhuan* tells of one Su Dan, who studied the art of transformation and finally turned himself into a crane who roosted in the lofts of the city. Huang says that perhaps Su Shi will return as well, but then he sighs—perhaps the crane that returns will be named Ding. This alludes to a poem in the *Soushen ji* about the famous Han dynasty Daoist Ding Lingwei: "There's a bird, there's a bird: it's Ding Lingwei. Departed from the house for eons, today he returns. The outer walls still exist, the people do not. Why not study to be a transcendent—see the burial mounds piled up?" The crane will not be Su Dan's, or Su Shi's, reincarnation, but someone else's. More important, even if Su were to return, he would find his friends dead and gone.

The quiet melancholy of the allusion to Xiang Xiu is augmented here by this irony, and this note of sadness is linked to another allusion embedded in Huang's poem. Su Shi, too, once spoke of seeing a crane, and in the "Rhymeprose on the Red Cliff," second of two, there is a tone of both wonder and alienation:

The night was half over and all around was deserted and still, when a lone crane appeared, cutting across the river from the east. Its wings looked like cart wheels, and it wore a black robe and a coat of white silk. With a long, grating cry, it swooped over our boat and went off to the west.

Soon afterwards, I left my friends and went to bed. I dreamed I saw a Taoist immortal in a feather robe come bouncing down the road past the foot of Linkao. He bowed to me and said, "Did you enjoy your outing to the Red Cliff?" I asked him his name, but he looked down and did not answer.

"Ah, wait—of course—now I know! Last evening, flying over our boat and crying—that was you, wasn't it?"

He turned his head and laughed, and I woke up with a start. I opened the door and peered out, but I could see no sign of him.[47]

Huang's poem plays on this notion of discovering immortality and yet being unable to control it. Immortality is of no use if it serves only to increase the distance between the living and the dead. The immortal returning from the dead finds himself alone: his friends have died, and there is no way to bring them back. This is not a simple exchange of places, for immortality has been shown to be an illusory form of salvation. Huang wants to believe that Su Shi transcended the limits of mortality, but he does not speak of this directly; he is too skeptical, and his laugh at the end of the poem is not without bitterness.

Huang's use of allusion in this poem is intimately tied to the conventions behind it. A visitor to a historic place commonly evokes the shadows of its prior inhabitants. Huang's use of allusion in the first couplet follows this convention, but his citations seem only to fill the form. An allusion to the history and historical figures associated with the place should resound; it should be emphatic. Here, Huang's allusions seem to be calculatedly weak, and, as we noted, the next couplet falls off into a kind of somnambulant wandering devoid of the historical echoes allusion should provide.

This shift in mood, I believe, complements the play on allusion in the second half of the poem. The poem traces the effacement of things, the slipperiness of mortality, and of immortality too. The echoes of the topos are incomplete, the return of the transcendents unpredictable, and even the mock solace that Huang allows himself in seeing Su Shi in the reincarnation of Su Dan is called into question. Once we understand this, we may re-read the Li Guang allusion. Li Guang's capricious cruelty negates the moral righteousness of the watchman and undermines an ethical system that rewards virtue. Worst of all, the act introjects an element of radical instability, and this instability informs the entire poem.

The eighth poem of the series again shows Huang's interest in playing with allusions, as well as with the stability of reference they are supposed to afford.

Allusion: Writing and Reading

Boring open the cavities of turbid, primal Chaos,	鑿開混沌竅
You spy into the mind of Fu Xi.	窺見伏羲心
There is something that preceded heaven and earth:	有物先天地
4 Possessing life; drowned on dry land.	含生盡陸沈
Cutting down mountains to build great edifices,	伐山成大廈
You beat the bellows to cast auspicious gold.	鼓橐鑄祥金
From this three-foot-long piece of wood without strings	三尺無絃木
8 I hope you will bring forth a perfect tone.⁴⁸	期君發至音

Line 1 alludes to the *Zhuangzi*:

> The emperor of the South Sea was called Shu [Brief], the emperor of the North Sea was called Hu [Sudden], and the emperor of the central region was called Hun-tun [Hundun; Chaos]. Shu and Hu from time to time came together for a meeting in the territory of Hun-tun, and Hun-tun treated them very generously. Shu and Hu discussed how they could repay his kindness. "All men," they said, "have seven openings so they can see, hear, eat, and breathe. But Hun-tun alone doesn't have any. Let's trying boring him some!"
> Every day they bored another hole, and on the seventh day Hun-tun died.⁴⁹

This dramatic and brutal allusion immediately sets the rhetorical tone of the poem.

Line 2 plays off the commentary to the *fu* hexagram of the *Classic of Changes*: "In the hexagram of 'return' one sees the mind of heaven and earth."⁵⁰ Huang substitutes the legendary sage Fu Xi for "heaven and earth" and brings in heaven and earth in the next line as the syntactic parallel to Fu Xi. The focus becomes what was in the legendary ruler's mind as he viewed primordial order and perceived the broken and unbroken patterns that came to inform the *Classic of Changes*.

The original sense behind this allusion is unequivocally positive, but its placement next to the *Zhuangzi* allusion negates that sense. The will to discern and analyze, to "spy into" things, takes on the status of a negative act. The conventional way of reading the allusion leads to a sense of dislocation; the initial, positive reading of the line is complicated by the example of the destructiveness of will in the first line.

Line 3 recalls *Laozi*:

> There is a thing confusedly formed,
> Born before heaven and earth.
> Silent and void
> It stands alone and does not change,
> Goes round and does not weary.
> It is capable of being the mother of the world.
> I know not its name
> So I style it "the Way."⁵¹

This primal unity, destroyed by the misguided intentions of Shu and Hu, is presented as the locus wherein we might recuperate our oneness with things.

In the final line of the first quatrain, Huang offers a way to begin to find that unity. The allusion is to the *Zhuangzi*:

> He [Yiliao] has buried himself among the people, hidden himself among the fields. His reputation fades away but his determination knows no end. Though his mouth speaks, his mind has never spoken. Perhaps he finds himself at odds with the age and in his heart disdains to go along with it. He is one who has "drowned in the midst of dry land."[52]

This line closes the argument of the first quatrain and reconciles the disjuncture of the first couplet.

The second quatrain follows a similar pattern. The first couplet of this quatrain alludes to the "Discourse on the Four Masters' Discussion of Virtue" by Wang Bao (fl. 552): "The material for a great edifice does not come from the wood of a single hillock."[53] As with its counterpart in line 2 of the poem, this verse seems to offer praise for ardent effort—this time to those who energetically gather lumber from mountaintops to construct great things. The next line parallels this line and thus seems to take on its positive virtue. But the two allusions that are combined here complicate the reading of the preceding line. The image of beating the bellows recalls *Laozi* V.14–16:

> Heaven and Earth are not humane [*jen*].
> They regard all things as straw dogs.
> The sage is not humane.
> He regards all people as straw dogs.
> How Heaven and Earth are like a bellows!
> While vacuous, it is never exhausted.
> When active, it produces even more.
> Much talk will of course come to a dead end.
> It is better to keep to the center.[54]

In Huang's line, the act of beating the bellows signifies drawing on an inexhaustible source of energy and an ardent application of the will. Wing-tsit Chan's discussion of the *Laozi* passage underscores the topic of vacuity and disinterestedness, of action *without* will. From this perspective, this is another example of the futility of ardently willing something. These pronouncements are complemented by the second allusion in Huang's line, which is to the *Zhuangzi*. As with the *Laozi* allusion, the sense of the *Zhuangzi* passage contradicts the first reading of the preced-

Allusion: Writing and Reading

ing line:

[Master Lai is speaking of reincarnation:] When a skilled smith is casting metal, if the metal should leap up and say, "I insist upon being made into a Mo-yeh!" [a famous sword of King Helu (r. 514–496 B.C.) of Wu], he would surely regard it as a very inauspicious metal indeed. Now, having had the audacity to take on human form once, if I should say, "I don't want to be anything but a man! Nothing but a man!", the Creator would surely regard me as a most inauspicious sort of person. So now I think of Heaven and Earth as a great furnace, and the Creator as a skilled smith. Where could he send me that would not be all right?[55]

The act of stripping the mountains of trees now takes on a different aspect; Huang uses the *Zhuangzi* passage to make an observation on our rampant will to achieve glory and to criticize Gao while seeming to bestow praise. To "beat the bellows to cast auspicious metal" is a mirror image of the metal jumping up to ask to be auspicious—both are acts of will that go against the nature of things.

As at the end of the first quatrain, Huang closes the poem by reconciling the ambiguity of the opening lines of the quatrain. He offers an alternative object to the "auspicious metal": the famous stringless zither mentioned in Xiao Tong's biography of Tao Qian: "Tao did not know about formal tonal rules; he had a stringless zither. Each time wine was good, he would strum the zither and convey his intent."[56] The stringless zither is again evoked by Li Bo: "A great tone becomes a song of itself; / One has but to play on a stringless zither."[57] The zither thus symbolizes all that the addressee of Huang's poem has forsaken. It is on this that Huang will refocus his spirit—the natural, spontaneous actions in harmony with our natural being, unhurried by zealous striving.

That lute might be used to produce a "perfect tone," one shared between intimate friends. The *Hou Han shu* (79.16) tells that the "perfect tone cannot be heard by the masses, and thus Bo Ya broke the strings [since his friend Zhong Ziqi, the only one who could truly appreciate Bo Ya's music had died]." Huang calls Gao Zimian back from his zealous efforts and asks him to consider the unity he has lost, a unity with things and with his friend. Huang carefully constructs this argument by manipulating the allusions and casting them against each other.

This poem is a good example of Huang's technique of playing with the wording of allusions to achieve specific effects. Behind this technique is Huang's keen perception of how allusions are read and how poetry signifies. He plays with the conventions of reading allusions and upsets the conventional response; here the tension between the conventional reading of the allusion and the "false" reading given the line by the context of Huang's construct is clear. Huang plays with this doubleness. He seems to catch his reader going the wrong way, as it were, and directs the reader back, away from the immediate reading. This redirection perfectly complements the argument of the piece as Huang transforms what first appear to be positive encouragements to strive into negative warnings against those very actions.

One of Huang's most famous poems again shows Huang's understanding of the mechanisms of convention and reading and his play on the very thing that allusion relies on for meaning—its source.

Rhyming in Response to Qian Mufu's "Song of the Apehair Brush"	和答錢穆父 詠猩猩毛筆
Fond of wine, its drunken soul remains.	愛酒醉魂在
Good at speech, yet muddled about strategies.	能言機事疏
In one lifetime, how many pairs of sandals?	平生幾兩屐
4 But after he dies, he produces five cartloads of books.	身後五車書
The excellence of this object was glimpsed at the Regal Assembly.	物色看王會
Its accomplishments exist recorded in the Stone Ditch.	勳勞在石渠
By pulling its hair, one can regulate the world;	拔毛能濟世
8 So in the end it repudiates Yang Zhu.[58]	端為謝楊朱

Every line in this poem contains at least one allusion, but Huang's construction makes it impossible to correlate the source and the significance of the allusion as it appears in his poem. The title announces that the poem is a *yongwu* poem on a brush; from that point on, Huang synthesizes allusions in metonymic and metaphoric play.

The first couplet recalls popular beliefs about apes. Ren Yuan says the first line is derived from the *Huayang guozhi* of the Eastern Jin writer Chang Qu: apes love to drink wine and to wear sandals; hunters often use these objects as lures. The "Quli" chapter of the *Liji* says that although these apes can speak, they do not differ from the other beasts. The two traits undercut one another—the apes' love of wine makes them incapable of speaking with any clarity.

The second couplet follows a similar pattern. Line 3 echoes a statement from the biography of Ruan Fu (278–326) in the *Jin shu* (49.1364). Famous for his love of sandals, a visitor once found him blowing the flames of a fire so that he could wax his own clogs. The visitor remarked, "I never knew how many pairs of sandals one could wear in one's lifetime." Ruan shared other attributes with apes: he was notorious for his drunkenness and sloth. The allusions thus complement each other.

Allusion: Writing and Reading 171

Just as line 2 of the poem plays on the apes' love of drink, which wastes their uncanny ability to speak and line 3 makes fun of Ruan Fu's misplaced energies, so line 4 plays on the notion of wasted talent. The allusion is to the *Zhuangzi* story of the logician Hui Shi. Hui is characterized as obsessed with intellect and lacking in imagination: "Hui Shih was a man of many devices and his writings would fill five carriages. But his doctrines were jumbled and perverse and his words wide of the mark."[59] Huang tells us that even though the ape never produces anything during its dissolute life, after it dies men pull its hair to make brushes, which in turn may be used to write texts. But the allusion retains the original sense—the books, however numerous, may be full of nonsense.

The next quatrain continues the playful lauding of the object. The "Regal Assembly" is the title of a section of the *Jizhong Zhoushu* that tells of a grand assembly of domestic and foreign ministers. Critics take this to mean that the brush was presented to the emperor from abroad. The next line continues this history of the brush: the "Stone Ditch" is the imperial library. The line also makes a pun: the brush is both the object and instrument of the record.

The last couplet again makes a pun. "Pulling its hair" alludes to a passage from the *Mencius*: "Mencius said, 'Yang Tzu [Yang Zhu] chooses egoism. Even if he could benefit the Empire by pulling out one hair he would not do it.'"[60] Huang inverts the allusion: one plucks a hair (albeit not one's own) and seizes the brush to govern the empire, and thus the brush refutes Yang Zhu. But this act of taking up the brush to govern the state still rings of the allusion to the five cartloads of useless texts. Throughout the poem, Huang maintains his sense of play and irony by carefully manipulating allusion and tropes.

Yokoyama Iseo notes that, for all its allusiveness, this poem cannot be understood by simply tracing the sources of the allusions.[61] This points out the idiomatic nature of Huang's use of allusion and indicates how the specific poetic context structures the role the allusions play. Although this is true of allusion in general, the examples in this chapter illustrate the conventions that governed the way allusions were read, the way that allusions generated meaning, and the extent to which Huang twisted and played on the semiotics of allusions.

The difficulty of reading Huang's allusive verse may thus be attributed to two things: his frequent use of relatively recondite allusions and his methods of using those allusions to ironize their former uses. Although the first aspect may be attributed to the valorization of learning during the late Northern Song and its place in Song poetics, this second aspect is consistent with the motives behind Huang's particular poetics and his notions of poetry: Huang sought to distinguish himself from his predecessors while using their own words. The creation of language was closed to him—what remained was invention on language, making the old signify new things. Poetic composition for Huang was inextricably tied to revision, but his notion of revision moved far beyond surface variations to comments on the act of writing poetry itself.

Conclusion: Signing the Palimpsest

Ultimately, what most distinguishes Huang Tingjian is his deep recognition of the necessary and ineffaceable presence of prior poetic language and his attempts to appropriate that presence to serve as an index to his own. In the Northern Song, there was a moment when the presumption of being able to totally assimilate the models of antiquity was played out. In the final moment of perfect assimilation, the latter-day poet challenged and eclipsed his predecessor, and the mark of origin became fainter. Indeed, the past's proprietorship of the word was nearly effaced.

The Aesthetic of the Unconscious: Poems Without Proprietors

Later poets had many ways to make their voice heard even as they articulated the phrases of others; part of their strategy required that manipulation not be immediately identifiable as such. Paradoxically they relied on the rich echoes of prior enunciations and sought distinction from them. To soften this contradiction, prior verse somehow had to be made either public property or an individual endowment from the former poets, thereby "naturalizing" its presence in the poem of the latter-day poet.

In the *Lengzhai yehua*, Huihong claims that in rhyming after Tao Qian, Su Shi received Tao's "left-behind intent" (*yi yi*).[1] Northern Song poets used a variety of strategies to claim their poetic inheritance and legitimize their use of existing lines. One way was to claim spontaneous acquisition. In a poem on a painter he much admired, Su Shi writes: "What is divinely imparted in a dream is retained by his mind. / When he awakes he relies on his hand, forgetting brush technique."[2]

Huang Tingjian plays off the notion of finding poetic inspiration in dream. He once composed two *yuefu* pieces because their tunes had fallen into disuse:

After I composed these two "Songs on the Bamboo Branch," I lodged overnight at Geluo Outpost. I dreamed that I met Li Bo in the mountains and he said to me, "In the past, when I was banished to Yelang prefecture,[3] I heard the sounds of a cuckoo and wrote three pieces to the tune of the 'Bamboo Branch.' Has the world recorded them or not?" I remembered that these poems were not in his collected works; I asked him to chant them for me and thereby obtained them.[4]

This is a wonderful conceit, and typical of Huang Tingjian—Huang here has proof that Li Bo, after hearing his poems, finds in him the one person who could be trusted with his "lost" compositions.

Others too claimed unconscious use of lines of prior poets. Stuart Sargent cites two examples: first, from the Song critic Ge Shengzhong (1072–1144): "In Tu Mu's poems, the words often take their meaning from Old Tu. [Examples are given.] It must be that when he so admired [Tu Fu] in his heart, he put the words down on paper and they naturally tallied [with Tu Fu]; it is not that he intended to plagiarize." Sargent's second example is a comment by Liu Bin (1022–88) on Su Shunqin's use of Du Fu: "How could [Su] Tzu-mei be a thief of poems? It must be that if [one] chants the ancients' poems so much, one often takes them as one's own accomplishment."[5] The unconscious use of prior poetry was proof one had truly assimilated that verse, a convenient way to avoid the charge of plagiarism. Witness this anecdote from the *Daoshan qinghua*:

Once Huang T'ing-chien wrote three quatrains which were respectively 65%, 40% and 50% identical to portions of three longer compositions by Po Chü-i [Bo Juyi], and very nearly identical even where they departed from Po. Tseng Yu [Zeng You], twenty years his junior, admired them and considered them an instance of "changing iron into gold." But shortly before Huang died, his last disciple, Fan Liao, asked him about it, and Huang told him he had recited these poems since he was young and no longer knew whose poems they were; he had simply written them down for fun while detained at Mt. Heng.... He thought it hilarious that poor Tseng had taken this as "changing iron into gold."[6]

Huang's denial of consciously crafting these poems is a good example of how the conceit of unconsciously employing another poet's lines could be used both as a way to make one's verse appear even more marvelous and as a defense against charges of plagiarism. Equally important, it was also a defense of "learned verse"; the result of ardent assimilation of texts is the unconscious, natural use of models.

Su Shi comes up with another defense against the charge of plagiarism; he simply says that no one owns poetry. He once recorded two poems by Du Fu as his own, and when asked about it he said:

> Now rice, hemp, grain and wheat originate from Shen Nung [Nong] and Hou Chi [Ji]. If at present a household has a granary and someone takes [grain] without its being given, this is theft. That which is purloined is a loss. [But] if the owner must trace it to its beginning, it is the property of Shen Nung and Hou Chi. In the present case, if we investigate into these poems, [we can see that] every word is a true record of the Retired Scholar [Su Shih]. This being so, they are the Retired Scholar's poems; how can [Tu] Tzu-mei forbid me to possess them?[7]

Implicit in Su Shi's comment is the feeling that by his age, Du Fu's poetry and that of other predecessors had become public domain. A prohibition against use of that reservoir of poetic language would leave one precious little to use. Su stretches that notion to the limit here, but its basic premise is one of the tacit presumptions of late Northern Song poetics.

In the following poem Su Shi comments on poetic borrowing:

Following the Rhymes of Kong Yifu's "Compiling Ancient Poets' Lines," Which He Presented to Me, first of five 　　次韻孔毅父集古人句見贈

I praise your playful gathering of other men's verse. 　　羨君戲集他人詩
Directing and shouting at the people of the market as though ordering about slaves. 　　指呼市人如使兒
If "A wild swan at the sky's border" is not easily obtained, 　　天邊鴻鵠不易得
4 Then make a parallel couplet by following it with a household chicken. 　　便令作對隨家雞
Tuizhi [Han Yu] gives a startled laugh and Zimei [Du Fu] weeps. 　　退之驚笑子美泣
I ask you, when will you return what you have borrowed for so long? 　　問君久假何時歸
The good lines in the world are shared by the men of the world; 　　世間好句世人共
8 A bright moon naturally fills the courtyards of a thousand homes.[8] 　　明月自滿千家墀

1/ Su Shi is playing with the connotations of *xian*, which can mean to praise or admire and to covet. In the second reading, Su Shi's use of Kong's own lines and rhymes become acts of playful appropriation on his part.

Su Shi is speaking here of the compositional method of "collecting poetic lines" (*ji ju*), in which one contrives poems by making a pastiche of lines from other poets.[9]

Su Shi's poem is humorous in its tone, but serious in its implications. First, it tells us that the ancients would be startled and even dismayed to witness the manipulation of their verses. This image plays off two pronouncements on the effect of fine verse: Du Fu, reflecting on his early project as poet, said, "If my lines don't startle others, in death I'll find no rest"; and He Zhizhang (fl. 720) on reading Li Bo's poem "Song of the Roosting Crows," said, "This poem could make gods and ghosts weep."[10] Here Su inverts these positive images to show the chagrin felt by the prior poets; they are startled precisely because they have not forgotten where those lines came from—they weep in dismay at what has happened to their lines.

Su Shi's sixth line plays off a passage from *Mencius* that again brings up the topic of ownership:

> Mencius said, "Yao and Shun [two legendary rulers, paragons of wisdom and virtue] had it [benevolence] as their nature. T'ang and King Wu embodied it. The Five Leaders of the feudal lords borrowed it. But if a man borrows a thing and keeps it long enough, how can one be sure that it will not become truly his?"[11]

Here the answer to Mencius' rhetorical question is that one *cannot* be sure that "it" is not his, and this becomes for Mencius a positive comment on the assimilation of the teachings of the ancients.

Su Shi's answer to this question is twofold. First, just as the thief of grain cannot return it to Shen Nong and Hou Ji, the latter-day poet can never "return" the lines of another once he has manipulated them, and this excuses him for his theft. Second, because the lines have been "borrowed so long," that is, because they have been assimilated so thoroughly by latter-day poets, they are now a legacy shared by all poets.

Su Shi ends his poem by evoking the naturalness of filling one's poem with the lines of other poets. The cliché of a "bright moon filling the courtyard" is portrayed as a universal experience with limited modes of articulation. If some things are universal and all share language, it is not plagiarism to repeat lines that convey that shared experience.

Huang Tingjian's famous remark on the superfluity of poetic language approaches this subject from another angle: even if poetic language is finite, its possible meanings are not: "The meaning of poetry is inexhaustible, yet the abilities of men are limited. In pursuing inexhaustible meaning through the use of limited talent, even Tao Yuanming and Du Fu could not achieve mastery in capturing it."[12]

In this vision, the meaning of words stands outside finitude. Any poetic utterance exudes a superfluity of significance, something uncontrollable in the context of any one creation.[13] Huang's reference to this inexhaustible quality is a twist on similar articulations of the theme. The *Shipin*'s description of *xing* speaks of a resonance of significance beyond the poetic trope—"The writing is exhausted yet the meaning contains a superfluity."[14] And the *Shiren yuxie* collects various references to the poetic significance beyond words.[15] Yet in these other pronouncements the "meaning" beyond the poetic word is still the creation of the original poet. It is his product, no matter how subtly and indirectly produced, and it is proof of his talent, rather than evidence of the inadequacy of all poets when faced with the task of controlling "inexhaustible meaning" by means of "limited talent."

For Huang, the resonances do *not* belong to the prior poet; they are fair game for later poets to appropriate, to embellish, to vary, or to refigure. By twisting the original intent of this notion of poetic superfluity and by asserting the inexhaustibility of poetic language, Huang opens up an immense field of poetic material and licenses a revolutionary and extremely self-conscious poetics.

Huang's pronouncement is also a conspicuous revision of a famous passage from the *Zhuangzi*: "Your life has a limit but knowledge has none. If you use what is limited to pursue what has no limit, you will be in danger. If you understand this and still strive for knowledge, you will be in danger for certain!"[16] That is, one should not dedicate one's life to the vain pursuit of what will always stand beyond one's power. Huang's manipulation of this phrase, an exemplary instance of "snatching the embryo," transforms it from a caution against overambition to an argument for a radical shift in poetic method and aim: the goal is no longer to *create* poetic language (a hopeless task), but to *invent on* the language of others.

But the blessing Huang contrives from the *Zhuangzi* is also a curse—the only way to stand out from the prior possessors of the poetic phrase is to do something markedly different and uniquely better with it. Furthermore, even if one does so, the condition of all poetry (which allows the appropriation in the first place) dictates that one's poem will not transcend that condition of inexhaustibility. One's own invention will become grist for someone else's mill. Despite playful attempts to erase the marks of ownership, late Northern Song poetics displays an endemic sense of melancholy, a sense that one's words will always be marked with the identity of other poets past and future.

"Spotting Critical Iron"

These comments on Huang Tingjian's poetics and poetry, particularly his views on the appropriation and transformation of poetic verse, reveal that Huang's "theory" results from a similar appropriation and manipulation of traditional critical discourses.

One key statement, which we have explored from various angles, offers alchemical transformation as a metaphor for the poetic process: "They [the great poets of antiquity] took the expressions of the ancients and entered them into brush and ink—it was like a pill of Spirit Cinnabar [*lingdan*], which spots iron and turns it to gold."[17] Huang's friend Su Shi draws on a similar metaphor: "Pure verse requires refinement and smelting; then one may obtain silver from lead."[18] Su is in turn echoing Sikong Tu (837–908): "Just as crude minerals put forth precious gold and lead ore silver, the transcendent mind smelts and refines."[19]

What differentiates Huang's pronouncement from Su Shi's and Sikong Tu's is that whereas the other two poets speak of refining and polishing one's own "crude" drafts, Huang explicitly focuses on revising *another's* language. Huang foregrounds the question of how the great poets of antiquity, coming as even they did into a condition of belatedness, transformed the deadened words of others into the vital elements of their art.

"Spirit Cinnabar," which Huang uses as an analogy for this process, is a Daoist element,[20] one of the five Spirit Cinnabars, each with its own use, which can lend one immortality.[21] The corollary of this is a poetic process that may revitalize language and perhaps even make it immortal. Huang changes the sad condition of being too late to create language to the hope that one may endow already created words with a transformed identity, an identity that bears one's own signature.

Transforming Primal Energy

Huang's most famous statements ("change the bone"; "seize the embryo") also derive from Daoist alchemy and arts of achieving immortality. In Chapter 6 we saw how these precepts are manifested in Huang's

Conclusion

poetic practice; here I focus on the particular manner in which Huang plays off other discourses to fabricate his critical metaphors.

"Changing the bone" is an obvious play on the term "bone" in traditional literary criticism. Its fullest exposition is in Liu Xie's *Wenxin diaolong*, section 28, "Feng gu" (The wind and the bone):

> The *Book of Poetry* contains six elements, and of these *feng*, or wind, stands at the head of the list. It is the source of transformation, and the correlate of emotion and vitality. He who would express mournful emotions must begin with the wind, and to organize his linguistic elements he must above all emphasize the bone. Literary expressions are conditioned by the bone in much the same way as the standing posture of the body is conditioned by its skeleton; feeling gives form to the wind very much as a physical form envelops the vitality which animates it. When expressions are organized on the right principles, literary bone is there; and when the emotion and vitality embodied are swift and free, there we find the purity of the literary wind.[22]

Although mutually distinct, the "wind" and the "bone" are interdependent; a lack of either results in a poem empty of energy. As Donald Gibbs points out, the emotional force described by the term *wind* relies on the structuring function of the bone to channel its energy (*qi*).[23] (As we shall shortly see, Huang's notion of "seizing the embryo" and his general project of revitalizing the language of the past have strong affinities to Liu Xie's concern for poetic vitality.) In a similar interpretation of "wind" and "bone," David Pollard notes: "Liu Hsieh says that 'wind' is the force that carries the feelings of the writer across to the reader (it is the 'basic source of influencing feelings'), while 'bone' is the quality that gives substance and strength to the thought structure and rhetorical scheme of the work (not the structure itself!)."[24] Pollard, following Xu Fuguan, claims that *feng* and *gu* refer here to complementary modes of manifesting *qi*.[25]

In later criticism, the term *gu* comes to refer more to the concrete rhetorical structure and diction of the poem. Certainly in his statement, Huang uses "bone" to describe the actual language of the poem and "wind" to symbolize the emotional force that both informs the poem and is conveyed in its language. Thus, by "changing the bone," Huang means altering or replacing the poetic line of a prior poet; he implies the "wind" is retained.

But even in seeming to leave the initial idea intact, Huang inevitably, albeit subtly, alters its significance and emotional register. In changing the bone, something happens to the original "wind," and this transformation of both form and content endows the poem with new and transcendent power. The suggestion, barely hidden, is that before this transformation the poetic line was somehow inadequate or, more precisely, that its full potential was unrealized.

In Daoist discourses on transformation and immortality, the idea of "changing the bone" refers to a mortal's acquiring immortal form.

> Wang [Kejiao] was rowing a fishing boat in a river when he spotted something that appeared to be a flowered boat in midstream. There were seven Daoists on that boat; one beckoned Wang to board and offered him wine. He tilted the goblet, but the wine did not come forth. One of the Daoists said, "As for this wine's spiritual properties, if you wish to have it enter your mouth, you must change your bones."[26]

In appropriating this imagery, Huang twists its logic significantly. It is not the original poet who desires to take on transcendent form; rather, it is Huang who benevolently appropriates the poem left behind and grants it immortality under his own name. Along with the bones, the entire "corpus" is changed, and thus to extend the metaphor, Huang's revision alters meaning as well as structure. As in the Daoist anecdote, the essential nature of the object is transformed, not merely prolonged.

As noted above, the more radical manner of appropriating prior verse is "seizing the embryo." Again, Huang creates a critical metaphor by playing off the dual functions of the terms in literary criticism and Daoist lore. Like "changing the bone," the "embryo" (*tai*) is mentioned often in Daoist texts, specifically with regard to *taixi*, a method of yogic breathing that is said to nourish vital energy (*qi*) and may help one achieve immortality. In the *Wenxin diaolong*, Liu Xie uses this practice as an analogue to poetic composition; in fact, Liu considers the proper regulation of *qi* in the expression of poetry to be a lesser form of *taixi*—both aim for the same nurturing of vital energy.

> Wang Chong [27–ca. 91] wrote a chapter on the theme of nourishing one's vitality.[27] ... Ears, eyes, nose, and mouth are organs which serve our physical life; thinking, pondering, speech, and linguistic expression are functions of our spirit. When all these operate spontaneously, in accordance with our nature and in perfect harmony, the principles of things are revealed and feeling finds unobstructed expression. But if a man works too hard, he becomes weary in spirit and sapped in vitality.
>
> ... During the time of the Three Sovereigns [Fu Xi, Nü Wa, and Shen Nong], the language was simple, and there was no desire to embellish it. The age of the [Five] Emperors [Tai Hao, Yan Di, Huang Di, Shao Hao, and Zhuan Xu] first witnessed the emergence of linguistic adornment, and there was a general emphasis on arranging the words in artistic patterns. Although this tendency to embellishment gradually grew throughout the period of the Three

Dynasties and the Spring and Autumn period, it remained always in perfect accord with the inner feelings of the writers, showing no sign of labor forcing the natural bounds of talent.

... The difference between a simple, sound language and a sophisticated, pretentious one is so apparent that it can still be recognized after a lapse of a thousand years. The one follows the nature of the mind, and the other exhausts the feelings; they are ten thousand miles apart, for one is spontaneous and the other laborious. In this way we may see the reason why the Ancients were always leisurely and at ease, and later writers so hurried and hasty.

... Now a man's capacity and natural parts are limited, but he may work his mind without limit. There are men who are ashamed of their short "wild duck" legs and aspire to those of the crane:[28] they will force themselves to write and their minds to function. In so doing, they wear out the vitality within, which fades away like the feeble waves of a stream, or make themselves as gaunt and emaciated as the trees on Mount Niu.[29]

Liu Xie is concerned primarily with assuring that the poem is not the product of forced, laborious composition but the natural and spontaneous manifestation of the writer's vital energy. He then speaks of the harm that laboring over writing may do to one's *qi*: first, attempting to tax one's inner spirit beyond its limits will strain it; second, whatever may be produced through this effort will doubtless be inauthentic. He ends by saying:

One should always try the sharpness of his talent at leisure, and spur on his literary courage when there is plenty of surplus energy, so that his knife may ever be as newly honed, and the circulation of the air through the veins to his muscles may be unobstructed. Although this method of achieving refreshment may not achieve the results obtained from the art of breath control [*taixi*], it is one way to protect our vitality.[30]

There are many compelling moments in these passages. The idea of "vitality" (*qi*) that we saw in the section on the "Wind and the Bone" as determining the emotional force of the poem reappears here strongly. Again, *qi* is manifested spontaneously; labor inevitably mars the poem. With his mention of a knife that ever appears newly honed, Liu Xie gestures toward a set of famous images of spontaneous and unlabored craft.

Most important, *qi* is inherently authentic; it is absolutely rooted in one's nature and cannot be transferred or inherited. This is perfectly in keeping with one of the term's earliest uses in literary criticism, Cao Pi's (187–226) "Dianlun lunwen":

Wen takes *qi* to be of prime importance. In clarity and murkiness *qi* has embodiments. It is not something that can be forced into being; it is just like music. Although the tune and the rhythm may be the same, when it comes to the drawing in of breath [*qi*], if that is not the same, the artfulness or clumsiness of the performance is predetermined. Although the father or elder brother may possess it, he cannot pass it on to his son or younger brother.[31]

If this is indeed the case and if *qi* is seen as the thing that passes in and out of the body as one practices *taixi*, then it seems strangely brutal to suggest "seizing" that embyronic entity, for it is through the careful nurturing of *qi* that one may prolong one's life.

Huang's use of this metaphor may be approached from two angles. First, as we have just discussed, "seizing the embryo" may be an act that interferes with the nature of the poem itself. That is, if *qi*, with all its connotations of emotional authenticity and immediacy, is the originating poet's alone and indeed part and parcel of his being, then to disturb the life-nurturing process of passing *qi* in and out of the body is an overt act of violence.[32] (And here we may supply the implicit correlation in Liu Xie's analogy—the poem stands as the outward expression of the poet's perception of and reflection on phenomena; that is, as *im*pressions enter the poet's mind, he spontaneously *ex*presses his emotional response.)

Second, the Daoist concept of *qi* and its role in the mind and body is tied to the notion of Primal Qi (*yuan qi*), the raw, unformed energy, without shape or direction, that preceded the creation of the phenomenal universe.[33] The course of cosmic history is a history of the ceaseless process of transforming *yuan qi*.

The dual characteristics of this *qi*—its raw energy and its continual transformation—have strong affinities to the nature of *wen* itself. *Wen* came about after *yuan qi* had begun to coalesce; as things evolved out of the primordial chaos, each was endowed with a particular identifying marking that correlated its being with the coming into being of the world.[34] The various manifestations of *qi* in discrete phenomena may be matched with the outward, particularizing sign of phenomena, *wen*. In literature (also designated as *wen*), poetry is both the outward manifestation of the inner nature (*qi*) of the poet and his apprehension of a facet of the world's *wen*.

The relationship between *qi* and *wen* cannot be overemphasized. For example, traditional critics held that as a culture's vital energy ebbs (a sure sign of a lax and corrupt ethos), the culture's *wen* (literature, art, and other cultural objects) reflects that weakness. What is true of a culture is equally true of an individual—writing reflects inner being. The manifestations of *qi* in time are an index to the "climate" of the age, its moral

Conclusion

character; the manifestations of *qi* in the individual are a sign of that person's style and manner of being in the world.

In the Tang, the cosmic process of transforming *yuan qi* came to be used as an analogy to the creative power of great poets. Han Yu, writing on the Southern Mountains, ends by paralleling their creation with his composing of a poem on those mountains.[35] Just as the creative and transformative force of the cosmos (*zao hua*) shapes primal energy, so the great poet forms his works of art. In a colophon Huang Tingjian adopts this correlation: "When one takes up brush and ink, one's achievement is the same as that of natural creation."[36]

We may thus draw forth the affinities between the transformation of *qi* and the creation of *wen*: as *qi* is transformed and molded, its outward corollary, *wen*, reflects this continual manifestation. If "seizing the embryo" means to appropriate the *qi* from another poet's work, then we have an image of Huang stepping into the role of cosmic/poetic regenerator, but in a particularly distinctive manner. Not only is he shaping the Primal Qi of the world, giving it a new manifestation (*wen*), but he is also appropriating an already formed *qi* and reshaping its articulation. The texts of the classical tradition are now correlated with Primal Qi.

This radically different image of poetic composition is reflected in the difference between Huang's notion of *qi* and that of the Wei and Jin dynasty critics. For the latter, *qi* cannot be learned or passed on. Liu Xie speaks more of how to conserve *qi*, but he gives no prescription for nurturing it. Huang, and other late Northern Song thinkers, emphasized that *qi* could be nurtured by immersing oneself in the *qi* of the natural world. The movement outward is vitally significant here; the relationship between man and external phenomena takes on a special significance.

As early as the *Lüshi chunqiu*, one finds the idea that all natural phenomena possess a certain *qi*: "When *qingqi* (quintessential *qi*) concentrates in something it must infuse it. When concentrated in birds it confers the ability to fly; in beasts, movement. In gems it confers brilliance; in trees, luxuriant growth. When concentrated in sages it confers great clarity."[37] This passage gives us an indication of why and how *qi* became, for Liu Xie, a sign of the potential energy behind the expression of emotion and thought.

Late Northern Song thinkers believed one could nurture *qi* by placing oneself near the *qi* of that which was great in the world. Su Che (1039–1112) makes this famous statement:

I consider writing [*wen*] to be the embodiment of one's vital force [*qi*]. However, writing is not something that one can learn to be capable of, while the vital force is something that one can acquire by cultivation. Mencius said, "I am good at cultivating my overflowing *qi*." Now, when we observe his writing, it is deep and wide, vast and grand, filling the space between heaven and earth, and matching the magnitude of his vital force. The Grand Historiographer [Sima Qian] travelled over the world, surveying all the famous mountains and great rivers within the four seas, and associating with the heroic and outstanding men of Yan and Zhao. Hence his writing is spacious and free, possessing to a remarkable degree an extraordinary air [*qi*]. Did these two masters ever, writing-brush in hand, learn to produce such writings? The vital force of each filled his inside, overflowed his countenance, stirred up his words, and manifested itself in his writing, without his knowing it himself.

I have lived for nineteen years. When I lived at home, those with whom I associated were only neighbors and fellow villagers, and what I saw was confined to a few hundred *li*, without high mountains I could climb or vast wilderness that I could view so as to broaden myself. And although among the books of the "hundred schools" there was none I did not read, these were all old traces left by the ancients, not sufficient to stimulate one's will and vital force. For fear these might trickle away, I left with determination, to seek the extraordinary events and grand views of the world, so that I might realize the greatness of the universe.[38]

Much here reminds one of the archetype of the youthful Romantic hero, off to the Alps to gaze on the sublimity of the peaks. But of great importance are the claim that, in contrast to Cao Pi's notion, *qi* can be "cultivated," and the method for doing so—by exposing oneself to as much firsthand experience as possible.

Again, although the last paragraph might be attributed to a young man's rejection of the dusty tomes of his father's library in favor of the unknown and as yet unexperienced wonders of the world outside, this rejection is in keeping with the implications in the Wei-Jin critics' writings on *qi* of the importance of primary experience. Yet one finds here an unmistakable shift of focus from the earlier critics' notion of the internal and inherent nature of *qi* to the particular relationship between the individual and external phenomena and their particularly manifested *qi*.

Huang Tingjian's notion of *qi* has some points in common with Su Che's. Shen Fu notes that for Huang Tingjian there were two kinds of *qi*. One kind could be obtained by cultivating literary talent; the other could come from direct experience of the world. Here we have the same dichotomy as in Su Che. Fu goes on to offer this statement by Huang on the second type of *qi*: "The late-style calligraphy of Mr. Dongpo [Su Shi] is especially monumental and strong; that is because he obtained the *qi* of the wind-blown crests of the sea."[39] Huang's notions of *qi* differ from those of Su Che in two important respects. First, unlike Su Che, Huang does not reject outright the notion that one might nurture *qi* through reading texts. In fact, that source of nourishment stands on par with direct experience. In this point of difference, we already see Huang's distance from Su Che's and Liu Xie's preference for direct experience.

Second, Su Che's and Huang's notions of direct experience are different. Whereas Su Che speaks of cultivating his *qi* through directly experiencing the world in an unwilled and spontaneous osmosis, Huang's pronouncement suggests that Su Shi has willfully appropriated *qi* from the natural world—he has somehow *made* it enter into his spirit and thereby cultivated his art. This difference is subtle, but it helps support the concept of "seizing the embryo" as we have begun to understand it.

If an artist can legitimately appropriate *qi* from external phenomena such as the crests of the sea and invent on that *qi*, fashioning it into a work of art as primal *qi* is fashioned and transformed by *zao hua* (Cosmic Transformation),[40] then a poet may appropriate the *qi* of another poet and transform it. The *qi* of a prior poet as manifested in a poem possesses no greater position of privilege than the *qi* of external phenomena, which may be "obtained" and reworked, transformed, and revised. The difference between the two objects of appropriation cannot but confound one; yet my sense is that for Huang the two acts of appropriation are not that dissimilar. It is this correlation that has astounded critics since his time.

Finally, if the linkage of "seizing the embryo" to the notion of *taixi* and *qi* seems weak, then let me point out that both Liu Xie and Huang allude to the same passage from the *Zhuangzi* regarding limited human abilities.[41] But although both men correlate nurturing *qi* with the poetic process, it is crucial to understand the difference in motives behind these citations.

Liu Xie follows the *Zhuangzi*'s pronouncement. Zhuangzi's point, and Liu Xie's, is that one should accept the limitations on one's abilities. Liu Xie extends the damage attempting to do so does to one's *qi* to the poem produced in the attempt.

But Huang challenges the condition of limitation. In his revision of the passage from the *Zhuangzi*, Huang concedes that a poet's abilities are limited—even the greatest poets are unable to contain and control the limitlessness of language, nor can they lay claim to having created any poetic word. But then Huang advises poets not to exhaust their *qi* in the attempt to create but to redirect that energy into mastering the art of appropriating the *wen* of others, seizing their manifested *qi*, and transforming it into something of one's own.

To mute the violence of this image, Huang portrays this transformation as both unavoidable (one cannot help but use the words of others'—that is all one has) and beneficent (it bestows immortality on prior verse, turning it into "gold"). This vision of poetic appropriation and revision becomes firmly established in exactly these terms in the discourse of Huang Tingjian's imitators. For example, Yu Cheng (fl. 1200) writes:

> A text must, of course, have a "live method." If it adheres to the worn tracks of earlier writers and cannot catalytically transform the language of their lines, then this is called a "dead method." If I merely copy, then what I say will have no life beyond the moment of my expression. But, if there is a "live method," if there is use of "appropriating the embryo" and "changing the bones," then the words will not be dead within the confines of my own expression. The death of my words gives birth to my words—thus it is a "live method." [42]

Huang's project absolutely contradicts the assumptions of Liu Xie's statement. Huang denies that by appropriating another's discourse one is negating the possibility of authentic verse. Simply put, *qi* is, for Huang, eminently transformable and transferable. "Seizing the embryo" might also be read "to snatch from the womb," to which Adele Rickett adds this paraphrase, "to drive off the soul of the foetus and take its place." [43] I believe that Huang is playing with both readings. Indeed, the poems that are cited as "seizing the embryo" exhibit a clear substitution of meaning in a similar form. It is clear how radical Huang's pronouncements were—in effect they seem to contravene all the basic values of the lyric tradition, namely, the direct expression of emotion and the authentic and spontaneous manifestation of a highly individual *qi*. Huang posited a poetics that foregrounded the mediation of prior texts and the appropriation and manipulation of what was thought to be untransferable and sacrosanct.

I end this discussion of Huang's metaphors for poetic appropriation and transformation by underscoring one of the essential premises of his poetics: the notion of extension and completion. These interrelated notions have both moral and aesthetic value. In previous chapters I spoke of the imperative to correlate the intent of the ancient sages with one's own life. The goal of the late Northern Song was not to replicate antiquity but to see the relationship between the ethos set forth in the Classics and their own age; above all, one was to make connections. The transformation of Primal Qi is another facet of extending and modifying culture.

The following comment on painting and literary composition is the corollary to this notion of extension and completion. Huang cites Li Gonglin: "Po-shih [Li Boshi] said with a smile: 'If a common painter had done this, he would have made the arrow hit the pursuing horsemen.' Through this I perceived that the art of painting and literary composition were essentially the same."[44] The implication is unmistakable: a poem, like a painting, should never give its reader everything; rather, it should lead the reader to "make" the poem himself. This aesthetic is more than simply a call for indirection and suggestiveness: it is a claim regarding the essential moral and aesthetic role of a work of art. The manifestation of this notion of incompleteness in Western Romantic discourse is, of course, the notion of the fragment, the ever-open lure of completion even in the face of radical incompletability—the demand for closure is played off the need for an ever-present and never-fulfilled desire.[45] But for the poet of eleventh-century China the notion of "completion" is radically different, and it is here, I believe, that we can delineate a major difference between classical Chinese and Western poetics.

Huang and the West

Stephen Owen neatly draws out the difference between the Western conception of literature and that in the classical Chinese tradition:

Concepts of imitation, representation, or even expression can never entirely free literature from its status as a secondary phenomenon, later and less than some "original" (in the case of expression, the "original" is a state of mind). . . . To escape the foredoomed failure, a most ingenious revision was devised: the "original" was displaced out of this world and became a hidden Something Else to which the poem gives unique access. By this strange inversion, the "original" significance becomes epistemologically contingent on the secondary representation.

. . . But if literature (*wen*) is the entelechy of a previously unrealized pattern, and if the written word (*wen*) is not a sign but a schematization, then there can be no competition for dominance. Each level of *wen*, that of the world and that of the poem, is valid only in its own correlative realm; and the poem, the final outward form, is a stage of fullness.[46]

In the Romantic tradition, the movement toward capturing that "origin" is correlated with the movement toward closure and plenitude but tainted by the skepticism found in Schiller's "sentimental." The Romantic poet has the entire realm of the abstract to feed his imagination, and yet the very infinitude of that realm constantly forestalls any actualization of completedness—that plenitude is both the privilege and limitation of the "naive."

Huang's stress on completion does not (and under the terms of his own concept of the limitlessness of words, cannot) involve a fixed closure. Rather, and this correlates with his notion of the transformation of *wen*, a poem may be the "complete" realization of the ever-immanent reality of the "intent" of the ancients' *wen for a particular moment* in history, but as time changes, history demands a re-articulation of that intent as it is meaningful and relevant to that new age.

This notion does not differ greatly from the pronouncements of traditional critics such as Liu Xie, who speaks of "flexible adaptability to varying situations."[47] What is distinctive in Huang's poetics is his particular mode of enacting that imperative to transform and renew *wen*. His enactment, as we have seen, runs counter to many of the basic premises of the lyric tradition regarding the unmediated, spontaneous nature of poetry.

I end this study of Huang Tingjian by raising the question of Huang's relevance to Western literary studies. In the Critical Introduction, I pointed out the affinities between Huang's concerns for originality and imitation and both ancient and Romantic literary criticism in the West. At present, there are two major views on the subject in literary critical discourse, and these views inform to one degree or another many of the remarks I have offered on Huang's poetry and poetics. These two views are found in the concept of intertextuality and in Harold Bloom's notion of poetic "anxiety."

The term *intertextuality* is fraught with vagueness. For some theorists it refers to the citation of prior texts in a later literary work.[48] To others, it designates the evocation of certain subgeneric or generic discourses within the frame of another discourse.[49] For still others, it refers to the imposition of one or more other semiotic systems on another.[50] All these variants of intertextuality define a text as a particular composite of other texts and discourses. In this definition one may sense the desire to displace the value of absolute origin and to champion a plurality of "origins."[51]

This seems to be a counterpart of Huang's pronouncement regarding our limited abilities in the face of the infinity of language. No one can claim to have created language; it is the common and necessary inheritance of all poets. One difference between Huang's statement and Western critical discourse is the pronounced absence of the nostalgia for a displaced and forever lost origin that haunts Western literature. The

Conclusion

compensatory reaction against the loss of the naive (in Schiller's terms) is emphasized in a seminal article on intertextuality:

> What is characteristic of intertextuality is that it introduces a new way of reading which destroys the linearity of the text. Each intertextual reference is the occasion for an alternative: either one continues reading, taking it only as a segment like any other, integrated into the syntagmatic structure of the text, or else one turns to the source text, carrying out a sort of intellectual anamnesis where the intertextual reference appears like a paradigmatic element that has been displaced, deriving from a forgotten structure. But in fact the alternative is only present for the analyst. These two processes really operate simultaneously in intertextual reading—and in discourse—studding the text with bifurcations that gradually expand its semantic space.
>
> Whatever the texts may be that are assimilated, the status of intertextual discourse is thus comparable to that of some super-parole in that the constituents of this discourse are not just words, but bits of the already said, the already organized, textual fragments. Intertextuality speaks a language whose vocabulary is the sum of all existing texts. There takes place a sort of release on the level of parole, a promotion to discourse of a power *infinitely superior* to that of everyday monologic discourse. [Italics added]

On intertextual discourse is, then, conferred "an exceptional richness and density." But in return the "cited" text must, as it were, give up its transitivity: "*it no longer speaks*, it is spoken" (italics added).[52] The desire to articulate a critical terminology that grants ascendancy to the latter-day text is unmistakable. The later text becomes the force that renders the prior text speechless. The last portion of this passage evolves in such a way that one could almost substitute "artistic language" or "literariness" for intertextuality—intertextuality becomes the sign of literature itself. The tension between the later writer and previous works is hard to miss here. (Recent discussions of the idea of postmodernity extend the intertextual critique radically, exploding even further the idealism of textual continuity and the integrity of origin, so much so that an absolute incommensurability between textual fragments characterizes the postmodern text.)[53]

Indeed, the strategies of intertextuality remind us of much in Huang Tingjian's poetry, but this similarity can be misleading. The basic premise of what literature *is* in the Western tradition and the classical Chinese tradition separates Huang Tingjian's poetics from the intertextual critique. As noted above, the Western literary tradition has valued the creative power of the poet to shape and fashion worlds that offer a vision of what is absent. Laurent Jenny evokes this notion in a strange manner, as he speaks of the informing, and yet forgotten (i.e., absent), paradigm behind the text.[54] For the poet writing in medieval China, the poem was seen not as a substitution but as a corollary. The poem was an attempt not to create a vision of another realm but to articulate the affinities between various realms of experience.

Another critical difference involves the relationship between the citation and the poem that cites it. Although Huang's revisions often involve a radical mode of playing with prior enunciations, this act was not performed in order to create something entirely different; rather, Huang's intent was to tap what he took to be the prior texts' potential and transform and extend it, not to displace or silence it. Indeed, Huang's poetic project hinges on the recognition of the prior text in the later work and a sense of a common project shared by all poets that lends the transformation coherence and ethical legitimacy.

Like the intertextual critique, Bloom's revisionary poetics has a stake in silencing texts of origin through a kind of misreading. This is brought about by subsuming the signifying function of the prior text(s) to the purposes of the latter-day poet. Instead of tracing out and restoring the semantic plenitude of the text as the intertextual critique attempts to do, Bloom is concerned with how Romantic and post-Romantic poetry reveals a continual struggle between a poet and his or her precursors. The poem is a scarred territory of misreading and revision. In the poet's search for a way to speak that does not call forth another's name, we find something similar to Huang Tingjian's project. Yet we can only be skeptical about the applicability of Bloom's theory to classical Chinese poetry.[55]

This skepticism derives, again, from the radical differences in literary traditions. Bloom's ratios cannot be taken as more than interesting parallels in the case of classical Chinese poetry. The notion of struggling with one's predecessors is, as pointed out in the introduction to this study, not new to the Western literary tradition. What is different in Bloom's psychoanalytically informed reading of Romantic poetry is the determining, radical act of misreading that allows the belated poet to appropriate and revise the words of his predecessors. Bloom sees this as an indication of the poet's desire to make a place for himself, to challenge the primacy and authority of those before him, and to elide the "anxiety of influence": "Poetic history, in this book's argument, is held to be indistinguishable from poetic influence, since strong poets make that history by misreading one another, so as to clear imaginative space for themselves."[56]

Conclusion 191

The Jin dynasty critic Wang Ruoxu (1174–1243) attributes Huang's poetic theories to a similar kind of anxiety:

> Huang's discourses on poetry contain the metaphors "seize the embryo and change the bone," and "spirit cinnabar spots iron and turns it into gold." The world takes these to be remarkable formulations, but as I see it, this refers to nothing more than clever plagiarism. Huang was fond of attaining superiority; he felt ashamed to have [his poetry] come forth from previous poets, and thus he came up with these formulas and made such new terms by himself.[57]

Here we find the essential difference between Bloom's notion of revision and the Chinese model: Bloom's theory is predicated on the claim that the later poet's revision improves, completes, or corrects the poem of his predecessor. In Huang Tingjian's poetics, and in classical Chinese poetics in general, these motives have quite different nuances. Each of these acts is subsumed to a larger vision of what literature is. By its very nature literature in the classical Chinese tradition not only lends itself to transformation but demands it. Furthermore, in the classical Chinese tradition in general and the late Northern Song in particular, like natural phenomena *wen* was not the absolute property of any one person. Rather, *wen* was something that achieved significance within an essentially collective discourse. To improve, complete, or correct a poem meant to draw forth what was latent rather than to invent something new.[58]

Again, Bloom's theory instructs us to recognize the suppressed, distorted presence of what was assumed to be absent or only benignly present—the prior text. Romantic poetics called for originality, not revision; Bloom shows how that value of originality was and always is threatened by the anxiety of influence. But the classical Chinese tradition had a very different notion of originality. A poet was unique in the explicit manner in which he wrote *within* the tradition or expanded on it, not in his power to create worlds that had never existed. Huang's critical and theoretical pronouncements are best understood as the most explicit articulations of that understanding. The presence of the past was a given element in literary texts; indeed, it was a necessary one.

The subconscious, evasive nature of Bloom's revisionary ratios is both a mark of the Romantic poet's need to conceal those enactments from the reader and to stake a claim to originality and a mark of the distinction between this vision and the classical Chinese poem, which openly relies on the reader's knowledge of both the prior text and the later text. Put succinctly, the nature of a citation, an intertextual fragment, differs radically in the Western and classical Chinese traditions precisely because of their different notions of textuality and its relation to cultural discourse.

The figure of the palimpsest illustrates this difference. In the Western Romantic tradition, the poet seeks to erase the mark of the prior writer in order, as Bloom puts it, to clear a space for himself. In the classical Chinese tradition, the poet seeks to adapt fragments of past texts to configurations of his own design. His poem achieves dimensionality and significance only insofar as it can both evoke and transform the past. In Huang Tingjian's poetics, we have one of the most emphatic acts of signing the palimpsest, of marking the poem with all its allusions to the past, as something of his own making. Most important, these acts of appropriation and extension are endorsed by a cultural tradition that is *continuous* between latter-day and present-day texts; indeed, the act of writing is here the sole means of preserving the ongoing significance of cultural discourse. In the West, this ideological continuity tends to be either suppressed in the name of aesthetic purity (e.g., the idea of art for art's sake) or denied in the name of individual creativity.

The questions I have raised regarding the essential nature of poetic composition in the West and China are obviously too large to answer in any sustained manner here—they give rise to knotty issues of, among other things, hermeneutics, the philosophy of language, and cultural semiotics. I have attempted in this study to illuminate a complex situation that faced Chinese poets at a point in literary history when they were particularly self-conscious of their situation and profoundly aware that that situation demanded a rethinking of the basic premises of literary composition and the nature of literature and to explore one poet's response to that condition, a response that came to characterize his age.

One final point remains to be made. Huang Tingjian's project, with all its complex contradictions, should not be regarded as an aberration in Chinese literary history. More than anything else, I have tried to show how his concerns are the concerns of the tradition. He drew forth and underscored the implicit problems that faced the classical Chinese poet, and his response underscored the problematic nature of the primary tenets of lyric poetry—spontaneous craft, immediate emotional response, and the fixed semantic authority of citation. Huang Tingjian deserves our attention because of the manner in which he articulated the paradox of originality, a paradox that runs deeply through both Chinese and Western poetics.

Appendixes

APPENDIX A

Short Biography of Huang Tingjian

Huang Tingjian, 1045–1105 (*zi* Luzhi, *hao* Shangu, also Fuweng), was born into a successful literati family. His father, Huang Shu (*zi* Yafu, 1018–58), was an accomplished poet in his own right, and, along with Huang's maternal uncle Li Chang (who raised the boy after his father's death in 1058), fostered in Huang Tingjian an interest in poetry. In particular, both Huang Shu and Li Chang were among the first in the Northern Song to revive interest in the poetry of Du Fu. Indeed, Huang carved his father's poems in stone in a gesture similar to that of his engraving and preserving Du Fu's poems (as told in "The Account of the Hall of the Great Odes"). Huang Shu's verse is collected in his *Fatan ji* (Hewing sandalwood collection) and appended to Huang Tingjian's collection (*SHSG*).[1] (It seems ironic that the poet most known for setting himself before his predecessors has his father's verse known through his.) Huang Shu's poetry is characterized by a penchant for the kind of astringent diction for which Huang Tingjian became famous, as well as a keen eye for visual detail and irony. Only two short *juan* of Huang Shu's poems remain; Huang Tingjian's extant poetry consists of some two thousand *shi* pieces, and one hundred *ci*.

Huang married twice, once in 1068, to Sun Jue's daughter, who died in 1070, and again in 1073, to the daughter of Xie Shihou (Jingchu, 1020–84). His second wife died in 1079. He had one daughter, Mu, who was born in 1076, and one son, Xiang, who was born in 1084 to a concubine.

In 1063 Huang unsuccessfully sat the *jinshi* examination in Kaifeng, but in 1067 he passed and was appointed sheriff of Ye *xian*. In 1072 he passed the examination for education officials and was appointed instructor at the National Academy of the Northern Capital, a position he held until 1077.

In 1078 he sent Su Shi two poems of introduction, in which he stated his great admiration for Su. This marked his entry into Su's group and the beginning of his serious poetic oeuvre. In 1079 he was stripped of his position as assistant staff author and fined for his support of Su Shi's attack on Wang Anshi's New Policies.

In 1085 he was appointed collator of the Imperial Library, and in 1086 Sima Guang asked that Huang join in the editing of the *Zizhi tongjian*. He was appointed assistant editor in the Office for the Veritable Records of Emperor Shenzong and, in 1087, was restored to his former status. Nevertheless, he was again attacked by the censor Zhao Tingzhi for immoral conduct and being a follower of Su Shi. His promotion in 1091 to recorder of the imperial movements was rescinded because of an attack on his conduct, and in 1094 he was accused of using his role as compiler of the Veritable Records to distort the records and attack the New Policies. He was banished to restricted residence first in Qianzhou and later in Rongzhou.

In 1100 he was restored to rank and appointed inspector of salt revenues and later signatory official of the Staff Supervisorate. In 1103 he retired with a temple sinecure. During this time the anti–New Policies faction came under severe attack, and woodblocks of their writings were ordered destroyed. Huang was banished to Yizhou, where he died in 1105.[2]

APPENDIX B

On Translating Huang Tingjian

Two problems confront the translator of Huang Tingjian's poetry. Aside from formidable gaps between ages and cultures, in translating such a highly allusive poet I have often had to choose among a number of possible registers of diction, allusive reference, and lyrical style, and, at the same time, keep in mind the fact that the lines have to approximate an effect that resists translation.

Wherever possible, I have tried to achieve a balance between linguistic accuracy and poetic style. This is not to say that Huang's poetry is always palpable—indeed, as we have seen, a "stringent" difficulty (a term employed by Chinese critics to describe Huang's poetry) was central to Huang's poetics. In my translations I have tried not to avoid that calculated difficulty but to present it as an essential part of the line, while capturing some of the "effect of spontaneity" that Huang sought to achieve.

It is nearly impossible to tell the specific force with which allusions were to be read, and here too I have tried to balance my rendering of the lines against some understanding of how the allusions might function within the larger context of the poem as a whole.

I have used a number of editions of Huang's poetry, most often the SBBY editions of his Inner Collection (annotated by Ren Yuan, ?–1144) and the Outer Collection (edited by Shi Rong, d. after 1201), to which is appended a Separate Collection. These annotations, as well as those of Qian Zhongshu, Arai Ken, and Kurata Junnosuke, are extremely helpful in tracking down Huang's allusions. Nevertheless, and this is particularly true for the SBBY annotations, one must weigh two factors before accepting the allusions cited.

First, the annotators often cite every possible source for even the most fragmentary images. Although obliged to consider each of these possibilities, one is often forced to reject some because of the interpretive "leap" necessary to fit them into the logic of the poem. This is not to say that some critics might not be able to find a way to use certain citations I have rejected.

Second, even given the plethora of citations that annotators have offered, some have escaped their notice, and here I have been fortunate to have had the advice of those mentioned in the Acknowledgments to add to my knowledge of classical Chinese poetry. Finally, it is important to recognize that, as I have tried to point out, Huang often gestures toward other poems, not by citing their lines, but by recreating their atmosphere, scenarios, or moods. Annotators often fail to remark on these sorts of allusions.

My last point is related to this issue; Huang undoubtedly plays with specific philosophical discourses in a similarly indirect manner. A firm grounding in Buddhist and Daoist lore would allow a deeper perception of densities of significance, as would a knowledge of popular lore and more specific sociopolitical circumstances. I hope that this study has provided a means of understanding the essential characteristics of Huang's poetics, so that other researchers can bring to light other aspects of the applications of these strategies.

Reference Matter

Notes

For complete author names, titles, and publication data for the works cited here in short form, see the Bibliography, pp. 227–38. For the abbreviations used here, see p. xiii.

PREFACE

1. See Mo, 23–24 and 291–92.

INTRODUCTION

1. Bate, 3–4; "Da Hong Jufu shu" (Letter in response to Hong Jufu), third of three, *YZ* 19.23b; second passage cited in Huihong, 1.5a–b.
2. Bate, 3–4; John Barth, "The Literature of Replenishment," *Atlantic Monthly*, Jan. 1980, 71.
3. Aristotle, *Rhetoric* 1.1354a; trans. Roberts and Bywater, 19.
4. Quintilian 10.2; trans. Russell and Winterbottom, 400–401. All citations of Quintilian are from this passage.
5. Aristotle, *Poetics* 4.1448b8; trans. Roberts and Bywater, 226–27.
6. Longinus, "On Sublimity," 2.1–2; trans. Russell and Winterbottom, 463. Subsequent citations of Longinus appear in the text and give chapter and verse followed after a semicolon by the page number in the translation.
7. See, e.g., Nitchie; and Monk.
8. Boileau, 338 (my trans.).
9. Monk, 36.
10. Young, 6. Subsequent citations of this work appear in the text.
11. For a discussion of the notion of "vegetable genius" in German Romantic discourse, see Abrams, 201–12.
12. Young (15) gives Swift as his example.
13. *Über das Naive* in no. 11 of 1795; *Die sentimentalischen Dichter* in no. 12, 1795; and *Beschluss der Abhandlung über naive und sentimentalische Dichter, nebst*

einigen Bemerkungen einen charakteristischen Unterschied unter den Menschen betreffend, no. 1, 1796. These are collected under one title, *Über naive und sentimentalische Dichtung*. References to this text give the page in the *Säkular-Ausgabe* followed after a semicolon by the page number in the English translation of Julias A. Elias.

14. At other points (see 85, 155, 160), Schiller adds another limitation to the naive—the naive poet's unity with nature can even taint his work, since there is such a thing as vulgar nature. The naive poet's absolute and necessary relation to nature prevents him from distancing himself from, or even from reflecting on, the vulgar.

15. Abrams, 213, citing *Vorlesungen über schöne Litteratur und Kunst*, in *Sämtliche Werke* (Leipzig, 1846), 6: 182.

16. This, of course, is the paradox that informs Kant's *Critique of Judgment*.

17. For this essay, see Eliot, *Sacred Wood*, 47–59. Subsequent citations of this work appear in the text.

18. Eliot, "The Metaphysical Poets" (1921), in *Selected Essays*, 247.

19. Ibid., 289.

20. I am aware that "Western / classical Chinese tradition" is a very rough, and reductive, distinction; I make no claim beyond a particular distinction between Western and classical Chinese presumptions about literary activity.

ONE

1. Huang Tingjian, "Yu Qin Shaozhang shu" (Letter to Qin Shaozhang), YZ 19.31a–b.

2. Rather than reading this as deeply haunted by a sense of belatedness and anxiety, as many modern critics do, I would suggest reading it as being written with a tone of false modesty and even bemusement, especially given what follows.

3. Qian Zhongshu, *Song shi xuanzhu*, 11–12.

4. Hu Yunyi, *Song shi yanjiu*, 11–12.

5. Both expressions refer to works that merely repeat earlier texts and are therefore worthless as literature.

6. Wu Zhizhen et al., Preface, 1a–6b.

7. Hu Yunyi, *Song shi yanjiu*, 19.

8. "Han Yu lun" (Discourse on Han Yu), Qin, 22.2a–3a.

9. I derive this scheme partially from Liang Kun, *Song shipai bielun*, which in turn is indebted to the work of the Jin critic Fang Hui (1227–1306). For an outline of the literary milieu of the early Northern Song using Liang Kun's work as a basis, see Chaves, *Mei Yao-chen*, chap. 2. For a short treatment of Song "schools" of poetry extending into and beyond Huang Tingjian's period, see Hightower, *Topics*, 84–89.

10. Hu Yunyi, *Song shi yanjiu*, 27–28.

11. See Liang Kun, 141.

12. The Nine Monks were Xizhou, Baoxian, Wenzhao, Xingzhao, Jianzhang, Weifeng, Huichong, Yuzhao, and Huaigu. Of these, Huichong is the most famous (Ouyang Xiu considered him the only truly important member of the group); the poems of the other monks have been lost. Their poetry was seen as the most representative corpus of the late Tang style.

13. Fang, section 21 ("Xue lei").

14. Zhu Bian, *Fengyuetang shihua, xia* 45; cited in Guo Shaoyu, *Zhongguo wenxue piping shi*, 182.

15. Wang Anshi, *Linchuan wenji*, 73.467; cited and trans. Lo, 41–53.

16. Bol, 108.

17. *Huaji*, iii; cited in Soper, 41.

18. See Li Gonglin's biography in Huizong, 7.197–204.

19. For Du Fu's line, see the first of his "Jueju manxing jiu shou" (Nine quatrains casually inspired), Du Fu, 788.

20. The term *an he* "unconsciously match" (lit.: "darkly match") comes from Lu Ji's "Wen fu," lines 139–40: "It must not be different from that which it takes as a model./Thus it will darkly match with former works." Cheng Huichang (92) interprets the lines to mean that the latter-day poet shares a similar spirit with the former: "Men are alike in this mind; the minds are alike in this inner principle."

21. Cai Juhou (fl. 1108) in *Cai Kuanfu shihua*; cited in Guo Shaoyu, *Song shihua jiyi*, 2: 31.

22. Wang is one of the major figures of early Northern Song verse. Often credited with being the first Song writer to be seriously interested in Bo Juyi's and Du Fu's poetry and the prose style of Han Yu, he set the stage for what is called the *fugu* ("reviving antiquity") movement in the Song, led by Ouyang Xiu.

23. Mei, 24.12b–13a; cited and trans. Chaves, *Mei Yao-ch'en*, 81–82.

24. Chaves, *Mei Yao-ch'en*, 82. For the poem, see Mei, 35.7a–8a.

25. Of course, the stage was set for this by the early Song poets, and we should differentiate explicit identification with Tang poets, which suggests an unimaginative repetition of models, and the actual poetics of the best poets of the time (Wang Yucheng, Su Shunqin, Ouyang Xiu, Mei Yaochen), whose works reveal their real difference from their self-desired prior incarnations. Nevertheless, as I argue throughout this study, the Yuanyou era (1086–94) marks a radical change in the degree and nature of that difference between former and latter poets.

26. Su Shi, "*Jushi ji* xu" (Preface to the *Collection of the Retired Scholar*), *Dongpo qiji, qian ji* 24.16a–17b.

27. Quoted in Guo Shaoyu, *Song shihua jiyi*, 47.

28. This critique is not as "modern" as it may appear. Even early Northern Song poets playfully imagined their predecessors following them. For example, Liu Bin (1023–89) relates an anecdote that neatly illustrates the audacity of

Northern Song poets in claiming primacy over their predecessors:

> The monk Huichong had a poem that read: "As the river splits, the power of the hillock is broken. / Spring enters, the scars of the burn turn green." These are old lines from Tang poets. Nevertheless, a disciple of Huichong's intoned a poem that he presented to his master:
>
> "As the river splits the hillock's power..." is Sikong Shu's [fl. 785–805];
> "Spring enters, scars of the burn..." is Liu Zhangqing's [709–80?].
> It is not that my master steals lines from the ancients;
> It is that the verses of the ancients resemble my master's!

For another perspective on Tang-Song (inverted) relations, see Yoshikawa's "To no Sōjin o manabu," *Kokoro* 26 (Nov. 1973): 89–92; reprinted in his *To shi ronshū*, 378–85. For Liu Bin's anecdote, see his *Zhongshan shihua*, 284. For a discussion of both passages, see Sargent.

29. Du Fu's poems at Kuizhou were late poems written between 766 and 768, while he was in exile. They traditionally have been regarded as his most poetically masterful and emotionally complex works. For a discussion of these poems, see Hung, 219–254; and Owen, *Great Age*, 212–14.

30. The term "this literature" (*si wen*) is used early on to denote a set of moral and cultural values (expressed in literary works, but in other cultural artifacts as well) always on the verge of extinction and dependent on righteous men for perpetuation. Here and elsewhere, "this literature" should be read to include the wider application "this culture." The locus classicus of this term is *Analects* 9.5: "The Master was put in fear of Kwang. He said, 'After the death of King Wen, was not the cause of truth lodged in me? If Heaven had wished to let this literature perish, then I, a future mortal, should not have such a relation to that cause. While Heaven does not let the cause of truth perish, what can the people of Kwang do to me?'" (trans. Legge, *Four Books*, 109–10). For a discussion of the changing concept of *wen* in pre-Song and Song texts, see Bol.

31. The terms "ascend the hall" (*sheng tang*) and "enter the room" (*ru shi*) occur in *Analects* 11.14 and refer to varying degrees of knowledge of the Sage's teachings. The closer one gets to the inner chamber(s), the more thorough one's understanding of the source of wisdom. Huang has fused the discourse of Du Fu's poetry with the Confucian canons the hall is named after.

32. This common locution in traditional Chinese criticism describes the ardent but misguided and blind reading of the Classics.

33. YZ 17.22b–23b.

34. Zhu Dongrun (278–79) believes that although Huang had the impulse to carve Du Fu's poems in stone early on, it was not until his own exile that he came to feel the affinity between his situation and Du Fu's. In his preface to Huang Tingjian's *Yizhou yi you jia sheng ji*, Fan Liao (fl. after 1101) remarks on how Huang was kept company in exile by the spirit of prior poets: "In the midst

Notes to Pages 37–42

of sorrow and evil, he never felt alone, he could see Han Zhitui [Yu] and Liu Zihou [Zongyuan; 773–819] with him."

35. Li Bo, 520.

36. In Ding, *Quan Han Sanguo Jin Nanbeichao shi*, "Quan Qi shi" 3.9a–9b.

37. "Qi ai shi: Xi jing luan wu xiang," in Ding, *Quan Han Sanguo Jin Nanbeichao shi*, "Quan Sanguo shi" 3.5a.

38. The tone of the line recalls the tone of poem no. 36 of the *Classic of Poetry*: "It's no use, it's no use, why not return; if it were not for the lord's sake, why be here in the dew? / It's no use, it's no use, why not return; if it were not for the lord's person, why be out here in the mire?" (trans. Karlgren, 23)

39. "Jingman fei wu xiang," in Ding, *Quan Han Sanguo Jin Nanbeichao shi*, "Quan Sanguo shi" 3.5a.

40. Chow Tse-tsung (pers. comm.) points out the precedent for this line in Du Fu's "Yu tai guan" (Monastery of the Jade Terrace): "Now I am even more willing to redden my visage [by drinking] and sprout wings [as a Daoist immortal]. / Now it is even more fitting to be a yellow-haired old fisherman or wood-gatherer" (Du Fu, 1090–91). Su Shi's poem is "Song Zhang Jiazhou" (Sending off Mr. Zhang of Jiazhou), *Su wenzhong gong shi* 32.17a–b.

41. The "floating clouds" derive from *Analects* 7.16 and refer to riches and honor gained unrighteously. "Carriages and ceremonial caps" are metonymies for court affairs; cf. *Zhuangzi*: "When the ancients referred to 'achieving one's intent,' they were not referring to carriages and ceremonial caps; [rather] they were referring to those for whom nothing could increase their happiness, this and nothing more. Today, when people refer to achieving one's intent, they are speaking of only carriages and caps" (*NHZJ* 6.9a–9b). By combining the two allusions in this fashion, Su Shi doubly renounces officialdom from two perspectives.

42. Huang Tingjian also uses this allusion in one poem, "Rivers and mountains aid the brush in moving freely back and forth" ("Yi Xing Dunfu" [Remembering Xing Dunfu], *Shi, nei* 10.8a–b).

43. Li Bo, 566.

44. "Carrying wine" is most likely an oblique reference to the biography of Yang Xiong (active at the end of the first century B.C.) in the *Han shu* (87A.1a–B.19b): "Liu Fen once studied how to do extraordinary calligraphy from Yang Xiong. Yang's family was very poor, and Yang was fond of drinking wine, so although visitors rarely came to his door, when one with good intentions [to learn] came, he brought wine with him for Yang to enjoy." In another poem Su Shi says, "I've heard tell that one carries a wine gourd when one asks about extraordinary calligraphy." The biography of Sima Xiangru (179–117 B.C.) in the *Shiji* (Sima Qian, 117.3070) refers to Sima as "one who would wander beyond the clouds" (cf. line 4). The term refers to a person of transcendent talent.

45. Cao Zhi (192–232).
46. Li Bo, 225.
47. For a translation by J. R. Hightower of Li Bo's letter, see Birch, 233–34.
48. "Feng song Zhou Yuanweng suo Jizhou sifating fu Libu shi," *Shi, wai* 9.14a.
49. Shi Rong, annotator of the "outer" (*wai*) collection of Huang Tingjian's *shi* poetry, suggests this borrowing.
50. *Shi, nei* 7.9a–b.
51. Yan Youyi, *Yiyuan cihuang*; cited in Wei, 7.147. For a discussion of this method, see Sargent, 177–82.
52. Egan, 444.

TWO

1. Hu Yunyi, *Song shi yanjiu*, 11–12.
2. Yoshikawa Kōjirō, *Sō shi gaisetsu*, 13; trans. Watson, *Introduction to Sung Poetry*, 9. See also Iritani, 13; and Ogawa, *Sō shi sen*, 287. For collections and analyses of comments by Chinese critics, see Ke, 88; and Liu Dajie, *Zhongguo wenxue fada shi*, 654. Ke feels that characterizing the Song as a period of philosophic poetry is inaccurate because such verse was written earlier (this defense, of course, does not disprove the charge); Liu concludes that not all Song poets wrote philosophical poetry. But his list of those who did includes most of the major figures—Su Shi, Wang Anshi, and Huang Tingjian. For the relevance of learning to Northern Song poetry and its relation to earlier attitudes toward learning and literature, see Goyama, "Sō shi no gakumonsei." For a survey of critical attitudes from the Southern Song to the Qing toward "learned" poetry, see Lynn, "The Talent–Learning Polarity."
3. Yan Yu, 24.
4. Yang Shen (1488–1559), cited in Hu Yunyi, *Song shi yanjiu*, 2. Hu Yunyi subscribes to this view to the extent of calling the Song poets cold and humorless (ibid., 10; and *Zhongguo wenxue shi*, 201).
5. For a discussion of the concept of *li* in the Song dynasty, see Fuller, 2–3 and *passim*.
6. See Yoshikawa, *Sō shi gaisetsu*, 12, 30.
7. *SHSG, wai* 14.9b.
8. "Qiang cun san shou" (Three poems on Qiang village), first of three, Du Fu, 391. Huang is fond of stretching this term. In one of his most famous poems, "Ti zhu shi mu niu" (Inscribed on the painting of the bamboo, rock, and herdboy), *Shi, wai* 9.12b, he opens with "Over in the field, crags and peaks." He is describing not a majestic peak but a weirdly shaped rock.
9. The line may also be read, "The chickens crow, (thus) I know it is time." I choose the other reading to accord with the images in lines 7–8, which show the strange effect of the light on the animals, and to complement line 10.
10. The image of "wrapping it to their bosoms" derives from *Analects* 15.7,

which advises that if one's capability is not put to use by the ruler, one should "press it to one's bosom" and keep it to oneself until a more enlightened ruler appears.

11. *Zhou Yi*, 7, "Xici zhuan" section. For "tian yun," see *NHZJ* 5.35a.
12. *NHZJ* 2.6a.
13. *NHZJ* 9.11a; trans. Watson, *Chuang Tzu*, 302.
14. *NHZJ* 1.26a; trans. Watson, *Chuang Tzu*, 39 (modified).
15. *NHZJ* 1.35b; trans. Watson, *Chuang Tzu*, 43.
16. "Zao xing" (*a*). This is a very early poem, written in 1068. In *SHSG, wai* 17.1a.
17. "Zao xing" (*b*), Bo, 20.452.
18. "Yue" (The moon), in Du Fu, 1476. Qiu Zhao'ao, the editor of this edition of Du's poems, notes that the lines derive from two other poems: Yu Xin's (512–80) "At the fourth watch, the sky is just about to brighten"; and Wu Yun's (d. 778) "The distant peaks at times spit forth the moon."
19. *Shi, nei* 16.7b–8a.
20. Zhou Zizhi (1082–after 1151) notes that Huang's couplet plays off a couplet by Mei Yaochen: "From antiquity poets and literati have generally taken those who came before them as their ancestors in making up language. Mei Yaochen has a couplet, 'As birds south of the dikes pass, birds north of the dikes call out, / The waters of the upper fields flow into the lower fields.' Ouyang [Xiu] chanted it often, not letting it leave his lips. . . . [Huang] uses [Mei's] structure, and yet, since the intent of his words is so lofty and marvelous, Huang can truly be called one who was expert in imitating his predecessors" (*Zhupo shihua*, 346–47).
21. This is the interlinear citation of Ren Yuan, editor of Huang's Inner Collection. Seng Zhao was one of the four philosophers of the Kumara (Jiumolo) sect. He first was a scholar of the Daoist texts of Zhuangzi and Laozi, but felt he had not completely penetrated their teachings. He then turned to the *Vimalakirti Sutra* (*Weimojing*) and found what he claimed was the key to Daoism.
22. "Xi tang yong ri xulun" (Preface to the Evening Hall of Perpetual Day), Wang Fuzhi, 64; cited in Qian Zhongshu, *Song shi xuanzhu*, 17.
23. Huang Tingjian, "You shi zhai," *YZ* 13.11a.
24. See Mo, 10–11, for data on the rise in the number of publishing houses and their increased productivity at this time, as well as the expansion of the literati class.
25. Arai Ken, *Kō Teiken*, 5–7. Goyama Kiwamu ("Sōdai bungei") traces the development of an aesthetic based on absolute opposition to the "vulgar" (*su*) to a similar interest in maintaining a clear difference from those who were perceived as intellectual and cultural parvenu.
26. "Jingxue liku shi shu zhang" (Essay on the poetry and prose of the *Principles of the Study of the Classics*), Zhang Zai, 5.98. The description of Mencius' ability to read poetry is from *Mencius*, 5A.4.

27. Huang Tingjian uses this phrase in describing those who he feels misread the Classics in exactly this manner; see the discussion of his "Account of the Hall of the Great Odes" in Chapter 1.

28. For the disdain in many of the central texts of literary criticism both preceding and during the Northern Song for "learned" verse, verse that identified itself as more than an immediate emotional response to a given scene, see Goyama, "Sō shi no gakumonsei," 3–14.

29. Ouyang Xiu, "Da Zuze zhi shu" (Response to Zuze's letter); cited in Qian Dongfu, 69.

30. Ouyang Xiu, "Da Wu Chong xiucai shu" (Response to candidate Wu Chong); cited in Qian Dongfu, 69.

31. Cf. Lu Ji, "Wen fu," lines 251–54 (Lu Ji, 17.239):

> As for the function of literature:
> Certainly it is that which the host of principles relies on.
> It expands over a myriad *li*, no obstacles remain;
> And spans over ten million years to form a ford.

32. James T. C. Liu, 87.

33. The growing doubt in the ability of texts to preserve meaning is a contributing factor in Huang's poetics, as will become clear in later chapters. Here it is important to note its general and pervasive nature in Northern Song intellectual history.

34. Shen Nong, Huang Di, and Qi Bo were mythical rulers and famous herbalists.

35. Huangfu Mi (215–82) and Zhang Ji (Eastern Han) were also famous herbalists. Huangfu Mi was well known for diligent study and his autodidactism. He wrote several books, including the *Gao shi zhuan*, and the *Lie nü zhuan*. Zhang Ji wrote the *Shang han za lun*.

36. Gao Ruona (997–1055) was a Song astrologer and medical scholar.

37. Yang Jie, *zi* Jilao, was another Song herbalist. For his biography, see *Song shi, juan* 38. The *Ben cao* and the *Su wen* are two famous treatises on medicine from the Han dynasty.

38. The Medicinal Stone (*yao shi*) is mentioned in "Cang gong zhuan" in the *Shiji* (Sima Qian, 105.2811). Su Shi uses the term as well in his "Fu yi xiansheng zhu ji shu": "Like the medicinal stone it must be able to cure illness" (*Dongpo qiji, qianji* 24.8a–b).

39. In present-day Sichuan, south of Mount Mei.

40. "Yang Zijian *Tong shen lun ji* xu" (Preface to Yang Zijian's *Discourse on Penetrating the Spirit*), *SHSG, bie* 2.3a–b.

41. It is no accident that Huang fuses the study of literature with that of medicine. In several essays, he uses medicine as a metaphor for literature's curative powers. (He himself was an amateur herbalist who often prescribed moxa—a sample prescription in his own handwriting is part of the collection of the Taiwan National Palace Museum.)

42. "*Lunyu* duan pian" (A fragment on the *Analects*), YZ 20.5a–b.
43. "Yu Pan Zizhen er shu" (Two letters written to Pan Zizhen), YZ 19.29b–30a. Huang's metaphor of learning as embarking on a journey for which one needs to seek direction plays off *Mencius* 6B. 2: "The Way is like a wide road. It is not at all difficult to find. The trouble with people is simply that they do not look for it" (Trans. Lau, *Mencius*, 172).
44. "Yu Xu Shichuan shu" (First letter to Xu Shichuan), *SHSG, zheng* 19.6a; cited and trans. Bol, 542.
45. "Yu Wang Ziyu shu" (Letter written to Wang Ziyu), YZ 19.15b–16a. Huang uses this image of effortless creation in his "He Zizhan xishu Boshi hua 'Hao tou chi'" (Following the rhymes of [Su] Zizhan playfully writing on [Li] Boshi's painting "Hao tou chi"): "Marquis Li paints the bone, he doesn't paint the flesh, his brush descends and horses are born as broken bamboo." The locus classicus for images of spontaneous ease in carrying out one's endeavors brought about by a special sensitivity for the object is in the "Nurturing Life" section of the *Zhuangzi* (*NHZJ*, 2.2a–b).
46. In poetic theory the corresponding notion is one of "live method"; Goyama, "Sō shi no gakumonsei," 9.
47. Cheng Yi, as cited in Zhu Xi, *Jinsi lu* 3.6a; trans. Wing-tsit Chan, 103.

Cheng Yi also makes explicit reference to using the *Classic of Poetry* in a similar manner:

"Being stimulated by poetry" [*Analects* 8.8] means that one expresses his own feelings and character, cultivates himself and functions smoothly in his moral life, gets the feeling of being stimulated and aroused, and thus has the disposition of which Confucius approved in Tseng Tien. (Trans. Chan, 105)

Cheng also comments on the application of one's understanding of poetry to one's actions:

People today do not know how to study books. Take the passage, "Though a man may be able to recite the three hundred odes, yet if, when he is given a governmental position, he does not know how to act, or if, when he is sent on missions to various states, he cannot give his own answers, although he has read much, what is the use? [*Analects* 13.5]" (Trans. Chan, 100)

One should not, however, take these passages as representing all of Cheng Yi's view on *wen*, which at other moments is extremely skeptical.

48. For further discussion on the idea of embodying the principles of the master, of integrating the knowledge of experience, see Tu, 104.
49. "*Mao shi* xu" (Preface to the Mao edition of the *Classic of Poetry*), WX 45.20; trans. James J. Y. Liu, *Chinese Theories of Literature*, 69.
50. *WXDL* 6.1b; trans. Shih, 216–17.
51. "Feng zeng Wei zuo chengzhang ershier yun" (Twenty-two rhymes respectfully bestowed on the Elder Left Councillor Mr. Wei), Du Fu, 73.
52. Fan Xiwen, *Duichuang yehua*, 494.

53. "Ba shu Liu Zihou shi" (Colophon on the poetry of Liu Zihou), *YZ* 26.4a; "Yu Wang Guanfu shu" (Letters to Wang Guanfu), first of two, *YZ* 19.18a. Guanfu is the *zi* of Wang Fan; for his biography, see *Song shi jishi buyi* 37.17 *xia*.

54. *SHSG, bie* 11.4a–6b.

55. "Da Hong Jufu shu" (Letter in response to Hong Jufu), third of three, *YZ* 19.23b. Goyama ("Sō shi no gakumonsei," 11) cites several precedents for the notion that all literature has prior sources, but claims that Huang was the first to advocate the idea widely and make it a central part of his poetics.

56. I discuss Huang's penchant for playing on Daoist metaphors in the Conclusion of this study.

57. Fan Zongshi was a Tang dynasty essayist greatly admired by Han Yu.

58. "Zixu fu" (Rhymeprose on Sir Fantasy), *WX* 7.119.

59. Tao Qian (Yuanming) is well known as the "poet of the field and garden" in Chinese literary history. His "Gui qulai ce" (The return; *WX* 45.636) is one of his most famous poems. The "Gui tian fu" (Rhymeprose on returning to the fields; *WX* 15.222–23) was written by Zhang Heng (1st c. A.D.).

60. This passage is from the *Mantanglu*, cited in *SRYX* 8.188.

61. "Du shi jian," *SHSG, bie* 4.11a–17a.

THREE

1. Wang Zhifang, "Shangu lun shi" (Shangu's discourses on poetry), 4. Wang is paraphrasing part of Huang's essay "Lun zuo shi wen" (see Chapter 2).

2. See Lu Ji, "Wen fu," line 60, for this expression.

3. "Dao Zhen shi hua zhu xu" (Preface to Master Dao Zhen's painting of bamboo), *YZ* 16.28a–b.

4. Su Shi, "Shu Chao Buzhi suo cang Yuke hua zhu" (Written on a painting of bamboo by Wen Yuke in Chao Buzhi's collection), first of three, in *SWGS* 29.2890.

5. See Lynn, "Orthodoxy and Enlightenment," for a discussion of *shen* and its various manifestations in theories of poetry.

6. Shen Gua (1030–94), *Mengqi bitan* 17.2a; cited and trans. in Bush, 49–50.

7. Bush, 64–65.

8. "Xici zhuan," *xia*/4; trans. Chan, 268.

9. One such example is Huang Tingjian's "Setting off at Early Morn"; see Chapter 2.

10. "Yundang gu yan zhu ji" (An account of Wen Yuke's painting of Yundang Valley leaning bamboo), in *Dongpo wenji shilue*, 49.1a–b; cf. Fuller, 88–89. A precedent for this notion can be found in Zhang Yenyuan, 2.23: "He [Wu Daozi] concentrated his spirit and harmonized it with the working of Nature, rendering the thing through the power of the brush. His ideas were...fixed before he took up the brush; when the picture was finished, it expressed them

all" (trans. Siren, 24). Though generally similar, the "expression" of the thing noted in this late Tang text differs in an important way from the manifestation of the principle of the thing referred to in Su Shi's text, which focuses precisely on the manifestation of the always immanent and always becoming state of things. Su Shi's conception links up importantly to ideas of poetic extension, as we will see in later chapters.

11. Du Zheng, 15.13a–b. For the importance of the concept of manifesting what is "inside the breast" in painting, see Ōno.

12. "Mountains and dragons" refer to ancient designs embroidered on clothes and flags. See Legge, *Book of Documents*, 80. Huang's text is "Ba shu Liu Zihou shi" (Colophon on the poetry of Liu Zongyuan), YZ 26.4a.

13. Compare Jiaoran, 308. 14. Schiller, trans. Elias, 98–99.
15. *Shi, wai* 7.6a. 16. Chen Shidao, 308.

17. Lu You, "Lao xue yan bi ji" (Notes on my old study hall); cited in Chen Yongzheng, 43.

18. Ouyang Xiu, *Liuyi shihua*, 268. See also Chaves, *Mei Yao-ch'en*, 126–27. The unpredictable nature of poetic inspiration and composition is a long-standing theme in Chinese poetics. The lines cited remind one of a couplet (lines 59–60) from Lu Ji's "Wen fu": "Sometimes one grasps the writing slip and dashes a line off; other times one chews on the brush and the thoughts remain distant"; and lines 244–48: "My thought is blocked as if I were trying to draw it out; and then I sometimes exhaust my feelings and still have regrets. Othertimes my thoughts move exceedingly lightly. Though this thing resides in me, it is not something I can force." By the Southern Song, Huang's poem is the object of much imitation. Zhang Bangji (?–after 1150), in his *Mozhuang manlu* 7.84–85, quotes Huang's poem and then cites an imitation of it by Cai Tianqi as well as two other imitations given to him, along with two cats, by Li Huangde. The manneredness of all three sets off Huang's elegant simplicity even more.

19. Mei, 11.9b; trans. Watson, *Chinese Lyricism*, 209.

20. Mei, 48.8a–8b; trans. Watson, *Columbia Book of Chinese Poetry*, 342.

21. See Mo (296) for another case of Huang's compressing longer poems in his revisions.

22. *Shi, wai* 11.6b–7a. For a translation into French, see Demiéville, 354.

23. Zhu Zeqing, 1: 73–77.

24. Demiéville translates the line according to the third reading, as a self-addressed imperative, "Imbecile, laisse la les affaires publiques!" This leads him to remove the poet completely from the opening couplet and therefore from the first half of the poem.

25. "Deng gao" (Climbing the heights), Du Fu, 1766.

26. *Liezi* 2.6a.

27. For his admiration for both the preceding poem and this one, see Hu Zi, *qianji* 47.320.

28. *Shi, nei* 9.12b.

29. Egan (434*n*53) also notes the opinions of Yoshikawa (125) and Chen (171).

30. The strangeness of Su Shi's paintings is well known. Huang has several poems on Su Shi's paintings; nearly all remark that the composition is eccentric yet captures the inner principle of the thing.

31. See the discussion of "The Account of the Wall of Great Odes" in Chapter 1.

32. *Shi, wai* 2.4a.

33. Her biography in the *Hou Han shu* (*juan* 110) tells us that she was "the wife of Cao Shishu [Cao Shou], her learning was extensive, her talent lofty. The emperor [He di; r. 89–106] summoned her to court numerous times and had the court ladies defer to her."

34. "Fengxian Liu Shaofu xin hua shan shui zhang ge" (A Song on Mr. Liu Shaofu of Fengxian's new paintings of mountains and rivers), in Du Fu, 275.

35. The classic example of a *zhi yin* is found in the famous story of Bo Ya and Zhong Ziqi noted above.

36. See also the Lotus Sutra: "Such is the wondrous Dharma: when all the Buddhas and Tathagatas explain it, it is like the *udumbara* flower that is manifest only once in an age" (trans. W. E. Soothill, 68).

37. *NHZJ* 3.33b–34a; trans. Watson, *Chuang Tzu*, 96.

38. Shi Rong, editor of Huang's Outer Collection, notes this in his commentary on the poem (*Shi, wai* 2.4a).

39. From Meng Jia's biography in the *Jin shu* (98.2581); cited in Liu Yiqing's (403–44) *Shishuo xinyu* (New Accounts of Tales of the World); trans. Mather, 205.

40. *NHZJ* 9.11a; trans. Watson, *Chuang Tzu*, 302.

41. Tao, 3.89.

42. *NHZJ* 1.19a–b; trans. Watson, *Chuang Tzu*, 36.

43. Bo, 12.241–43.

44. "Song sheng," Bo, 5.97–98; trans. Watson, *Columbia Book of Chinese Poetry*, 244.

45. *WX* 18.255; trans. Van Gulik.

46. Van Gulik, 69.

FOUR

1. In the Conclusion to this study I weigh the applicability of the concept of intertextuality to classical Chinese poetry. Here I scarequote it to signal that critique.

2. "Quewen" (lacunae) refers to a hiatus left in a text to await completion by one who knows the details. (For example, *Analects* 15.25: "Even in my early days [Confucius says], a historiographer would leave a blank in his text" (trans. Legge, *Four Books*, 230).

3. Lu Ji, lines 29–32.
4. *Analects* 11.19, trans. Waley, *Analects*, 157.
5. "Wang Bo ji xu" (Preface to the collection of Wang Bo), Yang Jiong, 3.1a–5b.
6. *WJ*, 139; trans. Bodman, 397. Collected by Kūkai (Henzō Kinkō) in his *Bunkyō hifuron* ("Nan juan"); I have used the Chinese annotation of this text by Zhou Weide, *Wenjing mifulun (WJ)*.
7. "Yunchao shi xu" (Preface to the collection of Yunchao), in Wu Yunjia, *Shenshi san xiansheng ji*; *Yunchao ji*. This anonymous Song compilation was re-edited in 1718 by Wu Yunjia. "Yunchao" is Shen Liao (1032–85).
8. Preface to "Zai ciyun Yang Mingshu shi" (Once again rhyming after a poem by Yang Mingshu), *Shi, nei* 12.38a.
9. "Shu Liu Zihou shi" (Colophon on a poem by Liu Zihou), in *Su Shi tiba*, *juan* 2; collected in *Songren tiba*, 37. Su Shi makes other statements resembling Huang's; for example, he once spoke of "spotting an earthenware tile turns [it] to gold" (see Qian Zhongshu, *Song shi xuanzhu*, 111). Liu Dajie ("Huang Tingjian de shilun") criticizes Huang for plagiarizing Su Shi, but it is hard to determine who originated what. Even if Su recorded a certain idea earlier than Huang, the two were in close contact on a number of aesthetic concerns; their discourses often shared similar figures. In this particular pronouncement, Su Shi himself is most likely borrowing from Sikong Tu (*Ershisi shipin*, 37): "As the future will never be exhausted, the old becomes the new."
10. *Ti* is translated in two ways here: as commonly used in poetics, as "style"; and as "frame," a concretization of something, an outward articulation. I choose to translate its second appearance as that, since Lü is commenting on the various ways that the tropes of *bi* and *xing* could be articulated, not on the kinds of "styles" they could be used in. *Bi* and *xing* were first defined in terms of the poems of the *Classic of Poetry*; there are no adequate terms in Western literary criticism to use as translations. Some loosely translate them respectively as "simile" and "metaphor"; the first is a much closer translation than the second. For a convincing argument against using "metaphor" as a translation for *xing*, see Pauline Yu, "Metaphor."
11. Lü Benzhong, 252. In his *Rongzhai suibi* (*juan* 15), Hong Mai refers to Huang as one who has "taken to the limit the marvelousness of *wenzhang*."
12. *Shi, nei*, preface 1.
13. Lu Ji, lines 53–54.
14. Yan Zhitui, *juan* 9 ("Wenzhang"); in *Zhuzi jicheng*, 8: 19.
15. YZ 19.18a–b.
16. Writing was thought to have evolved from the tracks of birds; Zhang Lei is saying that the person he is addressing aspires to the role of Primordial Author.
17. "Da Li tuiguan shu" (Letter in reply to Mr. Li, investigator of the Finance Commission), Zhang Lei, 58.4a–6b.

18. "Wang Jinggong chan jian" (On Wang Jinggong's [Anshi] Zen pieces), YZ 30.9a–b.

19. *Shi, nei* 17.4a–b.

20. "Bu jian [Jin wu Li Bo xiaoxi]," Du Fu, 858.

21. William Hung (187) conceives of the following scenario behind this poem: "'No Recent News of Li Po' was...no trivial matter. In the presence of the poetry-loving Yen Wu, many of the officials naturally would discuss poetry and poets. And they could not have avoided talking about the famous Li Po, who grew up in the K'uang Hills north of Mien-chou. Gossip could be very uncharitable and mean. Perhaps, even Tu Fu could not defend all the escapades of his friend Li Po. Hence he pleaded for consideration of the elder poet's extraordinary talents." This image seems to me only partially valid, for Du Fu's poem, while speaking of "no trivial matter," is clearly couched in a way that allows Du Fu, by playing the moralist in the beginning of his poem, to contrast the conservative literati and the brash Li Bo, whose bravado and tone he adopts himself in the second quatrain.

22. From "Bing hou guo Wang Yi yin zeng ge" (After an illness I encountered Mr. Wang Yi, and after drinking, I bestowed on him this song), Du Fu, 198.

23. "Gui yuantian ju wu shou" (Five poems on returning to live on the farm), Tao, 39. Su Shi's series is entitled "Dongpo ba shou" (Eight poems on the Eastern Slope), in *SWGS* 21.2512.

24. *Shi, nei* 1.1a–b. These two poems were presented by the then relatively unknown Huang to Su Shi to introduce himself to the famous poet. Su was impressed by the poems; he had heard of Huang before, and these pieces confirmed the high opinion others held of him. Su's collection contains two poems matching Huang's rhymes. The locus classicus for the image is in the *qian* hexagram of the *Classic of Changes*: "Similar tones respond to each other; similar temperaments seek each other out."

25. *SWGS* 28.2883. The Shoals are in Yichuan and are the subject of a number of poems by Bo Juyi. Wang Wen'gao interprets the last line as Su Shi saying that he wishes to divine a dwelling in the Yichuan mountains so as to be close to Wen Lugong (1006–97).

26. "Ciyun Zizhan ti Guo Xi hua qiu shan" (Rhyming after Zizhan's 'Guo Xi paints the autumn mountains level and distant'), in *Shi, nei* 7.6a–b.

27. The aesthetic of "level and distant" painting mentioned here is first remarked on in the *Xin Tang shu* (202.5765) biography of the Tang painter and poet Wang Wei: "Wang Wei's thoughts on painting perfected the skill of making mountains and waters level and distant, clouds full of force, and stone formations surpassing. It was only what the Natural Capacity [*tian ji*] could bring about, and nothing that an imitator could arrive at." This aesthetic was adopted by Five Dynasties and Northern Song painters.

28. Not much is known of this figure. A poem of his is mentioned in Hong Mai's *Rongzhai suibi wuji*, but more relevant here, Guo Xi mentions Wen Lugong's appreciation of landscape paintings in his *Linchuan gaozhi*, 29.

29. For the fusion of the viewer into the painted scene in Huang's verse, see Ōno, 34.

30. Guo Xi's comments on painting are collected in the *Linchuan gaozhi*. The above comment is from the *Linchuan*, 5; trans. Sakanishi, 33. Other remarks of a similar nature include: "It is the considered judgement of mankind that there are landscapes in which one can travel, landscapes which can be gazed upon, landscapes in which one may ramble, and landscapes in which one may dwell [Guo goes on to explain the superiority of the latter]" (trans. Sakanishi, 32). "The sight of such pictured mountains arouses in man exactly corresponding moods. It is as if he were actually in those mountains. They exist as if they were real and not painted" (trans. Sakanishi, 38).

31. "Tong zhugong deng Ci'en si ta," Du Fu, 103.

32. Guo Xi, p. 19; trans. Sakanishi, p. 53.

33. Han Yu's poem is: "Dong du yü chun" (In the Eastern Capital encountering the springtime), line 12, *Quan Tang shi*, 3804. Li Bo's poem is "Bring Forth the Wine," Li Bo, 225.

34. "Xi ti Wang Zai hua shan shui tu ge," Du Fu, 754.

35. *Guo Xi*, 24; trans. Sakanishi, 58.

36. Wang Anshi, *Wang Jingwen gong ji* 13.1a–b.

37. *Shi, wai* 16.5a–6b.

38. "Bing hou guo Wang Yi yin zeng ge" (After an illness I encountered Mr. Wang Yi, and after drinking, I bestowed on him this song), Du Fu, 198.

39. "Du Han Du ji" (Reading the collections of Han Yu and Du Fu), Du Mu, 2.19a–b.

40. In the *Liezi* 5.7a.

41. Li Bo, 1400.

42. *SWGS* 23.2644–45.

43. *Shi, nei* 17.2a–3a.

44. "Xuanzhou Xie Tiao lou jian bie jiaoshu Shuyun," Li Bo, 1077.

45. George Hatch (285) tells of Su Shi's interest in life-prolonging exercises and medicines: "Su Shi played at the alchemist's stove, and nearly burned his house down; he was also a connoisseur of natural substances of reputed preservative powers. Neither gained him the immediate gratification of yoga exercise, and he became disillusioned with the hobby. The famous masters had all finally died just like everybody else, though some lived to be a hundred; Su wondered if what had been written of 'wondrous men' [*yi ren*] in the past was really so, or just an embellishment of storytellers."

46. "Gu feng" ("Da ya jiu bu zuo") (Ancient Airs [The Great Odes have long not been composed]), Li Bo, 91.

47. This explicit play on metaphorical naming occurs in the *Classic of Poetry*, no. 203 (trans. Waley, *Book of Songs*, 320).

> In the south there is a Winnowing Fan;
> But it cannot sift, or raise the chaff.
> In the north there is a Ladle;
> But it cannot scoop wine or sauce.

The Winnowing Fan is the name of another constellation.

48. This may be a playful retort to Su Shi, who once said that Huang's poems were like fatty crabs—one could enjoy them immensely, but overindulgence could make one ill.

49. *WX* 29.6.

50. Diény, 129.

FIVE

1. See the Critical Introduction.

2. *SWGS* 2.1606; trans. Fuller, 59, modified. See Fuller, 59–60, for a discussion of this poem and its place in the development of Su Shi's style.

3. See note 47 to Chapter 4.

4. For a perceptive article on Song aesthetics tracing a movement that reflects this ambivalence, see Okamoto. Okamoto charts a progressively deepening skepticism regarding the adequacy of words. He finds that, particularly in the Song, this "inadequacy" is displaced onto an already established aesthetic that valorizes what is beyond words (*yan wai*). In Okamoto's view, in the Northern Song the locus of this aesthetic is the word *yin*, which signifies the subtleties of expression that are conveyed by, but not reducible to, words. This aesthetic dovetails with Huang's valorization of the "unlimited" power of words to evoke things. Both approaches reveal the desire to overcome the skepticism that informs them.

5. For Ren Yuan's comments on this poem, see *Shi, nei* 1.7b–9b.

6. Arai, "Kō Sankoku no 'Enga' no shi."

7. Ibid., 275–77; Ōno, 31–32; Ogawa, *Sō shi sen*, 301–5.

8. *Shi, nei* 1.7b–9b. In Arai, *Kō Teiken*, 52–60; and Kurata, 42–47.

9. For a discussion of allegory in classical Chinese poetry, see Pauline Yu, "Allegory," esp. 390.

10. The first annotator of this text was Guo Pu (276–324); in the early Northern Song Xing Bing (932–1010) revived interest in the work and wrote a new annotation that sought to clarify Guo' s text.

11. "Qinchong shi'er zhang," Bo, 857.

12. For this famous *Zhuangzi* passage, see Chapter 2. Here Bo Juyi is saying that the literal significance of the insects and birds is only a vehicle for the real significance of the parable-poem. Liu Xie (*WXDL* 4.86) uses these expressions to characterize the "discourse" (*lun*): "[Discourse] is the 'trap and snare' of the one hundred contemplations, the scale of the ten thousand matters."

13. "*Guan-guan* cry the ospreys" and "Now the magpie has a nest" (*Shijing* poems nos. 1 and 12) are the first poems, respectively, in the "Zhou nan" and

"Shao nan" sections of the "Guo feng" (Airs of the states) division of the *Classic of Poetry*. Bo Juyi probably has in mind Liu Xie's remarks on *bi* and *xing* ("simile" and "allegory," for want of more accurate terms in Western literary criticism), specifically with regard to the first poem: "Formally, the *pi* [*bi*] is a linguistic expression charged with accumulated indignation, and the *hsing* [*xing*] is an admonition expressed through an array of parables.... In the "Kuan-chü" [the first poem] the fishhawks understand the formal separation of the sexes.... Do not conjecture about these birds, for what is intended to be emphasized to us is chastity" (*WXDL* 8.1a–1b; trans. Shih, 276). The *kun* was a mythological fish of gigantic size; the *peng* was an equally enormous bird, and the *yan* a tiny quail-like bird contrasted in the *Zhuangzi* parable with the *peng*. See *NHZJ* 1.1a–4a.

14. "Record wonders" (*zhi guai*) comes from the *Zhuangzi* (*NHZJ* 1.2a): "The Universal Harmony records wonders." "Speak my mind" is a loose translation of *fang yan*, which has the sense of setting forth words in a free manner. Bo Juyi wrote five poems entitled "Speaking My Mind" in response to five seven-character regulated-verse pieces of the same name by his friend Yuan Zhen (779–831).

15. "Lüye shu huai" (Traveling at night, writing my feelings), Du Fu, 1228. For a translation and discussion, see Owen, *Traditional Chinese Poetry*, 12–17.

16. As discussed in Part I, the will to read Nature is characteristic of late Northern Song "philosophizing" in lyric poetry.

17. For *yongwu* conventions, see Owen, *Poetry of the Early T'ang*, 281; Kang-i Sun Chang, *Six Dynasties Poetry*, 122–25; and Fong, 78–90.

18. *Shi, nei* 15.6b. 19. Du Fu, 816.
20. Chen Changfang, *juan xia*. 21. Du Fu, 1566.
22. *WX* 19.269–72.

23. This kind of rhetorical twist was seen in the previous chapter, when Huang debunks the "peaches of immortality" and brews them for wine.

24. *SHSG, wai* 17.5b–6a.
25. "Dengtu zi hao se fu," *WX* 19.268–69.
26. *WXDL* 8.7b; trans. Shih, 297.
27. *Analects* 2.11; trans. Waley, *Analects*, 90.
28. See Yokoyama. Rather than repeat information given in this seminal article on Huang's use of allusion, I refer the reader to it, as well as to Chen Xiang's and Mo Lifeng's articles. These three studies are the best close analyses I have found of Huang's use of prior enunciations.
29. For a discussion of the history and various techniques of "verse eye," see Fisk, "The Verse Eye." For Huang's technique, see Mo, 49.
30. "Bishusheng dong ye su zhiji huai Li Desu" (In the Imperial Library on a winter's night cherishing Li Desu), *Shi, nei* 10.5b–6b.
31. For further discussion of Huang's shifts of focus, see Mo, 46–49.
32. *Shi, nei* 2.1b–2a.

33. The statement is made by a minister of the southern state of Chu who is attempting to dissuade the king of the northern state of Qi from attacking. See Chen Yongzheng, 94–96.

34. In a colophon on the piece, Huang explains that this borrowing was only part hyperbole—at the time Huang Jifu was in Guangzhou, to the south, and he was at the Dezhou garrison, to the north: "both were on the seashore."

35. This is Burton Watson's translation of the phrase (*Records of the Grand Historian*, 2: 299).

36. Huang Tingjian himself was banished to that area and by his own account fell victim to the diseases bred in those "miasmal vapors."

37. *Shi, wai* 8.15a.

38. The Old Man of Dragon Gallery is an ambiguous reference: some take it to refer to Huang's maternal uncle Li Chang (1027–90), who is considered to have influenced Huang's literary tastes and talents deeply; others take it to refer to Huang himself. In either case the point is the same: two acts are correlated, the first giving a home to both the meditations of the monk and the compositions of the poet.

39. See Mo, 38; and Duke, 448.

40. *Shi, wai* 6.1a–b.

41. "Liang shi zi fang deng zhuan," *Nanshi* 54.1344–45.

42. See Pan Boying, 80–81.

43. *Dai Kanwa jiten*, entry 39719.50.

44. "Yinzhong baxian ge," *Du Fu*, 81.

45. *Shi, nei* 8.4b–5a.

46. *Shi, nei* 9.8b–9b.

47. *Shi, nei* 13.2b.

48. The painting is entitled "The Priest of Xuansha Fears His Own Shadow Reflected in the Water." For more on this painting, see Meyer, 135.

49. *Shi, nei* 9.2a.

50. Another interpretation, offered by Stephen Owen, is that the fish will reproachfully remember the monk's past sins (pers. comm.).

51. *Shi, nei* 17.6a–b.

52. "Cleansing the ear" is a common image in poems on music and signifies a supreme tone that makes all other music inferior and superfluous. This beautiful music "washes out" the remnants of vulgar tones.

53. "Momiao tingji" (The account of the Hall of the Marvels of Calligraphy), Su Shi, *Dongpo wenji shilüe* 48.5b–6b; trans. Fuller, 187–88.

54. "Du shi," Wang Anshi, *Wang Jingwen gong shi*, 39.3a.

55. *Shi, wai* 8.5b.

56. Here I follow Chen Yongzheng (52).

57. This refers to service to the state.

58. The "*Lanting ji* xu" is recorded in Wang Xizhi's biography in the *Jin shu*, 50.2093.

59. Trans. Lattimore, 412.
60. Cited in Huihong, 1.5a–b.

SIX

1. Many critics see Huang Tingjian's use of allusion as a continuation of a trend begun by Wang Anshi and later Su Shi. See, e.g., Arai, *Kō Teiken*, 4–6; and Qian Zhongshu, *Song shi xuanzhu*, 113. Liang Qizhao (1873–1929) even claims that the rightful patriarch of the Jiangxi school is Wang Anshi:

After Ou-yang Hsiu and Mei Sheng-yü had improved on this style [the Xikun style] somewhat, a separate school was formed, of whom the most famous exponents were Wang An-shih, Su Tung-p'o, and Huang Shan-ku. But the one who made the biggest contribution to the improvement of the style was Wang An-shih. He transformed it from its high colouring and sickly conceits to a bold, concise, and direct style of composition.

The most illustrious poets of the Sung dynasty are Su Tung-p'o and Huang Shan-ku, and it is not claimed that Wang An-shih was their compeer. But it is wrong to regard Huang Shan-ku as the founder of the Hsi Chiang [*sic*] School, for that honour belongs to Wang An-shih.

In the ancient style of poetry Wang An-shih imitated Han Yü, and it is almost impossible to say of certain odes whether they are from the pen of Wang An-shih or Han Yü. In other poems he imitated Tu Fu, but he developed his own style which was based on Tu Fu, and which Huang Shan-ku adopted later. His style generally is characterized by variety, impressiveness, and richness of suggestion. (In *Yinbingshi heji*, pt. II, *zhuangji*, 7: 195; quoted from Williamson, 2: 291)

2. For translations and discussion of Luo's verse, see Owen, *Poetry of the Early T'ang*, 138.
3. See, e.g., Cai Juhou (fl. 1108): "I believe that there is something in Li Yishan's [Shangyin] poetry that surpasses other poets' verse. Perhaps it is in his profound and eccentric use of allusion. One could say that this language is crafted, and yet the ideas aren't really conveyed, and this is his shortcoming. Men of this generation, on the contrary, take this [style] to be extraordinary and bizarre and therefore imitate it. This is the corrupt practice of the Xikun style" (quoted in Cai Zhengsun, 99).
4. "Wang Jinggong Dongpo shi zhi miao" (On the marvelous aspects of Wang Anshi's and Du Fu's verse), Huihong, 4.19 *xia*.
5. For Huang's essay, see "Du shi jian," *SHSG*, *bie* 4.12b–20a.
6. "Ba Gao Zimian shi" (A colophon on Gao Zimian's verse), YZ 26.16a.
7. *WXDL* 8.5b; trans. Shih, 291.
8. The argument of the *Wenxin diaolong* is based on the idea of allusion as illustration. The figure awakened the reader to the relationship between past and present; that affinity was what the "key" unlocked.
9. Du Fu, 1506.
10. See, e.g., Huang Che, 396.
11. Yokoyama, 129.

12. *Quan Tang shi*, 6144; trans. Graham, 171 (modified).
13. *NHZJ* 1.47b–48b.
14. Dai Shulin's remark is quoted in Sikong Tu's "Yu Ji Pu tan shi shu" (Letter to Ji Pu discussing poetry), Sikong, *Shipin jijie*, 55.
15. For an interesting attempt that employs modern literary theory, see F. Cheng, 85–91.
16. He then says that Su Shi explained that the poem is structured around the four musical tones of the zither: *gan* [*shi*], *yuan*, *qing*, and *he*. This explication is supported by Xu Yi (?–after 1150), *LDSH*, 394. The Ming critic Wang Shizhen (1526–90) says that although the musical explanation is a popular one, it not only does not explain all the complexities of the poem but reduces it to a formula that robs the poem of its evocativeness (*see* Wang Shizhen, 1182). Another, even more reductive interpretation is put forward by the Qing critic Wang Shihan (1632–1705), who says it is a political allegory and the zither stands for Li Shangyin himself (*Shixue cuanwen*, 16b; cited in Tai, 257).
17. Shih, 287.
18. For a discussion of the use of allusion before the Song, see Lattimore; and also Kao and Mei, "Meaning, Metaphor and Allusion."
19. From Xu Gan, "Za shi" (Miscellaneous poem), in Ding, *Quan Han Sanguo Jin Nanbeichao shi*, "Quan Sanguo shi" 3.264.
20. From Cao Zhi, "Za shi" (Miscellaneous poem), *WX* 29.416.
21. The source of this quote is unknown. Xu Wenyun (*Wei Jin Nanbeichao wenxue shi*, 611 *n*10) claims that it is a misquotation that couples two sources: a line from Wu Yun and one from Shen Yue (441–513).
22. From Xie Lingyun, "Sui mu" (The year's end), in *Wei Jin Nanbeichao wenxue shi*, 478.
23. *LDSH*, 4; annotation from *Wei Jin Nanbeichao wenxue shi*, 597–616.
24. *WXDL* 8.4b; trans. Shih, 288.
25. *WXDL* 8.5a, trans. Shih, 289 (modified). Shih says that Zhang, Cui, and Du are not identifiable.
26. *WXDL* 8.5b, 6b; trans. Shih 290, 292.
27. Huihong, 1.5.
28. There are many discussions of these phrases and examinations of the examples that Huihong, Yang Wanli (1127–1206), and others use to illustrate their intent; see Mo, 283–305, for an extensive discussion. For analyses in English, see James J. Y. Liu, *Art of Chinese Poetry*, 78; Rickett, "Method and Intuition," 109–10; Tiang, 122; and Chaves, "'Not the Way of Poetry.'" The best discussion I have found, which places the passage in the context of the issue of intertextuality in Song writings on poetry, is in Fisk, "Formal Themes," 62.
29. *Shi, nei* 7.8a.
30. See Ren Yuan (ibid.) for the complete text of Xu Ling's poem.
31. Ibid.
32. Tiang, 180–81.

33. Yokoyama, 94.
34. *Shi, nei* 1.6a.
35. Sima Qian, 76.5b, also 79.13b.
36. This anecdote also appears in the *Nanshi* ("Biography of Wang Sengru"), 59.1459–63: "In antiquity a man sometimes no sooner had opened his mouth to speak than he became a minister or a lord; in the space of time it took to stand up to speak, a pale jade seal was given by the emperor."
37. The first stanza of the *Shijing* poem, "You you lu ming," reads:

> "*You you*," cry the deer,
> Nibbling the black southernwood in the fields.
> I have a lucky guest.
> Let me play my zithern, blow my reed again.
> Blow my reed again, trill their tongues,
> Take up the basket of offerings,
> Here is a man that loves me,
> And will teach me the ways of Zhou.

Trans. Waley, *Book of Songs*, 192 (modified).

38. *Shi, nei* 9.9b–10a.
39. "Danqing yin," Du Fu, 1147–52.
40. "Yulu," Xu Ji, 31. Guan and Bao are famous exemplars of true friendship; Xu is pointing out that alluding to them has become a worn-out device.
41. See *SRYX* 7.147.
42. Yang Wanli, 155. From the context of the quote it is clear that Yang is distinguishing "not using their meaning" (*bu yong qi yi*) from "negating their meaning" (*fan yong qi yi*), which means to contradict the original assertion of the allusion.
43. In *SHSG, zhengji* 3.1a–b.
44. *Shi, nei* 16.1b.
45. "Yi shi" (One room), Du Fu, 820.
46. "Sijiu fu," *WX* 16.7b–9a.
47. Trans. Watson, *Su Tung-p'o*, 92–93. For Su's text, see *Dongpo ji* (SBBY) 19.9b.
48. *Shi, nei* 16.3a.
49. *NHZJ* 3.36a; trans. Watson, *Chuang Tzu*, 97 (modified).
50. Trans. Wilhelm and Baynes, 505.
51. *Laozi* I.25; trans. Lau, *Lao Tzu*, 82.
52. *NHZJ* 8.50b–51a; trans. Watson, *Chuang Tzu*, 285–86.
53. "Sizi jiangde lun" (Discourse on the Four Masters' Discussions of Virtue), *WX* 51.711–16.
54. Trans. Chan, *Source Book*, 141–42. Compare Lau, *Lao Tzu*, 61: "Heaven and Earth are ruthless, and treat the myriad creatures as straw dogs." For explanations of their different renderings, see Lau, 165–66, and Chan, 142. My reading tends toward Professor Chan's view of cosmic indifference rather than of brutality.
55. *NHZJ* 3.17b; trans. Watson, *Chuang Tzu*, 85.

56. "Tao Yuanming zhuan," Xiao, 2.7b–8b.
57. "Zeng Linming xianling Hao di" (Bestowed on the magistrate of Linming prefecture, Mr. Hao), in Li Bo, 644.
58. *Shi, nei* 3.11a–b.
59. *NHZJ* 10.38a; trans. Watson, *Chuang Tzu*, 374.
60. *Mencius* 7A.26; trans. Lau, 187. Lau notes, "This is almost certain to be a distortion of Yang Chu's doctrine. What he taught was rather that one should not give a hair on one's body in exchange for the enjoyment of the Empire." For other comments by Mencius on Yang's egoism, see *Mencius* 3B.9.
61. Yokoyama, 96.

CONCLUSION

1. Huihong, 1.3, *xia*.
2. "Zeng xie yu rong Miaoshan shi" (Bestowed on the Imperial Painter, Master Miaoshan), *SWGS* 15.2245.
3. Yelang was a Tang prefecture; Huang's stop at Geluo Outpost is in the same region.
4. *Shi, nei* 12.1a–1b. Compare Liu Yuxi's account of composing poems to the same tune. He first, like Huang, tells of his appreciation for the tunes and then says:

Long ago, when Ch'ü Yüan lived near the Yüan and Hsiang rivers, the songs with which the common people summoned the spirits were vulgar and unrefined. Then he wrote the "Nine Songs" which are still sung and danced today in the regions of Ching and Ch'u. I have likewise written these nine bamboo branch pieces, so that good singers can make them known as additions to the tradition and later men who hear the songs of the districts of Pa and Yu will know from what the styles of these latter-day odes have developed. (*Quan Tang shi*, 4112; trans. Daniel Bryant in Wu-chi Liu and Lo, 199–200)

Huang may have had this account in mind when he wrote his preface: he adapts the theme of continuing a lost tradition but transforms following the lead of a former poet into being an absent poet's scribe. Huang may have also been taking up the motif of the power of the songs to "summon spirits"—his earlier poems have, indeed, summoned Li Bo.

5. For Ge's comment, see Ruan Yue, 25.315a.8; Liu Bin, *Kuanfu shihua* 1b–2a; cited and trans. Sargent, 193.
6. *Daoshan qinghua* (Baichuan xuehai ed.) 11b–12a. The author of this work is unknown. Cited and trans. Sargent, 194.
7. Su Shi, *Dongpo tiba* 2.15b–16a; cited and trans. Sargent, 194.
8. *SWGS* 22.2573.
9. Hu Zi (fl. ca. 1147), in his *Tiaoxi yuyin conghua* (35.239), claims that the practice began with Wang Anshi and was a product of his deep learning and automatic recall of the lines of prior poets. He then quotes the above poem by Su Shi. Huihong (3.2b–3a) recalls that Huang referred to this method as the "patchwork robe of a hundred poets' styles." He goes on to say that in "col-

lecting lines" Huang "prized 'clumsy' (*zhuo*) and hasty composition and not crafted and deliberate manner." Huang's writings contain several references to the aesthetic of the "clumsy," which, more often than not, finds its paradigm in Tao Qian's verse. It always denotes spontaneous and therefore genuine verse.

10. Du Fu's line comes from "Jiang shang zhi shui ru hai shi liao duan shu" (The waters set forth on the river are like the surging power of the sea; I casually make this account), Du Fu, 810; He's statement is cited in Fan Chuanzheng's "Tomb Inscription for Li Bo" (cited in Owen, *Great Age*, 120).

11. *Mencius* 7A.30; trans. Lau, *Mencius*, 188; cf. *Mencius* 7B.33 and 2A.3.

12. Cited in Huihong, 1.5a–b.

13. The notion of the incommensurability of ideas and words (which begins with the *Classic of Changes*) gives rise to a particular aesthetic of what lies "beyond words." In the Northern Song, this aesthetic becomes imbued with a strong skepticism with regard to language and its relation to things. This topic is treated in detail in previous chapters.

14. Zhong Rong (ca. 465–518), 3.

15. *SRYX* 6.128–29. For example, a line of Du Fu's is cited as "containing inexhaustible meaning"; and the comment that another poem has "meaning that lies beyond words" is followed by the question "If the meaning can be exhausted in one glance, how is it worth mentioning?"

16. *NHZJ* 2.1a–b; trans. Watson, *Chuang Tzu*, 50.

17. "Da Hong Jufu shu" (Letter to Hong Jufu), third of three, *YZ* 19.23b. See the epigraphs to the Critical Introduction for a fuller citation.

18. Cited in *SRYX* 8.176.

19. In Sikong, *Ershisi shipin*, 39.

20. *Yunji qiqian* ("Wu lingdan fa," 65.945) in *Daozang*, no. 1032.

21. In using this figure, Huang may also be playing with "cinnabar," which is used as a dye for paint and with *qing* forms the compound *danqing*, which signifies painting.

22. *WXDL* 6.4b; trans. Shih, 227.

23. For discussions in English on *feng* and *gu*, see Gibbs; Lin Wen-yüeh; and Pollard.

24. See Pollard, 53.

25. For an extensive study of Liu Xie's use of the terms *qi*, *feng*, and *qu*, see Xu Fuguan, *Zhongguo wenxue lunji*, 297–390.

26. The *Cihai* dictionary, s.v. *huan*[*gu*], attributes the passage to the *Liexian zhuan*. I have consulted several editions of the text but have not found this tale.

27. Wang Chong wrote the *Lunheng*, in which he mentions composing this treatise on nurturing nature.

28. Both the image of natural capacity, and the duck's short legs and the crane's long ones are from the *Zhuangzi* (*NHZJ* 2.1a–b and 4.4b).

29. See *Mencius* 6A.8, which likens the moral depravity of men to the weak condition of trees on Mount Niu, constantly at the mercy of axes and cattle.

30. *WXDL* 9.3a–4a; trans. Shih, 315–18. Fan Wenlan (2: 50), in a note on the term, cites Li Xiang's *Huang zhu bu zheng*: "In the 'Art of Prescriptions' ["Fang shu"] of the *Hou Han shu*, it says that Wang Zhen was able to enact embryonic breathing [*taixi*] and embryonic nurturing [*taiyang*]. Zhang Huai (Li Xian) explains that in the *Inner Biography of Han Wu* [*Di*] it says that Wang Zhen ... practiced closing up his breath [*bi qi*] and swallowing it, and he called this 'embryonic breathing.'"

31. *WX* 52.720–21. Pollard (49) notes the echo of *Zhuangzi* here. In the famous anecdote, the master wheelwright says, "The movement in the hand corresponds to the intention in the mind; it cannot be put into words. There is an art to it, but I cannot teach it to my son, and my son cannot receive it from me" (*NHZJ* 5.34b).

32. Indeed, Yokoyama Iseo (104) argues that the use of textual citation is diametrically opposed to the manifestation of individual personality that we witness in *qi*.

33. See, e.g., the account of *yuan qi* in the *Yunji qiqian* 56.771, *Daozang*, no. 1032.

34. For a discussion of the relation between the Way [*dao*] and *wen*, see Chow Tse-tsung, "Ancient Chinese Views."

35. For a discussion of this poem, see Owen, *Traditional Chinese Poetry*, 51; see also Schafer, 25–27.

36. Huang Tingjian, *Shangu tiba*, 3.18a; cited Cahill, 97–98.

37. *Lüshi chunqiu* (SKQS) 3.26; cited and trans. Pollard, 46.

38. Su Che, 22.1a–b; trans. in James J. Y. Liu, *Chinese Theories of Literature*, 130–31. Pollard also cites this essay (58) but omits the remarkable second paragraph.

39. Shen Fu, 254.

40. See Schafer, 23–24, for a discussion of this term, which he translates "Fashioner of Mutations."

41. Of course, we have no way of determining if Huang himself ever made this statement on "seizing the embryo." Our source is an indirect axiom from Huihong. Nevertheless, I strongly believe that the allusion to the *Zhuangzi* and of *tai*[*xi*] in both passages is striking and seems to confirm Huang's play on Liu Xie. It is particularly indicative of how exactly Huang departs from the presumptions of traditional literary criticism as expressed in the *Wenxin diaolong*.

42. Yu Cheng, A.7a–7b; cited in Fisk, "Formal Themes," 65. For further discussion of the "live method" in Southern Song poetics, derived again from Huang Tingjian, see Schmidt, 56–77.

43. Rickett, 109 n28.

44. "Ti mo yan Guo shangfu tu" (On copying the swallows in Guo's painting) in *YZ* 27.15a; cited and trans. in Bush, 44. Li is speaking of one of his own paintings. For a discussion of this painting and Huang's understanding of Li Gonglin's statement, see Barnhart, 58.

45. This notion has strong affinities with a basic premise of ancient Western rhetoric—the audience is to be led to believe that they themselves have arrived at the truth. But the purpose behind this rhetorical lure and the Chinese notion of incompleteness is absolutely different. In Western rhetoric, having the audience believe that they had arrived at the truth and therefore have a vested interest in the orator's case made it possible for the orator to lead them into untruths. For the links between rhetoric and literature in these and other terms, see Barthes.

46. Owen, *Traditional Chinese Poetry*, 21.

47. This is Vincent Shih's (232) rendering of *tong bian*.

48. See, e.g., Michael Riffaterre's work on the various subtleties of textual citation wherein a textual fragment serves as an interpretant, especially *Semiotics of Poetry* and *La production du texte*.

49. See Genette, *Introduction à l'architexte* and *Palimpsestes*.

50. See Kristeva, *Texte du roman*, 139–76, and *Semioteké*. Issue no. 27 of *Poétique* (1976) is devoted to intertextuality. The work of Mikhail Bakhtin informs nearly all modern concepts of intertextuality.

51. The presence or absence of a guiding and conscious Will behind such invention varies according to one's reading of the critical term.

52. Jenny, 266–67; trans. R. Carter in Todorov, 44–45. Jenny is speaking in general terms. I do not mean to suggest that Riffaterre, Genette, and Kristeva share equally in this nostalgia for original plenitude; rather, I use Jenny's statements to point out the motives underlying the general intertextual critique as it is perceived in Jenny's review of the literature.

53. See especially Appignanesi; Harvey; Jameson; and Lyotard.

54. This informing paradigm is akin to Riffaterre's notion of the hypogram; both terms operate as disjunctures from "ordinary" discourse and evolve from the artistic matrix of the text. Both this "paradigm" and the hypogrammatic model involve the same sort of displacement, the same attachment to an originating point of potential richness.

55. Sargent (165–98) has pointed out the similarities between the revisionary ratios Bloom enumerates and Song modes of rewriting Tang poetry. As compelling as these similarities are, Sargent himself warns against taking the parallels too far: "I have used Bloom cautiously as a means of organizing the Sung material on this problem. He provides some interesting parallels for some of the more bizarre texts we shall encounter, and his framework brings into perspective important aspects of Sung poetic practice. This does not mean, of course, that his scheme is universal in application."

56. Bloom, *Anxiety of Influence*, 5. For the precise nature of misreading, see Bloom, *Map of Misreading*.

57. Wang Ruoxu, 3; as collected in *XLDSH*, 632.

58. As I have argued throughout this study, these notions of literature by no means account for all the ways in which Chinese poets sought to establish

their poetic identity. But one can argue that the proprietary nature of Romantic poetry is fundamentally alien to the classical Chinese tradition. Of course, as we have seen, Northern Song poets played off the notion of a shared tradition to endorse quite dramatic departures from it.

APPENDIX A

1. "Hewing Sandalwood" is the title of *Shijing* poem no. 112. See Huang's account, "Ke xian dafu shi ba" (Colophon on carving my late father's poems in stone), *Shangu tiba*, 8.7j.

2. This information is from Bol, 592–97. Bol synthesizes material from Huang Tingjian's *nianpu*, written by Huang Tian, as well as information provided by Ren Yuan and Shi Rong in Huang Tingjian, *Shi*. See also Arai, *Kō Teiken*; Bieg; and Kurata; as well as Huang's biography in *Song shi, juan* 444; and Duke.

Bibliography

For the abbreviations used here, see p. xiii.

Abrams, M. H. *The Mirror and the Lamp*. London: Oxford University Press, 1953.
Appignanesi, Lisa, ed. *Postmodernism: ICA Documents*. London: Free Association Books, 1989.
Arai Ken 荒井健. *Kō Teiken* 黄庭堅. Chūgoku shijin senshū 中國詩人選集, 2nd series, no. 7. Tokyo: Iwanami, 1963.
———. "Kō Sankoku no 'Enga' no shi" 黄山谷の演雅の詩. *Tachibana Joshi Daigaku kenkyū nenpō* 橘女子大学研究年報 2. Reprinted in *Chūgoku kankei ronsō shiryō* 中国関係論叢資料. 12.2 (1970): 271–78.
Aristotle. *Rhetoric and Poetics*. Trans. W. Rhys Roberts and Ingram Bywater. New York: Modern Library, 1954.
Barnhart, Richard. "Li Kong-lin's Assimilation of Past Styles." In Murck, *Artists and Traditions*, 51–71.
Barthes, Roland. "L'ancienne rhetorique." *Communications* 16 (1970). Trans. as "The Old Rhetoric: An Aide-memoire." In idem, *The Semiotic Challenge*. New York: Hill & Wang, 1988, 11–94.
Bate, William Jackson. *The Burden of the Past and the English Poet*. New York: Norton, 1970.
Bieg, Lutz. *Huang T'ing-chien: Lieben und Dichtung*. Heidelberg: Bläschke, 1971.
Birch, Cyril, ed. *Anthology of Chinese Literature from Early Times to the Fourteenth Century*. New York: Grove, 1965.
Bloom, Harold. *The Anxiety of Influence*. Oxford: Oxford University Press, 1973.
———. *A Map of Misreading*. Oxford: Oxford University Press, 1975.
Bo Juyi 白居易. *Bo Juyi ji* 白居易集. Ed. and annot. Gu Xuejie 顧學頡. Beijing: Zhonghua, 1979.
Bodman, Richard. "Poetics and Prosody in Early Mediaeval China." Ph.D. dissertation, Cornell University, 1978.

Boileau, Nicholas. *Oeuvres complètes*. Paris: Gallimard, 1966.
Bol, Peter. "Culture and the Way in Eleventh Century China." Ph.D. dissertation, Princeton University, 1982.
Bush, Susan, comp. *The Chinese Literati on Painting: Su Shih (1037–1101) to Tung Ch'i-ch'ang (1555–1636)*. Cambridge, Mass.: Harvard University Press, 1971.
Buxbaum, David C., and Frederick W. Mote, eds. *Transition and Permanence: A Festschrift in Honor of Dr. Hsiao Kung-ch'üan*. Hong Kong: Cathay, 1972.
Cahill, James. "Confucian Elements in the Theory of Painting." In Wright, *Confucianism and Chinese Civilization*, 77–102.
Cai Zhengsun 蔡正孫. *Shilin guangji* 詩林廣記. Beijing: Zhonghua, 1981.
Cao Pi 曹丕. "Dianlun lunwen" 典論論文. In *WX* 52: 720–21.
Chan, Wing-tsit, comp. *A Source Book of Chinese Philosophy*. Princeton: Princeton University Press, 1963.
Chan, Wing-tsit, *see also under* Zhu Xi.
Chang, Carsun. *The Development of Neo-Confucian Thought*. 2 vols. New York: Bookman Associates, 1957.
Chang, Kang-i Sun. *The Evolution of Chinese Tz'u Poetry*. Princeton: Princeton University Press, 1980.
———. *Six Dynasties Poetry*. Princeton: Princeton University Press, 1986.
Chao Buzhi 晁補之. *Jile ji* 雞肋集. SBCK.
Chaves, Jonathan. "The Legacy of Ts'ang Chieh: The Written Word as Magic." *Oriental Art* 23.2 (1977): 200–214.
———. *Mei Yao-ch'en and the Development of Early Sung Poetry*. New York: Columbia University Press, 1976.
———. "'Not the Way of Poetry': The Poetics of Experience in the Sung Dynasty." *CLEAR* 4 (1982): 199–212.
Chen Changfang 陳長方. *Buli ketan* 步里客談. In *Shuofu* 説郛, Hanfenlou ed. 1927, *juan* 9.
Chen, Diana Yu-shih. "Change and Continuation in Su Shih's Theory of Literature." *Monumenta Serica* 31 (1974): 375–92.
———. "The Literary Practice of Ou-yang Hsiu." In Rickett, *Chinese Approaches to Literature*, 67–96.
Chen Shidao 陳師道. *Houshan shihua* 後山詩話. In *LDSH*, 1: 301–16.
Chen Xiang 陳香. "Huang Tingjian shizhong de guaidan xingrongci" 黃庭堅詩中的怪誕形容詞. *Chun wenxue* 純文學 7.1 (1970): 61–73.
Chen Yongzheng 陳永正. *Huang Tingjian shi xuan* 黃庭堅詩選. Hong Kong: Joint Publishing, 1980.
Cheng, François. *Chinese Poetic Writing*. Trans. Donald A. Riggs and Jerome P. Seaton. Bloomington: Indiana University Press, 1982.
Cheng Huichang 程會昌. *Wenlun yaoquan* 文論要詮. Shanghai: Kaiming, 1948.
Chow Tse-tsung. "Ancient Chinese Views on Literature, the Tao, and Their Relationship." *CLEAR* 1 (1979): 3–29.
———. "The Early History of the Chinese Word 'Shih.'" In idem, ed., *Wenlin:*

Studies in the Chinese Humanities. Madison: University of Wisconsin Press, 1968, 151–209.

Chuci sizhong 楚辭四種. Taipei: Huazheng, 1974.

Daozang 道藏. Shanghai: Shangwu, 1923–26. Reprinted—Taipei: Shangwu, 1977.

De Bary, W. T., ed. *The Unfolding of Neo-Confucianism*. New York: Columbia University Press, 1975.

Demiéville, Paul, trans. *Anthologie de la poésie chinoise classique*. Paris: Gallimard, 1962.

DeWoskin, Kenneth. "Early Chinese Music and the Origins of Aesthetic Terminology." In Susan Bush and Christian Murck, eds., *Theories of the Arts in China*. Princeton: Princeton University Press, 1983, 187–214.

Diény, Jean-Pierre. *Les dix-neuf poèmes anciens. Bulletin de la Maison Franco-Japonais*, n.s. 7.4. Paris: Presses Universitaires de France, 1963.

Ding Fubao 丁福保, comp. *Quan Han Sanguo Jin Nanbeichao shi* 全漢三國晉南北朝詩. 1959. Reprinted—Taipei: Yiwen, n.d.

———. *Xu lidai shihua* 續歷代詩話. 1969. Reprinted in 2 vols.—Taipei: Yiwen, 1974 [the Taiwan reprint lists the author as Ding Zhonghu].

Du Fu 杜甫. *Du shi xiangzhu* 杜詩詳註. Annot. and ed. Qiu Zhao'ao 仇兆鰲. Beijing: Zhonghua, 1979.

Du Mu 杜牧. *Fanchuan shi jizhu* 樊川詩集注. SBBY.

Du Zheng 度正. *Xingshan tang gao* 性善堂稿. Shanghai: Shangwu, 1935.

Duke, Michael. "Huang T'ing-chien." In William H. Nienhauser, ed. *The Indiana Companion to Traditional Chinese Literature*. Bloomington: Indiana University Press, 1986, 447–48.

Egan, Ronald. "Poems on Paintings: Su Shih and Huang T'ing-chien." *HJAS* 43 (1983): 413–51.

Eliot, Thomas Stearns. *On Poetry and Poets*. London: Faber & Faber, 1957.

———. *The Sacred Wood*. New York: Barnes & Noble, 1960.

———. *Selected Essays*. London: Faber & Faber, 1932.

Fan Wen 范溫. *Qianxi shiyan* 潛溪詩眼. In Guo Shaoyu, *Fragments*, 1: 389–411.

Fan Xiwen 范晞文. *Duichuang yehua* 對牀夜話. In *XLDSH*, 1: 481–540.

Fang Hui 方回. *Ying-Kui lüsui* 瀛奎律髓. SKQS.

Fisk, William Craig. "Formal Themes in Medieval Chinese and Modern Western Literary Theory: Mimesis, Intertextuality, Figurativeness and Foregrounding." Ph.D dissertation, University of Wisconsin, Madison, 1976.

———. "The Verse Eye and the Self-Animating Landscape in Chinese Poetry." *Tamkang Review* 8 (Apr. 1977): 123–53.

Fong, Grace. *Wu Wenying and the Art of Southern Ci Poetry*. Princeton: Princeton University Press, 1987.

Franke, Herbert, ed. *Sung Biographies*. Wiesbaden: Franz Steiner Verlag, 1976.

Frankel, Hans. "The Contemplation of the Past in T'ang Poetry." In Wright and Twichett, *Perspectives on the T'ang*, 345–66.

———. *The Flowering Plum and the Palace Lady: Interpretations of Chinese Poetry*. New Haven: Yale University Press, 1976.

Fu, Shen. "Huang T'ing-chien's Calligraphy and His 'Scroll for Chang T'a-tung': A Masterpiece Written in Exile." Ph.D. dissertation, Princeton University, 1976.

Fu Xuancong 傅璇琮. *Huang Tingjian he Jiangxi pai juan* 黄庭堅和江西派卷. Beijing: Zhonghua, 1978.

Fuller, Michael A. *The Road to East Slope: The Development of Su Shi's Poetic Voice*. Stanford: Stanford University Press, 1990.

Genette, Gérard. *Introduction à l'architexte*. Paris: Editions du Seuil, 1979.

———. *Palimpsestes*. Paris: Editions du Seuil, 1982.

Gibbs, Donald. "Notes on the Wind: The Term 'Feng' in Chinese Literary Criticism." In Buxbaum and Mote, *Transition and Permanence*, 285–93.

Goyama Kiwamu 合山究. "Sōdai bungei ni okeru zoku no gainen" 宋代文芸における俗の概念. *Kyūshū Chūgoku gakkaihō* 九州中国学会報 13 (1967): 39–55.

———. "Sō shi no gakumonsei" 宋詩の学問性. *Kyūshū Daigaku Chūgoku bungaku kai* 九州大学中国文学会 1 (1970): 3–14.

Graham, A. C. *Poems of the Late T'ang*. Harmondsworth, Eng.: Penguin, 1965.

Guillory, John. "The Ideology of Canon Formation: T. S. Eliot and Cleanth Brooks." *Critical Inquiry* 10.1 (1983): 147–72.

Guo Shaoyu 郭紹虞. *Song shihua kao* 宋詩話考. 1971. Reprinted—Beijing: Zhonghua, 1979.

———. *Zhongguo wenxue piping shi* 中國文學批評史. 1950. Reprinted—Hong Kong: Hongzhi, n.d.

Guo Shaoyu 郭紹虞, ed. and comp. *Song shihua jiyi* 宋詩話輯佚. English title: *Fragments of Sung Criticism of Poetry*. Yenching Journal of Chinese Studies, Monograph series no. 14, vols. 1 and 2. Beijing: Harvard-Yenching Institute, 1937.

Guo Xi 郭熙. *Linchuan gaozhi* 林泉高致. Comp. Guo Si 郭思. In Deng Shi 鄧實, comp., *Meishu congshu* 美術叢書. 1928–36. Reprinted—Taipei: Yiwen, 1964, 2nd series, vol. 9. Trans. Shio Sakanishi, *An Essay on Landscape Painting*. London: John Murray, 1935.

Han shu 漢書. Shanghai: Wuzhou tongwen, 1903.

Han Yu 韓愈. *Han Changli wenji jiaozhu* 韓昌黎文集校注. Annot. and ed. Ma Tongbo 馬通伯. Beijing: Zhonghua, 1972.

Harvey, David. *The Condition of Postmodernity*. Oxford: Oxford University Press, 1989.

Hatch, George. "Brief on *T'ung-p'o Chih-lin*." In Hervouet, *Sung Bibliography*, 280–88.

Hawkes, David, trans. *Ch'u Tz'u: The Songs of the South*. Oxford: Clarendon Press, 1959.

He Wenhuan 何文煥, ed. *Lidai shihua* 歷代詩話. 1740. Reprinted in 2 vols.—Beijing: Zhonghua, 1982.

Henzō Kinkō [Kūkai] 遍照金剛. *Bunkyō hifuron* 文鏡秘府論. Trans. and annot. Zhou Weide, *Wenjing mifulun*. Beijing: Renmin, 1975.
Hervouet, Yves, ed. *A Sung Bibliography*. Hong Kong: Chinese University Press, 1978.
Hightower, James Robert. *The Poetry of T'ao Ch'ien*. Oxford: Clarendon Press, 1970.
———. *Topics in Chinese Literature*. Cambridge, Mass.: Harvard University Press, 1950.
Hong Mai 洪邁. *Rongzhai suibi wuji* 容齋隨筆五集. Shanghai: Shangwu, 1935.
———. *Rongzhai tiba* 容齋題跋. Changsha: Shangwu, 1939.
Hou Han Shu 後漢書. Shanghai: Wuzhou tongwen, 1903.
Hu Yunyi 胡雲翼. *Song shi yanjiu* 宋詩研究. 1959. Reprinted—Taipei: Hongye, 1973.
———. *Zhongguo wenxue shi* 中國文學史. Shanghai: Beixin, 1932.
Hu Zi 胡仔, comp. *Tiaoxi yuyin conghua* 苕溪漁隱叢話. Beijing: Renmin wenxue, 1981.
Huang Che 黃徹. *Gongxi shihua* 䂬溪詩話. In *XLDSH*, 1: 389–478.
Huang Shang 黃裳. *Yanshan ji* 演山集. Taipei: Shangwu, 1983.
Huang Tingjian 黃庭堅. *Shangu shi zhu* 山谷詩注. SBBY. Inner collection, 20 *juan*, annot. Ren Yuan 任淵 (fl. 1133); Outer collection, 17 *juan*, annot. Shi Rong 史容 (d. after 1201); Separate collection, 2 *juan*.
———. *Shangu tiba* 山谷題跋. In *Songren tiba*.
———. *Song Huang Shangu xiansheng quanji*. 宋黃山谷先生全集 Fenning: Jixiang Tang, 1765.
———. *Yizhou yi you jia sheng ji* 宜州乙酉家乘集. Shanghai: Shangwu, 1936.
———. *Yuzhang Huang xiansheng wenji* 豫章黃先生文集. SBCK.
Huihong 惠洪. *Lengzhai yehua* 冷齋夜話. Changsha: Shangwu, 1939.
Huizong 徽宗 (attrib.). *Xuanhe huapu* 宣和畫譜. 2 vols. Shanghai: Shangwu, 1936.
Hung, William. *Tu Fu: China's Greatest Poet*. Cambridge, Mass.: Harvard University Press, 1952.
Iritani Sensuke 入谷仙介. *Sō shi sen* 宋詩選. Chūgoku koten sen 中國古典選, vol. 33. Tokyo: Asahi Shinbun, 1979.
Jameson, Fredric. *Postmodernism, or, The Cultural Logic of Late Capitalism*. Durham, N.C.: Duke University Press, 1991.
Jenny, Laurent. "La strategie de la forme." *Poétique* 27 (1976): 257–81.
Jiaoran 皎然. *Shi shi* 詩式. In *LDSH*, 1: 25–36.
Jiao Xun 焦循. *Jiao Litang diaogu ji* 焦里堂雕菰集. Shanghai: Shangwu, 1936.
Jin shu 晉書. Ed. Fang Xuanling 房玄齡. Beijing: Zhonghua, 1974.
Jiu Tang shu 舊唐書. Ed. and comp. Liu Xu 劉昫. Beijing: Zhonghua, 1975.
Kao Yu-kung and Mei Tsu-lin. "Meaning, Metaphor and Allusion in T'ang Poetry." *HJAS* 38.2 (1975): 281–356.
———. "Syntax, Diction and Imagery in T'ang Poetry." *HJAS* 31 (1970): 49–136.

———. "Tu Fu's 'Autumn Meditations': An Exercise in Linguistic Criticism." *HJAS* 28 (1968): 44–80.

Karlgren, Bernhard, trans. *The Book of Odes*. Stockholm: Museum of Far Eastern Antiquities, 1974.

Ke Dunbo 柯敦伯. *Song wenxue shi* 宋文學史. Shanghai: Shangwu, 1934.

Kobayashi Katsundo 小林勝人, trans. and annot. *Mōshi* 孟子. Tokyo: Iwanami, 1968.

Kracke, Edward A. *Translations of Sung Civil Service Titles, Classifications, Terms, and Government Organ Names*. San Francisco: Chinese Materials Center, 1978.

Kristeva, Julia. *Semioteké*. Paris, 1968.

———. *Le texte du roman*. Paris: Mouton, 1970.

Kūkai—*see* Henzō Kinkō.

Kurata Junnosuke 倉田淳之助. *Kō Sankoku* 黄山谷. Tokyo: Shūeisha, 1967.

Lattimore, David. "Allusion in T'ang Poetry." In Wright and Twichett, *Perspectives on the T'ang*, 405–40.

Lau, D. C., trans. *The Analects*. Harmondsworth, Eng.: Penguin, 1979.

———. *Lao Tzu: Tao Te Ching*. Harmondsworth, Eng.: Penguin, 1963.

———. *Mencius*. Harmondsworth, Eng.: Penguin, 1970.

Ledderose, Lothar. *Mi Fu on the Classical Tradition of Chinese Calligraphy*. Princeton: Princeton University Press, 1979.

Legge, James, trans. *Book of Documents*. The Chinese Classics, vol. 3. 1865. Reprinted—Hong Kong: Hong Kong University Press, 1979.

———. *The Four Books*. 1923. Reprinted—New York: Paragon, 1966.

Li Bo 李白. *Li Bo ji jiaozhu* 李白集校注. Ed. and annot. Qu Tuiyuan 瞿蜕園 and Zhu Jincheng 朱金成. Shanghai: Guji, 1980.

Li Yuanzhen 李元貞. *Huang Shangu de shi yu shilun* 黄山谷的詩與詩論. Taipei: Guoli Taiwan Daxue, Wenxueyuan, 1972.

Liang Kun 梁昆. *Song shipai bielun* 宋詩派別論. Taipei: Dongsheng, 1980.

Liang Qichao 梁啟超. *Yinbingshi heji* 飲冰室合集. Shanghai: Zhonghua, 1937.

Liezi 列子. SBCK ed.

Lin, Shuen-fu, and Stephen Owen, eds. *The Vitality of the Lyric Voice*. Princeton: Princeton University Press, 1986.

Lin Wen-yüeh. "The Decline and Revival of *Feng-ku* (Wind and Bone): On the Changing Poetic Styles from the Chien-an Era Through the High T'ang Period." In Shuen-fu Lin and Owen, *Lyric Voice*, 130–66.

Liu Bin 劉攽. *Kuanfu shihua* 寬夫詩話. Baichuan xuehai 百川學海 ed.

———. *Pengcheng ji* 彭城集. Wenyuange 文淵閣 SKQS. 5 vols. Reprinted—Taipei: Shangwu, 1975.

———. *Zhongshan shihua* 中山詩話. In *LDSH*, 1: 283–300.

Liu Dajie 劉大杰. "Huang Tingjian de shilun" 黄庭堅的詩論. *Wenxue piping* 文學批評 1 (1964): 64–72.

———. *Zhongguo wenxue fada shi* 中國文學發達史. 1958. Reprinted—Taipei: Zhonghua, 1974.

Liu, James J. Y. *The Art of Chinese Poetry*. Chicago: University of Chicago Press, 1962.

———. *Chinese Theories of Literature*. Chicago: University of Chicago Press, 1975.

Liu, James T. C. *Ou-yang Hsiu: An Eleventh-Century Neo-Confucianist*. Stanford: Stanford University Press, 1967.

Liu Kezhuang 劉克莊. *Houcun shihua* 後村詩話. Taipei: Guangwen, 1971.

Liu, Wu-chi, and Irving Lo, eds. *Sunflower Splendor*. New York: Doubleday, Anchor, 1975.

Liu Xie 劉勰. *Wenxin diaolong* 文心雕龍. SBCK. Trans. Vincent Shih, *The Literary Mind and the Carving of Dragons*. Taipei: Chunghwa, 1970.

———. *Wenxin diaolong zhu* 文心雕龍注. Annot. Fan Wenlan 范文瀾. Hong Kong: Shangwu, 1986.

Liu Yiqing 劉義慶. *Shishuo xinyu* 世說新語. Trans. Richard Mather, *New Accounts of Tales of the World*. Minneapolis: University of Minnesota Press, 1976.

Lo, Winston. "Wang An-shih and the Confucian Ideal of Inner Sageliness." *Philosophy East and West* 26.1 (1976): 41–53.

Longinus. "On Sublimity." In Russell and Winterbottom, *Ancient Literary Criticism*, 460–503.

Lu Ji 陸機. "Wen fu" 文賦. In *WX* 17.239–44.

Lü Benzhong 呂本中. *Tongmeng shi xun* 童蒙詩訓. Collected in Guo Shaoyu, *Fragments*, 2: 234–52.

Lü Simian 呂思勉. *Song dai wenxue* 宋代文學. Hong Kong: Shangwu, 1964.

Luo Genze 羅根澤. *Zhongguo wenxue piping shi* 中國文學批評史. 1943. Reprinted—Taipei: Xuehai, 1980.

Lynn, Richard John. "Orthodoxy and Enlightenment: Wang Shih-chen's Theory of Poetry and Its Antecedents." In DeBary, *Unfolding of Neo-Confucianism*, 215–69.

———. "The Talent–Learning Polarity in Chinese Poetics." *CLEAR* 5 (1983): 157–84.

Lyotard, Jean-François. *La condition postmoderne: Rapport sur le savoir*. Paris: Minuit, 1979. Trans. *The Postmodern Condition*. Minneapolis: University of Minnesota Press, 1984.

Mather, Richard, *see under* Liu Yiqing.

McFarland, Thomas. *Originality and Imagination*. Baltimore: Johns Hopkins University Press, 1985.

McKeon, Richard. "Literary Criticism and the Concept of Imitation in Antiquity." *Modern Philology* 34.1 (1936): 1–36.

McMullen, David. "Historical and Literary Theory in the Mid-Eighth Century." In Wright and Twichett, *Perspectives on the T'ang*, 307–42.

Mei Yaochen 梅堯臣. *Wanling xiansheng ji* 宛陵先生集. SBCK.

Meyer, Agnes E. *Chinese Painting as Reflected in the Thought and Art of Li Lung-mien*. New York: Duffield, 1923.

Mo Lifeng 莫礪鋒. *Jiangxi shipai yanjiu* 江西詩派研究. Ji'nan: Qilu, 1986.
Monk, Samuel H. *The Sublime: A Study in Critical Theories in 18th Century England*. Ann Arbor: University of Michigan Press, 1960.
Murck, Christian, ed. *Artists and Traditions: Uses of the Past in Chinese Culture*. Princeton: Princeton University Press, 1976.
Nanshi 南史. Ed. Li Yanshou 李延壽. 5 vols. Beijing: Zhonghua, 1975.
Nitchie, Elizabeth. "Longinus and the Theory of Poetic Imitation in 17th and 18th Century England." *Studies in Philology* 32 (1915): 580–97.
Ogawa Tamaki 小川環樹. *Kaze to kumo: Chūgoku bungaku ronshū* 風と雲中國文学論集. Tokyo: Asahi Shinbun, 1972.
Ogawa Tamaki 小川環樹, ed. and comp. *Sō shi sen* 宋詩選. Tokyo: Chikuma, 1967.
Okamoto Fujiaki 岡本不二明. "'In' 'shu' hyōgen no chikaku gengoteki kentō" 隱秀表現の知覚言語的檢討. *Chūgoku bungakuhō* 中国文学報 28 (1977): 71–111.
Ōno Shūsaku 大野修作. "Kō Teiken shi ni okeru 'mono' ni yoru shikō" 黄庭堅詩におけるものによる思考. *Kagoshima Daigaku bunka hōkoku* 鹿児島大学文科報告 18.1 (1984): 29–46.
Ouyang Xiu 歐陽修. *Liuyi shihua* 六一詩話. In *LDSH*, 1: 262–72.
———. *Ouyang Wenzhong gong ji* 歐陽文忠公集. SBCK.
Owen, Stephen. *The Great Age of Chinese Poetry: The High T'ang*. New Haven: Yale University Press, 1981.
———. *The Poetry of the Early T'ang*. New Haven: Yale University Press, 1977.
———. *Remembrances*. Cambridge, Mass.: Harvard University Press, 1986.
———. *Traditional Chinese Poetry and Poetics: Omen of the World*. Madison: University of Wisconsin Press, 1985.
Pan Boying 潘伯鷹, ed. and comp. *Huang Tingjian shi xuan* 黃庭堅詩選. Shanghai: Gudian wenxue, 1957.
Pan Zhonggui 潘重規, ed. and comp. *Yuefu shi jiaojian* 樂府詩校箋. Beijing: Jiulong Rensheng, 1963.
Pollard, David. "Ch'i in Chinese Literary Theory." In Rickett, *Chinese Approaches to Literature*, 43–65.
Qian Dongfu 錢冬父. *Tang Song guwen yundong* 唐宋古文運動. Shanghai: Shanghai Guji, 1962.
Qian Mu 錢穆. *Song Ming lixue gaishuo* 宋明理學概說. Taipei: Xuesheng, 1977.
Qian Zhonglian 錢仲聯 and Qian Xuezeng 錢學增. *Song shi san bai shou* 宋詩三百首. Hangzhou: Zhejiang Guji, 1987.
Qian Zhongshu 錢鍾書. *Tanyi lu* 談藝錄. Shanghai: Kaiming, 1948.
Qian Zhongshu 錢鍾書, ed. and comp. *Song shi xuanzhu* 宋詩選注. Beijing: Renmin Wenxue, 1982.
Qin Guan 秦觀. *Huaihai ji* 淮海集. SBCK.
Quan Deyu 權德輿. *Quan Zaizhi wenji* 權載之文集. SBCK.
Quan Song ci 全宋詞. Ed. Tang Guichang 唐圭璋. Beijing: Zhonghua, 1965.
Quan Tang shi 全唐詩. Beijing: Zhonghua, 1960.
Rickett, Adele Austin. "Method and Intuition: The Poetic Theories of Huang T'ing-chien." In Rickett, *Chinese Approaches to Literature*, 97–119.

Rickett, Adele Austin, ed. *Chinese Approaches to Literature*. Princeton: Princeton University Press, 1978.
Riffaterre, Michael. *La production du texte*. Paris: Editions du Seuil, 1979.
———. *The Semiotics of Poetry*. Bloomington: Indiana University Press, 1978.
Ruan Yue 阮閱. *Zengxiu shihua zonggui* 增修詩話總龜. SBCK.
Russell, D. A., and M. Winterbottom, eds. and trans. *Ancient Literary Criticism*. Oxford: Clarendon Press, 1972.
Saddharmapundarika. *The Lotus of the Wonderful Law*. Trans. W. E. Soothill. London: Curzon Press, 1975.
Sargent, Stuart. "Can Latecomers Get There First? Sung Poets and T'ang Poetry." *CLEAR* 4 (1982): 165–98.
Schafer, Edward H. *Pacing the Void: T'ang Approaches to the Stars*. Berkeley: University of California Press, 1977.
Schiller, Friedrich. *Über naive und sentimentalische Dichtung*. In Eduard von den Hellen et al., eds., *Säkular-Ausgabe*. Stuttgart and Berlin: Cotta, 1904–5. Trans. Julias A. Elias, *Naive and Sentimental Poetry*. New York: Ungar, 1966.
Schmidt, J. D. *Yang Wan-li*. Boston: G. K. Hall, 1976.
Shao Yong 邵雍. *Yichuan xirangji* 伊川擊壤集. SBCK.
Shih, Vincent, *see under* Liu Xie.
Shijing 詩經. *Mao shi zhushu* 毛詩主疏. Ed. Zheng Xuan 鄭玄, with subcommentary by Kong Yingda 孔穎達. Beijing: Zhonghua, 1957. *For translations, see* Karlgren; Waley.
Shio Sakanishi, *see under* Guo Xi.
Sikong Tu 司空圖. *Ershisi shipin* 二十四詩品. In *LDSH*, 1: 37–44.
———. *Shipin jijie* 詩品集解. Comp. and annot. Guo Shaoyu 敦紹虞. Shanghai: Shangwu, 1965.
Sima Guang 司馬光. *Wenguo wenzheng Sima gongji* 溫國文正司馬公集. SBCK.
Sima Qian 司馬遷. *Shiji* 史記. 5 vols. Tainan: Pingping, 1975. Trans. *Records of the Grand Historian of China*. 2 vols. New York: Columbia University Press, 1961.
Siren, Oswald, trans. and comp. *Chinese on the Art of Painting*. New York: Schocken, 1963.
Song Qi 宋祁. *Song Jingwen gong biji* 宋京文公筆記. Shanghai: Shangwu, 1936.
Songren tiba 宋人題跋. Ed. Yang Jialuo 楊家駱. Taipei: Shijie, 1974.
Song shi 宋史. Comp. Tuo Tuo 脫脫 et al. Beijing: Zhonghua, 1977.
Song shi jishi 宋詩紀事. Comp. Li E 厲鶚. Shanghai: Guji, 1983.
Song shi jishi buyi 宋詩紀事補遺. Comp. Lu Xinyuan 陸心原. 1908–9. Reprinted—Taipei: Zhonghua, n.d.
Song Yuan Xue'an 宋元學案. Ed. Huang Zongxi 黃宗羲 et al. SBBY.
Soothill, W. E., *see under* Saddharmapundarika.
Soper, Alexander C. "The Relationship of Early Chinese Painting to Its Own Past." In Murck, *Artists and Traditions*, 21–47.
Su Che 蘇轍. *Luanchengji* 欒城集. SBCK.
Su Shi 蘇軾. *Dongpoji* 東坡集. SBBY.
———. *Dongpo qiji* 東坡七集. Ming Chenghua ed. Reprinted—1908–9.

———. *Dongpo tiba* 東坡題跋. In *Songren tiba*.
———. *Dongpo wenji shilüe* 東坡文集事略. SBCK.
———. *Su Wenzhong Gong shi bian zhu ji cheng*. Comp. Wang Wen'gao 王文誥. 1822. Reprinted—Taipei: Xuesheng, 1967.
Su Shunqin 蘇舜欽. *Su Shunqin ji* 蘇舜欽集. Beijing: Zhonghua, 1961.
Tai Jingnong 臺靜農, ed. *Baizhong shihua leipien* 百種詩話類編. 3 vols. Taipei: Yiwen, 1974.
Tao Qian 陶潛. *Tao Yuanming ji* 陶淵明集. Ed. and annot. Lu Qinli 逯欽立. Beijing: Zhonghua, 1979.
Tiang, Seng-yong. "Huang T'ing-chien and the Use of Tradition." Ph.D. dissertation, University of Washington, 1976.
Todorov, Tzvetan, ed. *French Literary Theory Today*. Cambridge, Eng.: Cambridge University Press, 1982.
Tu Wei-ming. "'Inner Experience'": The Basis of Creativity." In Murck, *Artists and Traditions*, 9–15.
Van Gulik, R. H., trans. *Hsi K'ang and His Poetical Essay on the Lute*. Monumenta Nipponica monograph. Tokyo: Sophia University, 1941.
Waley, Arthur, trans. and annot. *The Analects of Confucius*. New York: Vintage, 1938.
———. *The Book of Songs*. New York: Grove Press, 1960.
Wang Anshi 王安石. *Linchuan wenji* 臨川文集. SBCK.
———. *Wang Jingwen gong ji* 王荊文公集. Annot. Li Yinghu 李應湖. SBCK.
Wang Fuzhi 王夫之. *Chuanshan yishu* 船山遺書. Shanghai: Taipingyang, 1935.
Wang Ruoxu 王若虛. *Hunan shihua* 滹南詩話. In *XLDSH*, 1: 607–40.
Wang Shizhen 王世貞. *Yiyuanzhiyan* 藝苑卮言. In *XLDSH*, 2: 1095–282.
Wang Wei 王維 (701–61). *Xuxi xiansheng jiaoben Tang Wang Youcheng ji* 須溪先生校本唐王右丞集. SBCK.
Wang Wei 王暐 (fl. 1510). *Daoshan qinghua* 道山清話. Baichuan xuehai 百川學海 ed.
Wang Zhifang 王直方. *Wang Zhifang shihua* 王直方詩話. In Guo Shaoyu, *Fragments*, 1: 1–115.
Wang Zhijian 王志堅. *Biao yi lu* 表異錄. In Wang Yunwu 王雲五, comp., *Congshu jicheng* 叢書集成, vol. 194. Shanghai: Shangwu, 1937.
Watson, Burton. *Chinese Lyricism*. New York: Columbia University Press, 1971.
Watson, Burton, ed. and trans. *Columbia Book of Chinese Poetry: From Early Times to the Thirteenth Century*. New York: Columbia University Press, 1984.
Watson, Burton, trans. *Chuang Tzu: Complete Works*. New York: Columbia University Press, 1968.
———. *Su Tung-p'o: Selections from a Sung Dynasty Poet*. New York: Columbia University Press, 1965.
———. *See also under* Sima Qian; Yoshikawa Kōjirō.
Wei Jin Nanbeichao wenxue shi cankao ziliao 魏晉南北朝文學史參考資料. Ed. and annot. Beijing University, Research Group in Literary History. Beijing: Zhonghua, 1962.
Wei Qingzhi 魏慶之, comp. *Shiren yuxie* 詩人玉屑. Taipei: Jiusi, 1979.

Wen xuan 文選. Comp. Xiao Tong 蕭統. Beijing: Zhonghua, 1977.
Wilhelm, Richard, and Cary Baynes, trans. *The I-Ching or Book of Changes.* Princeton: Princeton University Press, 1967.
Williamson, H. R. *Wang An-shih: Chinese Statesman and Educationalist of the Sung Dynasty.* 2 vols. London: Probsthain, 1935, 1937.
Workman, Michael. "Huang T'ing-chien: His Ancestry and Family Background as Documented in His Writings and Other Sung Works." Ph.D. dissertation, Indiana University, 1982.
Wright, Arthur, ed. *Confucianism and Chinese Civilization.* Stanford: Stanford University Press, 1959.
Wright, Arthur, and Denis Twichett, eds. *Perspectives on the T'ang.* New Haven: Yale University Press, 1973.
Wu Ceng 吳曾. *Nenggai zhai manlu* 能改齋漫錄. Shanghai: Guji, 1960.
Wu Yunjia 吳弁嘉, ed. *Shenshi san xiansheng ji* 沈氏三先生集. Hangzhou: Zhejiang, 1896.
Wu Zhizhen 吳之振, Lü Liuliang 呂留良, and Wu Eryao 吳爾堯, eds. and comps. *Song shi chao* 宋詩鈔. Shanghai: Shangwu, 1935.
Xi Kang 嵇康. "Qin fu" 琴賦. In *WX* 18.255.
Xiao Tong 蕭統. *Liang Zhaoming taizi ji* 梁昭明太子集. Wenyuange 文淵閣 SKQS. Reprinted—Taipei: Shangwu, 1983.
Xin Tang shu 新唐書. Comp. Ouyang Xiu 歐陽修 et al. Beijing: Zhonghua, 1975.
XLDSH, see Ding Fubao.
Xu Fuguan 徐復觀. "Huang Shangu zai Song shi de diwei" 黃山谷在宋詩的地位. *Mingbao* 14.7 (1979): 21–25.
———. *Zhongguo wenxue lunji* 中國文學論集. Taipei: Xuesheng, 1980.
Xu Ji 徐積. *Jiexiao ji* 節孝集. SKQS.
Xu Yi 許顗. *Yanzhou shihua* 彥周詩話. In *LDSH,* 1: 377–402.
Yan Youyi 嚴有翼. *Yiyuan cihuang* 藝苑雌黃. Collected in Guo Shaoyu, *Fragments,* 2: 181–234.
Yan Yu 嚴羽. *Canglang shihua* 滄浪詩話. Ed. and annot. Guo Shaoyu 郭紹虞. 1962. Reprinted—Taipei: Dongsheng, 1980.
Yan Zhitui 顏之推. *Yan shi jiaxun* 顏氏家訓. Shanghai: Shijie, 1936.
Yang Jiong 楊烱. *Yang Yingchuan ji* 楊盈川集. SBCK.
Yang Wanli 楊萬里. *Chengzhai shihua* 誠齋詩話. In *XLDSH,* 1: 149–80.
Yang Zhizhuang 楊志莊. *Liang Song wenxue yanjiu* 兩宋文學研究. Renren wenku 人人文庫, no. 279. Taipei: Shangwu, 1973.
Yokoyama Iseo 橫山伊勢雄. "Kō Teiken shiron kō, tenko no yōhō o chūshin to shite" 黃庭堅詩論考典故の用法を中心として. *Tōkyō Kyōiku Daigaku kanbungaku ronsō* 東京教育大学漢文学論叢 82 (1971): 93–130.
Yoshikawa Kōjirō 吉川幸次郎. *Sō shi gaisetsu* 宋詩概說. Chūgoku shijin senshū 中国詩人選集, 2nd series, no. 1. Tokyo: Iwanami, 1962. Trans. Burton Watson, *An Introduction to Sung Poetry,* Cambridge, Mass.: Harvard University Press, 1967.
———. *To shi ronshū* 杜詩論集. Tokyo: Chikuma, 1980.

Young, Edward. *Conjectures on Original Composition*. Ed. Edith J. Morley. Manchester: University Press, 1918.
Yu Cheng 俞成. *Yingxue congshuo* 螢雪叢説. Baichuan xuehai 百川學海 ed.
Yu, Pauline R. "Allegory, Allegoresis, and the *Classic of Poetry*." *HJAS* 43 (1983): 377–412.
———. "Metaphor and Chinese Poetry." *CLEAR* 3 (1981): 205–24.
Yuan Zhen 元稹. *Yuan shi Changqing ji* 元氏長慶集. SBCK.
Zhang Bangji 張邦基. *Mozhuang manlu* 墨莊漫錄. Shanghai: Shangwu, 1939.
Zhang Bingquan 張秉權. *Huang Shangu jiaoyou ji zuopin* 黃山谷交遊及作品. Hong Kong: Zhongwen daxue, 1978.
Zhang Jian 張健. *Song Jin sijia wenxue piping yanjiu* 宋金四家文學批評研究. Taipei: Liaojing, 1975.
Zhang Jie 張戒. *Suihantang shihua* 歲寒堂詩話. In *XLDSH*, 1: 541–75.
Zhang Lei 張耒. *Zhang Youshi wenji* 張右史文集. SBCK.
Zhang Yenyuan 張顏遠. *Lidai minghua ji* 歷代名畫記. Beijing: Renmin meishu, 1963.
Zhang Zai 張載. *Zhang Hengqu ji* 張橫渠集. Beijing: Shangwu, 1936.
Zhong Rong 鍾嶸. *Shipin* 詩品. In *LDSH*, 1: 1–24.
Zhou Weide 周維德, *see under* Henzō Kinkō.
Zhou Zizhi 周紫芝. *Taicang timi ji* 太倉稊米集. SBCK.
———. *Zhupo shihua* 竹坡詩話. In *LDSH*, 1: 337–58.
Zhu Bian 朱弁. *Fengyue tang shihua* 風月堂詩話. Taipei: Guangwen, 1973.
Zhu Dongrun 朱東潤. "Huang Tingjian de zhengzhi taidu ji chi lun shi zhuzhang" 黃庭堅的政治態度及其論詩主張. 1963. Reprinted in idem, *Zhongguo wenxue lun ji* 中國文學論集. Beijing: Zhonghua, 1983, 259–82.
Zhu Xi 朱熹, comp. *Jinsi lu* 近思錄. Taipei: Shijie, 1967. Trans. Wing-tsit Chan, *Reflections on Things at Hand*. New York: Columbia University Press, 1967.
Zhu Ziqing 朱自清. *Gudian wenxue lunwen ji* 古典文學論文集. 2 vols. Shanghai: Guji, 1980.
Zhuangzi 莊子. *Nanhua zhenjing* 南華真經. SBCK.
Zhuzi jicheng 諸子集成. 8 vols. Shanghai: Shijie, 1936.

Character List

Entries are alphabetized letter by letter, ignoring word and syllable breaks. Not listed here are titles and authors that appear only in the Notes and for which characters are given in the Bibliography.

anhe 闇合
aolü 拗律
aoti 拗體
"Ba ai shi" 八哀詩
"Ba Gao Zimian shi" 跋高子勉詩
ban 半
Ban Gu 班固, Mengjian 孟堅, 32–92
Ban Zhao 班昭, 1st c. A.D.
Bao Shuya 鮑叔牙, 7th c. B.C.
Baoxian 保暹
Bao Zhao 鮑照, Mingyuan 明遠, 414?–66
"Ba shu Liu Zihou shi" 跋書柳子厚詩
Bei zheng 北征
Ben cao 本草
bi 比
Bie Ling 鼈靈
"Bing hou guo Wang Yi yin zeng ge" 病後過王倚飲贈歌
bi qi 閉氣
"Bishusheng dong ye su zhiji huai Li Desu" 祕書省冬夜宿直寄懷李德素

Bo Juyi 白居易, Letian 樂天, 772–846
Bowu zhi 博物志
Bo Ya 伯牙, 6th c. B.C.
"Bujian: Jin wu Li Bo xiao xi" 不見近無李白消息
"Bu ju" 卜居
bu yong qi yi 不用其意
Cai Juhou 蔡居厚, Kuanfu 寬夫, fl. 1108
Cai Kuanfu shihua 蔡寬夫詩話
Cai Tianqi 蔡天啟, jinshi 1080
Cai Yong 蔡邕 (Eastern Han)
Cai Ze 蔡澤, 3rd c. B.C.
Cao Cao 曹操, Mengde 孟德, 155–220
Cao Pi 曹丕, Zihuan 子桓, 187–226
Cao Shen 曹參, fl. 200 B.C.
Cao Shou 曹壽, Shishu 世叔, ca. 1st c. A.D.
Cao Xuequan 曹學佺, Nengshi 能始, 1574–1647
Cao Zhi 曹植, Zijian 子建, 192–232
Cen Shen 岑參, 715–70

"Changge xing" 長歌行
Changli 昌黎
Chang Qu 常璩 (Eastern Jin)
chan xin 禪心
Chao Buzhi 晁補之, Wujiu 無咎,
  1053–1110
Chen Changfang 陳長方, Qizhi 齊之,
  1108–48
Cheng Yi 程頤, Zhengshu 政叔,
  Yichuan 伊川, 1033–1107
Chen Shidao 陳師道, Lüchang 履常,
  Wuji 無己, 1053–1101
chen yan 陳言
Chen Zi'ang 陳子昂, Boyu 伯玉,
  661–702
chi'er 痴兒
Chuandenglu 傳燈錄
chu chu 出處
Chuci 楚辭
"Chun ye xi yu" 春夜喜雨
ci 詞
ci bian 伺便
ciyun 次韻
Cui Bo 崔白, Zixi 子西, 1050–80
Cui Yin 崔駰, ?–92

da dao 大道
"Da Hong Jufu shu" 答洪駒父書
Dai Shulun 載叔倫, 732–89
Da Jia 大家
"Da Li tuiguan shu" 答李推官書
"Da Liu Zhengfu shu" 答劉正夫書
danqing 丹青
"Danqing yin" 丹青引
dao 道
Daoshan qinghua 道山清話
Dao Zhen 道臻, late 11th c.
"Dao Zhen shi hua zhu xu"
  道臻師畫竹序
"Daren fu" 大人賦

"Da Wu Chong xiucai shu"
  答吳充秀才書
"Da ya jiu bu zuo" 大雅久不作
"Da Zuze zhi shu" 答祖擇之書
"Deng gao" 登高
"Dengtu zi hao se fu" 登徒子好色賦
dian 點
dian gu 典故
"Dianlun lunwen" 典論論文
Ding Lingwei 丁令威 (Western Han)
Ding Wei 丁謂, Weizhi 謂之, 962–1033
Di Ya 狄牙 (Eastern Qi)
"Dong du yu chun" 東都遇春
"Dongpo ba shou" 東坡八首
Dong Zhongshu 董仲舒, ca. 179–ca.
  104 B.C.
Du Fu 杜甫, Zimei 子美, 712–70
"Du gu shi" 讀古詩
"Du Han Du ji" 讀韓杜集
Du Mu 杜牧, Muzhi 牧之, 803–52
duo tai 奪胎
"Du shi" 讀史
"Du shi jian" 杜詩箋
Du Zheng 度正, Zhouqing 周卿, *jinshi*
  1190

Erya 爾雅

Fang Hui 方回, Wanli 萬里, 1227–1306
"Fang shu" 方術
fangyan 法言
Fan Liao 范寥, Xinzhong 信中, fl.
  after 1101
Fan Xiwen 范晞文, Jingwen 景文, fl.
  1266
fan yong qi yi 反用其意
Fan Zhongyan 范仲淹, Xiwen 希文,
  989–1052
Fan Zongshi 樊宗師, late 8th c.
Fatan ji 伐檀集

Character List

Fayan 法言
"Fa yuan wen" 發願文
feng 風
"Feng gu" 風骨
"Feng song Zhou Yuanweng suo Jizhou sifa ting fu Libu shi" 奉送周元翁鎮吉州司法廳赴禮部試
"Fengxian Liu Shaofu xin hua shan shui zhang ge" 奉先劉少府新畫山水障歌
"Feng yu kan zhouqian luohua xi wei xinju" 風雨看舟前落花戲爲新句
"Feng zeng Wei zuo chengzhang ershier yun" 奉贈韋左丞丈二十二韻
fu (hexagram) 復
fu (rhymeprose) 賦
fu gu 復古
Fu Xi 伏羲 (myth.)
Fu Xian 傅咸, fl. 300
"Fu yi xiansheng zhu ji shu" 鳧繹先生諸集叙

gan 感
Gao Cheng 高丞, fl. mid-12th c.
Gao He 高荷, Zimian 子勉, fl. 1086
Gao Ruona 高若訥, Minzhi 敏之, 997–1055
Gao shi zhuan 高士傳
Geluo 歌羅
Ge Shengzhong 葛勝仲, Luqing 魯卿, 1072–1144
Guan Zhong 管仲, d. 645 B.C.
"Gu feng" 古風
"Gui qulai ci" 歸去來辭
"Gui tian fu" 歸田賦
"Gui yuantian ju wu shou" 歸園田居五首
Gu Kaizhi 顧愷之, Changkang 長康, 345?–406?
Gu Longzhen 顧龍振

Guo Pu 郭璞, Jingchun 景純, 276–324
Guo Si 郭思, Dezhi 得之, *jinshi* 1082
Guo Xi 郭熙, ca. 1020–90
Guo Xiang 郭象, d. 312
gushi 古詩

Han Gan 韓幹, b. ca. 710
"Han shi" 寒食
Han shu 漢書
Han Yu 韓愈, Tuizhi 退之, 768–824
"Han Yu lun" 韓愈論
hao 號
he 和
He di 和帝, r. 89–106
He Zhizhang 賀知章, fl. 720
"He Ziyu bingqi you shuzhai" 和子由病起遊書齋
"He Zizhan xishu Boshi hua hao tou chi" 和子瞻戲書伯時畫好頭赤
Hong Mai 洪邁, Jinglu 景廬, Rongzhai 容齋, 1123–1202
Hou Han shu 後漢書
huai gu 懷古
Huaigu 懷古, 9th c.
Huainantzu 淮南子
Huang Binlao 黃斌老, late 11th c.
Huang Che 黃徹, Changming 常明, *jinshi* 1124
Huang di 黃帝 (myth.)
Huangfu Mi 皇甫謐, Shi'an 士安, 215–82
Huang Mu 黃睦, b. 1076
Huang Shang 黃裳, Mianzhong 冕仲, 1044–1130
Huang Shu 黃庶, Yafu 亞父, 1018–58
Huang Tian 黃甶, 1150–1212
Huang Tingjian 黃庭堅, Luzhi 魯直, Shangu 山谷, Fuweng 涪翁, Yuzhang 豫章, 1045–1105
huan gu 換骨

Huang Xiang 黃相, b. 1084
Huang zhu bu zheng 黃注補正
Huang Zongxi 黃宗羲, Taizhong 太沖, 1610–95
Huan Wen 桓溫, Yuanzi 元子, 312–73
Huan Yi 桓伊, Shuxia 叔夏, d. 392
Huayang guozhi 華陽國志
Hu Dongwei 胡洞微, 11th c.
Huichong 惠崇, late 9th c.
Huihong 惠洪, Yuanming chanshi 元明禪師, 1071–1128
Huinan 惠南, late 9th c.
huofa 活法
huoyong 活用

Jia Dao 賈島, Langxian 浪仙, 779–849
jiang 將
"Jiang shang zhi shui ru hai shi liao duan shu" 江上值水如海勢聊短述
Jiangxi pai 江西派
"Jiangzhou fu Zhongchuan zhi Jiangling yilai zhou zhong shi shedi wushi yun" 江州赴忠川至江陵以來舟中示舍第五十韻
Jianzhang 簡長, late 9th c.
"Jiaoliao fu" 鷦鷯賦
Jiao Xun 焦循, Litang 理堂, 1763–1820
ji ju 集句
jin 今
Jin dynasty 晉, 265–420
Jin dynasty 金, 1115–1234
"Jingman fei wu xiang" 荊蠻非吾鄉
"*Jingxue liku* shi shu zhang" 經學理窟詩書章
Jin shu 晉書
"Jiu bian" 九辯
"Jiu ge" 九歌
Jiumolo 鳩摩羅
Jizhong Zhoushu 汲冢周書
Ji Zhu 季主 (Eastern Han)

"Jueju manxing jiu shou" 絕句漫興九首
"*Jushi ji* xu" 居士集序
ju yan 句眼

ke ren 可人
"Ke xian Dafu shi ba" 刻先大夫詩跋
Kong Yingda 孔穎達, Zhongda 仲達, 574–648
Kongzi jiayu 孔子家語
kun 鯤

"*Lanting ji* xu" 蘭亭集序
"*Lao xue an bi ji*" 老學庵筆記
lei 類
leng ran 冷然
li 理
Liang dynasty 梁, 502–57
"Liang Shi Zifang deng zhuan" 梁世子方等傳
Li Bo 李白, Taibo 太白, 701–62
Li Chang 李常, Gongze 公擇, 1027–90
Li Chongde 李崇德, 12th c.
Lie nü zhuan 列女傳
Liexian zhuan 列仙傳
Liezi 列子
Li Gonglin 李公麟, Boshi 伯時, 1049–1106
Li Guang 李廣 (Eastern Han)
Li Guang 李廣, Taifa 泰發, d. 1155
Li He 李賀, Changji 長吉, 791–817
Li Huangde 李璜德 (Southern Song)
Liji 禮記
Li Ling 李陵, ?–74 B.C.
Lin Bu 林逋, 967–1028
lingdan 靈丹
"Li sao" 離騷
Li Shan 李善, 630–89
Li Shangyin 李商隱, Yishan 義山, 813?–58
Liu Bang 劉邦, 256–195 B.C.

Liu Bei 劉備, 162–223
Liu Bin 劉攽, Gongfu 貢夫, 1023–89
Liu Chang 劉敞, 1019–68
Liu Kezhuang 劉克莊, Qianfu 潛夫, 1187–1269
Liu Xiang 劉向, Zizheng 子政, 77–6 B.C.
Liu Xie 劉勰, Yanhe 彥和, 465–522
Liuyi shihua 六一詩話
Liu Yun 劉筠, 971–1031
Liu Yuxi 劉禹錫, Mengde 夢得, 772–842
Liu Zhangqing 劉長卿, Wenfang 文房, 709–80?
Liu Zhen 劉楨, Gonghan 公幹, ?–217
Liu Zongyuan 柳宗元, Zihou 子厚, 773–819
Li Xiang 李詳, Shenyan 慎言, 1859–1931
Lixue 理學
Li Yannian 李延年, ca. 140–87 B.C.
Li Zonge 李宗諤, 965–1013
Lü An 呂安, Zhongti 仲悌, d. 262
Lü Benzhong 呂本中, Juren 居仁, 1084–1145
Lu Gong 魯恭, 2nd c. A.D.
Lu Ji 陸機, Shiheng 士衡, 261–303
lun 論
Lunheng 論衡
"*Lunyu* duan pian" 論語斷篇
"Lun zuo shi wen" 論作詩文
Luo Binwang 駱賓王, ca. 640–84
"Luo shen fu" 洛神賦
Lü Shang 呂尚 (myth.)
Lüshi chunqiu 呂氏春秋
Lu Tong 盧仝, Yuchuanzi 玉川子, d. 835
"Lüye shu huai" 旅夜書懷
Lu You 陸游, Wuguan 務觀, Fangweng 放翁, 1125–1209
Lu Zhi 陸贄, Jingyu 敬輿, 754–805

Mantanglu 漫塘錄
"*Mao shi* xu" 毛詩序
Maoshi zhushu 毛詩注疏
"Mao wu wei qiu feng suo po ge" 茅屋爲秋風所破歌
Mei Yaochen 梅堯臣, Shengyu 聖俞, 1002–60
Meng Jia 孟嘉, Wannian 萬年, mid-4th c. A.D.
Meng Jiao 孟郊, Dongye 東野, 751–814
Mengqi bitan 夢溪筆談
Mi Fu 米芾, Yuanzhang 元章, 1051–1107
"Minggao ge song Cen Zhengjun" 鳴皋歌送岑徵君
"Momiao tang ji" 墨妙堂記
"Mu qiu Wang Pei Daozhou shouzha shuai er qian xing ji di cheng Su Huan shi yu" 暮秋枉裴道州手札率爾遣興寄遞呈蘇渙侍御

Nanshi 南史
nianpu 年譜
Nü Wa 女媧 (myth.)

"Ouyang sheng ai ci hou" 歐陽生哀辭後
Ouyang Xiu 歐陽修, Yongshu 永叔, Wenzhong 文忠, 1007–72

pai 派
pangtong 旁通
Pan Yue 潘岳, Anren 安仁, 247–300
peng 鵬
pin 聘
pipa 琵琶
"Pipa xing" 琵琶行

qi (energy, vital breath, force) 氣
qi (strange) 奇

"Qi ai shi: Xi jing luan wu xiang"
  七哀詩:西京亂無象
qian 乾
"Qiang cun san shou" 羌村三首
Qian Qianyi 錢謙益, 1582–1664
"Qian xing" 遣興
Qi Bo 岐伯 (myth.)
qin 琴
"Qinchong shi'er zhang" 禽蟲十二章
"Qin fu" 琴賦
qing 清
qingqi 清氣
qingtan 清談
Qin Guan 秦觀, Taixu 太虛, Shaoyu 少游, 1049–1100
qisi qiju 奇思奇句
"Qiu ren" 求人
"Qiu shui" 秋水
"Qiu xing" 秋興
"Qiu xing fu" 秋興賦
"Qi wu" 齊物
Qi Yu 耆域, 5th c. B.C.
qi yun 氣韻
Quan Deyu 權德輿, Zaizhi 載之, 759–818
quewen 闕文
"Quli" 曲禮
Qu Yuan 屈原, 4th. c. B.C.

"Renjian shi" 人間世
Ren Yuan 任淵, Ziyuan 子淵, ?–1144
ru 入
Ruan Fu 阮孚, 278–326
Ruan Ji 阮籍, Sizong 嗣宗, 210–63
Ruan Xian 阮咸, Zhongrong 仲容, 234–305
Ruan Yue 阮閱, Hongxiu 閎休, fl. 1126
ru shen 入神
ru shi 入室

ru shou 入手
ru yu shen 入于神

sa lo 灑落
Seng Zhao 僧肇, d. 415
Shang han za lun 傷寒雜論
"Shanglin fu" 上林賦
"Shangu lun shi" 山谷論詩
Shao Hao 少昊 (myth.)
Shao Yong 邵雍, Yaofu 堯夫, 1011–77
she gong 射工
shen 神
Shen Deqian 沈德潛, 1693–1769
sheng tang 昇堂
Shen Gua 沈括, Cunzhong 存中, 1031–95
shen hui 神會
Shen Liao 沈遼, Yunchao 雲巢, 1032–85
Shen Nong 神農 (myth.)
Shen Quanqi 沈佺期, Yunqing 雲卿, 650–713
shen tong li 神通力
Shenxian zhuan 神仙傳
Shen Yue 沈約, Xiuwen 休文, 441–513
She xun hu 射訓狐
shi (allusion) 事
shi (poetry) 詩
shi (tone of zither) 適
Shiji 史記
shi lei 事類
Shi Manqing 石曼卿, Yannian 延年, 994–1041
Shipin 詩品
Shiren yuxie 詩人玉屑
Shi Rong 史容, ?–after 1201
Shi wei 式微
Shi xue cuan wen 詩學纂聞
shi yan zhi 詩言志

Shi zhou ji 十洲記
"Shu Chao Buzhi suo cang Yuke hua zhu" 書晁補之所藏與可畫竹
"Shu Liu Zihou shi" 書柳子厚詩
"Shu Luzhi ti Gao Qiu Fu qing ting shi hou" 書魯直題高求父清亭詩後
"Shuo lin xun" 說林訓
Shuowen jiezi 說文解字
Shu shi 書史
si chen 司晨
Sihuiliao 死灰寮
"Sijiu fu" 思舊賦
Sikong Shu 司空署, fl. 785–805
Sikong Tu 司空圖, Biaosheng 表聖, Zhifeizi 知非子, Nairu jushi 耐辱居士, 837–908
Sima Guang 司馬光, Junshi 君實, 1019–86
Sima Qian 司馬遷, Zichang 子長, 145–90 B.C.
Sima Xiangru 司馬相如, Changqing 長卿, 179–117 B.C.
Siming shihua 四溟詩話
si wen 斯文
"Sizi jiangde lun" 四子講德論
Song dynasty 宋, 960–1279; Northern Song, 960–1126
Song Jingwen gong biji 宋京文公筆記
Song Qi 宋祁, Zijing 子京, 998–1061
"Song sheng" 松聲
Song shi chao 宋詩鈔
Song Ying shi 送雁氏
"Song you ren gui shan ge" 送友人歸山歌
Song Yu 宋玉, 3rd c. B.C.
"Song Zhang Jiazhou" 送張嘉州
Song Zhiwen 宋之問, Yanqing 延清, d. 712
Soushen ji 搜神記

su 俗
Su Che 蘇轍, Ziyou 子由, 1039–1112
suhe 蘇和
"Sui mu" 歲暮
Sui shu 隋書
Sun Jue 孫覺, 1028–90
Su Qin 蘇秦, ?–317 B.C.
Su Shi 蘇軾, Zizhan 子瞻, Dongpo 東坡, 1037–1101
Su Shunqin 蘇舜欽, Zimei 子美, 1008–48
Suwen 素問
Su Wu 蘇武, 2nd c. B.C.

tai 胎
Tai Hao 太昊 (myth.)
taixi 胎息
taiyang 胎養
Tang dynasty 唐, 618–907
"Tang gu Gongbu yuan wailang Du jun muxi ming" 唐故工部員外郎杜君墓係銘
Tang Ju 唐舉, 3rd c. B.C.
"Tang zhu gang" 湯祝綱
tao (chan) 逃禪
Tao Qian 陶潛, Yuanliang 元亮, Yuanming 淵明, Shenming 深明, 365–427
Tao yinju 陶隱居
"Tao Yuanming zhuan" 陶淵明傳
ti 體
tian ji 天幾
Tianrui 天瑞
"Tianwen zhi" 天文志
Tian yun 天運
Tian zi fang 田子方
"Tiba Dongpo yuefu" 題跋東坡樂府
"Ti da yun cang da guan tai" 題大雲倉達觀臺

"Ti mo yan Guo shangfu tu"
題摹燕郭尚父圖
"Ting yun" 停雲
"Ti Shangu shiniudong" 題山谷石牛洞
"Ti zhu shi mu niu" 題竹石牧牛
tong bian 通變
"Tong zhugong deng Ci'en si ta"
同諸公登慈恩寺塔
tu 吐

"Wai wu" 外物
Wang Anshi 王安石, Jiefu 介甫,
   1021–86
Wang Bao 王豹 (Spring and Autumn
   period)
Wang Bao 王褒, Ziyuan 子淵, fl. 552
Wang Bo 王勃, Zi'an 子安, 648–75
"*Wang Bo ji* xu" 王勃集序
Wang Can 王粲, Zhongxuan 仲宣,
   177–217
Wang Changling 王昌齡, Shaobo 少伯,
   690–756
Wang Chong 王充, 27–ca. 91
Wang di 望帝 (Zhou dynasty)
Wang Fan 王蕃, Guanfu 觀復, 11th c.
Wang Fuzhi 王夫之, Ernong 而農,
   1619–92
"Wang Jinggong chan jian"
   王荊公禪簡
"Wang Jinggong Dongpo shi zhi
   miao" 王荊公東坡詩之妙
Wang Kejiao 王可交
Wang Pin 王蘋, Xinpo 信伯,
   1082–1153
Wang Qiang 王嬙, Zhaojun 昭君, 1st
   c. B.C.
Wang Qiao 王喬 (Spring and Autumn
   period)
Wang Ruoxu 王若虛, 1174–1243

Wang Sengru 王僧孺, 465–522
Wang Shihan 汪師韓, 1632–1705
Wang Shizhen 王世貞, Yuanmei 元美,
   1526–90
Wang Wei 王維, Mojie 摩詰, 701–61
Wang Xizhi 王羲之, Yishao 逸少,
   303–79
Wang Yucheng 王禹偁, Yuanzhi 元之,
   954–1001
Wang Zhen 王真 (Eastern Han)
Wang Zhifang 王直方, Lizhi 立之,
   1069–1109
Weifeng 維鳳, late 9th c.
Weimojing 維摩經
Weiqing 惟清, 11th c.
Wei Yingwu 韋應物, 737–?
wei you 唯有
wen 文
"Wen fu" 文賦
Wen Lugong 文潞公, 11th c.
Wen Tong 文同, Yuke 與可, 1018–79
wenzhang 文章
Wenzhao 文兆, late 9th c.
"Wu bu qian" 物不遷
Wu Ceng 吳曾, Huchen 虎臣, 1127–60
Wu Daoxuan 吳道玄, Daozi 道子,
   ?–792
"Wu lingdan fa" 五靈丹法
Wu Qing 吳慶 (Western Han)
Wu Yun 吳筠, d. 778
Wu Yunjia 吳允嘉, fl. 1718
wu zhi wai 物之外
Wu Zhizhen 吳之振, Mengju 孟舉,
   1640–1717

xian 羨
Xiang Xiu 向秀, Ziqi 子期, ca.
   221–ca. 300
Xiangyangji 襄陽記

Character List

xiao 小
Xiao He 蕭何, ?–193 B.C.
xiaoshuo 小說
Xiao Tong 蕭統, Deshi 德施, 501–31
"Xici zhuan" 繫辭傳
"Xida Chen Yuanyu" 戲答陳元輿
Xie Lingyun 謝靈運, Kangle 康樂, 385–433
Xie Shihou 謝師厚, Jingchu 景初, 1020–84
Xie Tiao 謝朓, Xuanhui 玄暉, 464–99
"Xi jiao" 西郊
Xi Kang 嵇康, Shuye 叔夜, 223–62
Xikun chouchang ji 西崑酬唱集
xin 心
xing 興
Xing Bing 邢昺, Shuming 叔明, 932–1010
"Xing mai pian" 幸邁篇
Xingzhao 行箒, late 9th c.
Xin Tang shu 新唐書
xiong zhong 胸中
Xiqing shihua 西清詩話
"Xi tang yong ri xulun" 夕堂永日緒論
"Xi ti Wang Zai hua shan shui tu ge" 戲題王宰畫山水圖歌
Xizhou 希畫
Xuansha 玄沙
"Xuanzhou Xie Tiao lou jian bie jiaoshu Shuyun" 宣州謝朓樓餞別校書叔雲
"Xue lei" 雪類
Xu Gan 徐幹, 170–217
Xu Ji 徐積, Zhongche 仲車, 1028–1103
Xu Ling 徐陵, Xiaomu 孝穆, 507–82
xunhu 訓狐
Xunzi 荀子
Xu Shen 許慎, 30–124
Xu Yi 許顗, Yanzhou 彥周, ?–1150
Xu Yin 許尹, fl. 1140

yan 顏
Yan di 炎帝 (myth.)
"Yan ge xing" 艷歌行
Yang Jie 楊介, Jilao 吉老, fl. 1113
Yang Jiong 楊炯, 650–92
"Yangliu zhi ci" 楊柳枝詞
yang qi 養氣
Yang Shen 楊慎, Yongxiu 用修, 1488–1559
Yang sheng zhu 養生主
Yang Suweng 楊素翁, 11th c.
Yang Wanli 楊萬里, Tingxiu 廷秀, 1127–1206
Yang Xiong 揚雄, Ziyun 子雲, 53 B.C.–A.D. 18
Yang Yi 楊億, Danian 大年, 974–1020
"Yang zhi shui" 揚之水
Yang Zhu 楊朱 (Warring States period)
Yang Zijian 楊子建
"Yang Zijian tong shen lun ji xu" 楊子建通神論集序
yan wai 言外
Yan Wu 嚴武, 726–65
Yan Yanzhi 顏延之, Yannian 延年, 384–456
Yan Yu 嚴羽, Yiqing 儀卿, Canglang buke 滄浪逋客, 1180–1235
Yan Zhitui 顏之推, Jie 介, 531–91
yan zhong 眼中
Yao Cha 姚察, 533–606
yao shi 藥石
Yao Silian 姚思廉, Jianzhi 簡之, 557–637
Yelang 夜郎
"Ye wen bili" 夜聞觱篥

"Ye xing guan xing" 夜行觀星
yi 意
yi cai 逸才
Yijing 易經
Yiliao 宜僚, 5th c. B.C.
yin 隱
ying zhuan wan 硬轉彎
"Yinzhong ba xian ge" 飲中八仙歌
Yiqiejing yiyi 一切經意義
yiren 異人
Yi shi 一室
"Yi Xing Dunfu" 憶邢惇夫
yi yi 遺意
Yi Yin 伊尹 (myth.)
Yiyuan 異苑
yi zhuo 已拙
yong dian 用典
yong shi 用事
yongwu 詠物
"You huai Banshan laoren zai ciyun er shou" 有懷半山老人再次韻二首
you shen 有神
"You shi zhai" 優士齋
"You you lu ming" 呦呦鹿鳴
yu 蝝
yuan 怨
Yuan Jie 元結, Cishan 次山, 719–72
Yuanming 淵明 (Tao Qian)
yuan qi 元氣
"Yuanyang fu" 鴛鴦賦
"Yuan you" 遠遊
Yuanyou period 元祐, 1086–94
Yuan Zhen 元稹, Weizi 微之, 779–831
"Yuanzhuan xing" 宛轉行
Yu Cheng 俞成, Yuande 元德, fl. 1200
"Yue" 月
yuefu 樂府
"Yu fu" 漁夫
"Yu He Wengjing shu" 與何翁靜書
"Yu Ji Pu tan shi shu" 與極浦談詩書

"Yulu" 語錄
"*Yunchao shi* xu" 雲巢詩序
"Yundang gu yan zhu ji" 篔簹谷偃竹記
Yunji qiqian 雲笈七籤
"Yu Pan Zizhen er shu" 與潘子真二書
"Yu Qin Shaozhang shu" 與秦少章書
"Yu tai guan" 玉台觀
"Yu Wang Guanfu shu" 與王觀復書
"Yu Wang Ziyu shu" 與王子予書
"Yu Wu Zhi shu" 與吳質書
Yu Xin 庾信, Zishan 子山, 512–80
"Yu Xu Shichuan shu" 與徐師川書
Yuzhao 宇昭, late 9th c.

"Zai ciyun Yang Mingshu shi" 再次韻楊明叔詩
zao hua 造化
zao qi yu 造其語
"Zao xing" (a) 早行
"Zao xing" (b) 早興
zao yu 造語
"Za shi" 雜詩
Zeng Gong 曾鞏, Zigu 子固, 1019–83
"Zeng Linming xianling Hao di" 贈臨洺縣令皓弟
"Zeng xie Yurong Miaoshan shi" 贈寫御容妙善師
Zeyang 則陽
Zhang Bangji 張邦基, Zixian 子賢, ?–1150
Zhang Dun 章惇, 1035–1105
Zhang Heng 張衡, 1st c. A.D.
Zhang Hua 張華, Maoxian 茂先, 232–300
Zhang Huai 章懷 (Li Xian 李賢), 651–84
Zhang Ji 張機 (Eastern Han)
Zhang Ji 張籍, Wenchang 文昌, 765–830
Zhang Jie 張戒, *jinshi* 1124

Zhang Lei 張耒, Wenqian 文潛, 1054–1114
Zhang Xu 張旭, Bogao 伯高, fl. 700–750
Zhang Yi 張儀, ?–309 B.C.
Zhang Yue 張說, Daoji 道濟, 667–730
Zhang Zai 張載, Zihou 子厚, 1020–77
Zhao Tingzhi 趙挺之, Zhengfu 正夫, 1040–1107
zhengrong 崢嶸
Zheng Zhanyin 鄭詹尹, 4th c. B.C.
zhen xing 真性
"Zhenzhong ji" 枕中記
zhi guai 志怪
zhi yin 知音
Zhong Rong 種嶸, Zhongwei 仲偉, ca. 465–518
Zhong Ziqi 種子期, 6th c. B.C.
Zhou Dunyi 周敦頤, Lianxi 濂溪, 1017–73
Zhou Fang 周昉, Zhonglang 仲朗, ca. 730–ca. 800
Zhou Zizhu 周紫芝, Shaoyin 少隱, 1082–after 1151
Zhuang Zhou 莊周, 369 B.C.–?
Zhuan Xu 顓頊 (myth.)
Zhuge Liang 諸葛亮, Kongming 孔明, 181–234
Zhulin qixian 竹林七賢
zhuo 拙
Zhuo Qi 卓玘, 11th c.
Zhuo Wangsun 卓王孫, 11th c.
Zhu Xi 朱熹, Yuanhui 元晦, 1130–1200
"Zi jing fu Fengxian yonghuai wu bai zi" 自京赴奉先詠懷五百字
Zi shuo 字說
"Zixu fu" 子虛賦
Zizhi tongjian 資治通鑑
"Zongwu shengri" 宗武生日
Zuo Qiuming 左丘明 (Warring States period)
Zuxin 祖心

Index

In this index an "f" after a number indicates a separate reference on the next page, and an "ff" indicates separate references on the next two pages. A continuous discussion over two or more pages is indicated by a span of page numbers, e.g., "57–59." *Passim* is used for a cluster of references in close but not consecutive sequence. Entries are alphabetized letter by letter, ignoring word breaks, hyphens, and accents.

alchemy, 178ff
allegory, 123–28 *passim*
ambiguity, 78f
Analects, 51, 63, 92, 131, 161, 204*n*30, 205*n*41
anxiety of influence, 3, 188–92 *passim*
aolü (unregulated tonal patterns), 136
aoti (unregulated style), 136
Arai Ken, 58, 119–23 *passim*, 197, 207*n*25
Aristotle, 3f, 9
art and artifice, 70, 82; and nature, 17, 22, 83, 85ff; disappearance of, 17, 73
authenticity, 59

Bakhtin, Mikhail, 225*n*50
Ban Gu, 28, 83, 154
Ban Zhao, 83
Baoxian, 203*n*12
Bao Zhao, 28
Barth, John, 2
Bate, William Jackson, 2
belatedness, 25
Ben cao, 61, 121f
bi, 93, 213*n*10
Bie Ling, 153

Bloom, Harold, 188–92 *passim*
Boileau, Nicolas, 9
Bo Juyi, 28–34 *passim*, 123, 174
— works, 86, 121; "Early Rising," 52ff; "Pine Sounds," 86; preface to "Twelve Pieces on Birds and Insects," 123f
Bo Juyi style, 29
Bol, Peter, 31, 226*n*2
Bowu zhi, 121, 129, 157
Bo Ya, 79f, 109, 169
Buddha, 33

Cai Juhou, 219*n*3
Cai Yong, 154
Cai Ze, 110
Canglang shihua, 48
Cao Cao, 154f
Cao Pi, 139; "Dianlun lunwen," 181f, 184
Cao Shen, 151
Cao Zhi, 28, 128
Chan, Wing-tsit, 221*n*54
Changli style, 29
Chang Qu, 170
Chao Buzhi, 25, 31
Chaves, Jonathan, 33, 220*n*28

Chen Changfang, 127f
Cheng Yi, 63, 209n47
Chen Shidao, 25, 75
Chen Xiang, 217n28
chen yan, 117
Chen Yongzheng, 81, 132
Chow, Tse-tsung, 75, 205n40
Chuandeng lu, 141
Chu ci, 25, 107, 161; "Encountering Sorrow," 35; "Nine Songs," 35; "Divination," 113
Classic of Changes, 50f, 167; "Xici zhuan," 71, 75, 214n24
Classic of Documents, 28, 67
Classic of Poetry, 25, 28, 35, 39, 48, 58, 63f, 83, 107, 118–24 *passim*, 159, 213n10, 217n13, 221n37
conventions of reading, 130, 134, 166–69 *passim*
craft, 86, 104
Cui Bo, 31
Cui Yin, 154
culture, activity of, 83; continuity of, 4, 31, 59f, 182, 186, 191f

Dai Daochun, 54ff
Dai Shulun, 152
Da Jia, 83
Daoshan qinghua, 174
Dao Zhen, 70
Demiéville, Paul, 211n24
dian (to spot, dot), 67
dian gu (allusion to the Classics), 154
diction, 75–80 *passim*, 94, 137
Diény, Jean-Pierre, 116
difference and identity, 74, 91, 97, 104, 125, 177
Ding Lingwei, 165
Ding Wei, 29
Di Ya, 87
Dong Zhongshu, 61
Du Fu, 1, 28–32 *passim*, 64f, 67, 109, 131, 156, 174–77 *passim*; poems on, 104ff; and allusion, 149–53 *passim*
— poems, 49, 53, 79, 83, 96, 102f, 107f, 111f, 121, 124, 138, 161, 164, 205n40; "On the Riverbank I Pace Alone Searching for Blossoms," 127; "Poem on the Bound Chickens," 127f; "Poems on Ancient Sites" (fifth of five), 150
Duke, Michael, 136
Du Mu, 109, 174
duo tai (seize the embryo), 156, 163–71 *passim*, 177–86 *passim*, 224n41
Du Zheng, 72

Egan, Ronald, 45, 81
Eliot, T. S., 17–21 *passim*
"Encountering Sorrow," 112
Erya, 123
extension and completion, 186

Fan Liao, 174, 204n34
Fan Wenlan, 224n30
Fan Xiwen, 64f
Fan Zongshi, 67
Fatan ji, 195
Fayan, 122
feng gu (wind and bone), 179–83 *passim*
Fisk, Craig, 220n28
Fuller, Michael, 206n5
Fu Xi, 50, 152, 167
Fu Xian, 78

Gao Ruona, 61, 208n36
Gao Zimian, 149, 164f
Ge Shengzhong, 174
Gibbs, Donald, 179
Goyama Kiwamu, 57, 63, 210n55
Graham, A. C., 152
Guo Xi, 99–104 *passim*, 215n30
Guo Xiang, 122
gushi (ancient-style poetry), 159

Han shu, 164, 205n44
Han Yu, 1, 28–34 *passim*, 61, 67, 103, 107, 183, 219n1
Hatch, George, 215n45
He Zhizhang, 176
High Tang technique, 55
Hong Mai, 67, 213n11
Hou Han shu, 121, 139, 169
Huaigu, 203n12
Huainanzi, 122, 146

Huang Di, 61, 208*n*34
Huangfu Mi, 61
Huang Mu, 195
Huang Shu, 195
Huang Tingjian, 36, 219*n*1; on using prior verse, 1; as Yuanyou poet, 30; on integrating past models, 66ff; as imitating Xu Ling, 67; on Su Shi's calligraphy, 184f; as herbalist, 208*n*41; introduction to Su Shi, 214*n*24
— colophons: "On Liu Zihou's Poetry," 65; "On Gao Zimian's Verse," 149
— essays: "The Account of the Hall of the Great Odes," 34f; "Fragment on the *Analects*," 62; "On Composing Poetry and Prose," 65ff; "Commentary on Du Fu's Verse," 67; "On Wang Jinggong's [Anshi] Zen pieces," 95
— letters: 57, 66; to Hong Jufu, 1, 66f, 178; to Qin Shaozhang, 25; to Xu Shichuan, 62; to Pan Zizhen, 62; to Wang Ziyu, 63; to Wang Guanfu, 65
— lines: 44, 97, 209*n*45
— poems: "On Chao Yidao's Painting of Wild Geese in Snow," 44; "Rising at Early Dawn at Linru," 48ff, 54; "Setting off at Early Morn," 52; "From Baling on a Calm Yangtze, I Approached the Xiang Tributary . . .," 54ff; "Begging for a Cat," 74; "Climbing Kuai Gallery," 78; "Inscribed on the Painting of the Bamboo, Rock, and Herdboy," 80ff; "Listening to [Li] Chongde Play the Zither," 82; "On Su Shi's Rhyming After Tao Qian," 95; "Rhyming After Zizhan's 'Guo Xi Painting the Autumn Mountains Level and Distant,'" 98–104 passim; "On Du Fu's Portrait at Wanhua Stream," 105–8; "Following Su Shi's Rhyming After Li Bo's 'A Poem on Being Moved by Autumn at the Palace of Purple Extremity in Xunyang,' Cherishing Li Bo and Su Shi," 112f; "Elaborating on the *Erya*," 119–23; "Wang Chongdao Sent Me Fifty Stems of 'Water Transcendent Blossoms' . . ." 126f; "Following the Rhymes of 'Appreciating Plums,'" 129; "A Poem Sent to Huang Jifu," 132; "On the 'Room of Rising Mountain Mists Rippling' of the Falling Star Temple" (third of four), 134f; "Following the Rhymes of Senior Secretary Gai Leading Senior Secretary Guo to Retire from Office," 136f; "Playfully Responding to Chen Yuanyu," 138f; "Rhyming After Zizhan, Sent to Wang Xuanyi of Mount Omei," 140; "Rhyming After Huang Binlao, Wandering in the Evening by the Pond by the Pavilion" (second of two), 141; "On Boshi's Painting of a Monk Gazing at a Fish," 141; "The Gallery of Pine Winds at Wuchang," 142f; "Lingering in the Wind and Rain by the Pond for Three Days," 145f; "Sleeping Ducks," 157f; "Rhyming After Uncle Gongze," 159; "Song on Listening to Song Zengru Play the Ruan Lute," 160f; "Ten Poems Rhyming After Gao Zimian" (third of ten), 164; idem, (eighth of ten), 167; "Rhyming in Response to Qian Mufu's 'Song of the Apehair Brush,'" 170
— prefaces: "To Yang Zijian's 'Discourse on Penetrating the Spirit,'" 60f; "To Master Dao Zhen's Painting of Bamboo," 70; "To the Collection of Yunchao," 92
huan gu (changing the bone), 156–63 passim, 178–82 passim
Huang Xiang, 195
Huang Zongxi, 27
Huan Wen, 84
Huayang guozhi, 170
Hu Dongwei, 110f
Huichong, 203*n*12, 204*n*28
Huihong, 156, 173, 220*n*28
Huinan, 55
Huishi, 171
Hung, William, 214*n*21
Hu Yunyi, 27f, 30, 206*n*4

Hu Zi, 222*n*9

intent, 59–65 *passim*, 163, 173, 188
intertextuality, 87, 91, 188f
irony, 79f, 96f, 112–28 *passim*, 134–36

Jenny, Laurent, 189, 225*n*52
Jia Dao, 29f
Jiangxi school, 29f
Jianzhang, 203*n*12
ji ju (collecting poetic lines), 176
Jin shu, 78, 121, 165, 170
Jizhong Zhoushu, 171

Karlgren, Bernhard, 123
Ke Dunbo, 206*n*2
Khakheperresenb, 1
Kongzi jiayu, 123
Kurata Junnosuke, 113, 122, 197

Laozi, 33, 113, 167, 221*n*54
Late Tang style, 29f
Lau, D. C., 222*n*60
learned poetry, 57–69 *passim*, 73, 175
lei (textual reference), 153f
Lengzhai yehua, 156, 173
li (inherent principle), 48, 71, 94, 206*n*5
Liang Kun, 30
Liang Qizhao, 219*n*1
Li Bo, 28, 34, 39, 43ff, 96, 176, 214*n*21;
  lines alluded to, 103, 161ff, 169
— works, 78, 107; "Intoned Beneath the
  Moon atop the West Tower of the
  Walled City of Jinling," 37; "Letter to
  Mr. Han of Jingzhou," 40ff, 44;
  "Urging Forth the Wine" (segment),
  43; "A Poem Being Moved by Autumn
  at the Palace of Purple Extremity in
  Xunyang," 110, 114f
Li Chang, 159, 195
Li Chongde, 82–85 *passim*
Liezi, 28, 79, 123
Li Gonglin, 31, 80f, 187
Li Guang 41, 164ff
Li He, 28
Liji, 107f, 170

Li Ling, 28
Lin Bu, 29
Linchuan gaozhi, 102
Li Shangyin, 28ff, 148–53 *passim*, 220*n*16;
  "The Pattern Lute," 152
literary models, assimilation of, 68–73
  passim
Liu Bang, 150
Liu Bei, 150
Liu Bin, 174, 203*n*28
Liu Chang, 61
Liu Dajie, 206*n*, 213*n*9
Liu, James J. Y., 220*n*28
Liu, James T. C., 59f
Liu Xiang, 61
Liu Xie, 64, 131, 149, 154, 179–88 *passim*,
  216*n*12. See also *Wenxin diaolong*
Liu Yun, 29f
Liu Yuxi, 112, 222*n*4
Liu Zhen, 28
Liu Zongyuan, 61
live usage (*huoyong*), 63
Li Xiang, 224*n*30
Lixue school, 30
Li Zonge, 29
Longinus, 3, 6ff
Lotus Sutra, 212*n*36
Lü An, 165
Lü Benzhong, 93, 164
Lu Ji, 91f, 203*n*20, 208*n*31, 211*n*18. See also
  "Wen fu"
Lunheng, 121
Luo Binwang, 148f
Lü Shang, 150f
Lüshi chunqiu (Spring and autumn annals
  of Mr. Lü), 79, 121, 132f, 183
Lu Tong, 33
Lu You, 75
Lu Zhi, 34

Mei Yaochen, 29, 33, 75, 77, 203*n*25; lines
  alluded to, 207*n*20
— poems: "Sharing Lodging with Xie
  Shishou," 76; "An Offering for a Cat,"
  76
Meng Jia, 84ff

Index

Meng Jiao, 29, 33
Mengzi (Mencius) 33, 61, 63, 81, 107, 122, 171, 176, 184
metaphor, 213*n*10
models, 5ff, 69
modernism, 2
Mo Lifeng, 136, 217*n*28, 220*n*28
Monk, Samuel, 9
moral action, 71

naive and sentimental poets, 13–17, 20
Nanshi, 137, 221*n*36
naturalness, 9, 59. *See also* spontaneity
nature, 125, 146
Nine Monks, 30, 203*n*12
"Nineteen Poems in the Ancient Style," 83, 115f
Northern Song, cultural and historical milieu of, 47, 57
Northern Song poets, relationship to past, 26–36 *passim*, 57
Northern Song poetry, philosophic nature of, 47–57 *passim*, 84, 91

Ogawa Tamaki, 119
Okamoto Fujiaki, 216*n*4
"Old Fisherman," 161
Ōno Shūsaku, 119, 126
originality, 1ff, 8, 17
Ouyang Xiu, 29, 33f, 59, 61; *Liuyi shihua*, 75, 203*n*12, 203*n*25, 219*n*1
Owen, Stephen, 187, 218*n*50

painting, 31, 81f, 98–104 *passim*, 187, 214*n*27, 223*n*21; technique, 67, 70
Pan Boying, 138
Pan Yue, 110
paradox of originality, 8, 12, 21
parody, 77
"Pipa xing," 86
plagiarism, 32, 173–79 *passim*
poetic identity, 97. *See also* difference and identity
poetic language, 117, 119, 130f, 136; its "exhaustibility," 2; twisting, 92, 176f
poetic sensibility, 12

poetic will, 10, 13, 19, 83, 124
poetry as craft, 26, 77, 79. *See also* art and artifice
poetry, schools of (*pai*), 29ff
Pollard, David, 179, 224*n*31
postmodernity, 189
Purple Jade, 152

qi (vital energy), 179–87 *passim*
Qian Qianyi, 27
Qian Zhongshu, 26, 122, 197
Qi Bo, 61, 208*n*34
qing qi (quintessential *qi*), 183
Qing Shen, 61
Qin Guan, 25, 61
qin poems, 82ff
Qiu Zhao'ao, 207*n*18
Qi Yu, 160ff
Quintilian, 4–12 *passim*
Qu Yuan, 28, 67, 113, 161, 222*n*4

Recluse Tao, 122
Ren Yuan, 96, 102, 112f, 121, 123, 157, 170, 197, 207*n*21
Rickett, Adele, 186, 220*n*28
Riffaterre, Michael, 225*n*48, 225*n*54
Romantic aesthetics, 8, 12, 187f, 191f
Ruan Fu, 170f
Ruan Ji, 28, 79f, 137f
rushen (entering the spirit), 70f

Sargent, Stuart, 174, 225*n*55
Schiller, Friedrich von, 12–17 *passim*, 20f, 74, 187, 189, 202*n*14
Schlegel, August von, 17
Seng Zhao, 55, 207*n*21
Seven Sages of the Bamboo Grove, 137, 165
Shakespeare, 17
Shen Fu, 184
shenhui (joining in spirit), 71
Shen Liao, 213*n*7
Shen Nong, 61, 208*n*34
Shenxian zhuan, 165
shi (lyric poetry), 1, 26
Shih, Vincent, 153

Shiji (Records of the Historian), 41, 110, 133, 159, 205*n*44. *See also* Sima Qian
Shi Manqing, 33
Shipin, 154, 177
Shiren yuxie, 67, 177
Shi Rong, 84, 197, 206*n*49, 212*n*38
shi yan zhi (poetry speaks the intent of the poet), 58
Shi Zhou ji, 111
Shuowen jiezi, 122
Shu shi, 102
Sikong Tu, 178
Sima Guang, 196
Sima Qian, 28, 34, 61, 184. *See also Shiji*
Sima Xiangru, 42f, 61, 67, 133, 205*n*44
siwen (this literature), 34f, 93, 204*n*30
Six Dynasties: rhetoric, 148; allusion in, 151
Song Qi, 160ff
Songshi chao, 27
Song Yu, 28, 129
Soper, Alexander, 31
Soushen ji, 165
Spirit Cinnabar, 1, 117, 178
spontaneity, 1f, 13, 35, 59, 64, 69–75 *passim*, 83, 87, 173, 188. *See also* naturalness
Sublime, 8f
Su Che, 183ff
Su Dan, 165
Sui shu, 113
Sun Jue, daughter of, 195
Su Qin, 28
Su Shi, 26, 36, 45, 61, 63, 67, 80f, 122, 143, 163–66 *passim*, 173–78 *passim*, 184f, 196, 213*n*9, 219*n*1, 220*n*16; as Yuanyou poet, 30, 33f; synthetic style, 31; on transforming prior verse, 93; exile of, 96; and allusion, 148; on plagiarizing Du Fu, 175f
— works: "Sending off Mr. Zhang of Jiazhou," 40; "Written on a Painting of Bamboo by Wen Yuke...," 70f; essays by, 71, 144; "Guo Xi Painting the Autumn Mountains Level and Distant," 98–104 *passim*; "Matching Li Bo," 110, 113–15; "Traveling at Night, Observing the Stars," 118; "Rhymeprose on the Red Cliff" (second of two), 165f; "Following the Rhymes of Kong Yifu's 'Compiling Ancient Poets' Lines'" (first of five), 175
Su Shunqin, 29, 33, 174, 203*n*25
Suwen, 61, 110
Su Wu, 28

tai (embryo), 180
taixi (yogic breathing), 180ff
Tang: and Song contrasted, 26–29 *passim*, 48, 204*n*28
Tang Ju, 110
Tang shu (Tang history), 41
Tao Yuanming (Tao Qian), 1, 30, 34, 67, 95, 111, 114, 156; poems alluded to, 85, 97, 173, 177, 210*n*59, 223*n*9
technique, 5, 8, 12
temple poems, 135
ti (frame, style), 213*n*10
Tiang Seng-yong, 158, 220*n*28
transcendence of self, 119, 124ff

verse eye, 131f

Wang Anshi, 30f, 61, 95f, 148f, 219*n*1; "On Du Fu's Portrait," 104f; "Studying Historical Texts," 144f
Wang Bao, 87, 168
Wang Bo, 92
Wang Can, 38, 111
Wang Changling, 92
Wang Chong, 121, 180
Wangdi, 152
Wang Guanfu, 73
Wang Qiang, 161
Wang Qiao, 87
Wang Ruoxu, 191
Wang Shizhen, 220*n*16
Wang Wei, 102, 113, 214*n*27
Wang Wen'gao, 214*n*25
Wang Xizhi: "Preface to the *Lanting Collection*," 146
Wang Yucheng, 29, 32, 203*n*22, 203*n*25
Wang Zhifang, 25

Index

Weifeng, 203n12
Weiqing, 55
Wei Yingwu, 67
wen, 35, 59, 66f, 72, 92ff, 182–88 *passim*, 191, 209n47
"Wenfu," 91, 94. See also Lu Ji
Wen Lugong, 100
Wen Tong, 70
Wenxin diaolong, 69, 94, 131, 149, 155, 180; "Feng gu" (The wind and the bone), 179–83 *passim*. See also Liu Xie
Wen xuan, 67, 123
Wenzhao, 203n12
Western rhetoric, 225n45
Western theory, 3, 187–92 *passim*
Wu Daoxuan (Daozi), 31, 70
Wu Qing, 159

Xiang Xiu, 165
Xiao He, 151
Xiao Tong, "Biography of Tao Yuanming," 161, 169
Xie Lingyun, 28
Xie Shihou, daughter of, 195
Xie Tiao, 37–44 *passim*; "Late in the Evening I Ascend 'Three Mountains' and Turn to Gaze on the Capital District," 38
Xi Kang, 137, 165; "Rhymeprose on the Zither," 86f
Xikun chouchang ji, 29
Xikun school, 30; style, 29, 219n1
xing, 93, 177, 213n10
Xin Tang shu (New Tang history), 214n27
Xizhou, 203n12
Xongzhao, 203n12
Xuansha, 141
Xu Fuguan, 179
Xu Ji, 163
Xu Ling, 28, 67; "Rhymeprose on the Mandarin Ducks," 157f
Xunzi, 61f
Xu Wenyun, 220n21
Xu Yi, 220n16
Xu Yin, 93

"Yange xing," 107

Yang Jie, 61, 208n37
Yang Minshu, 93
Yang Wanli, 163, 220n28, 221n42
Yang Jiong, 92
Yang Xiong, 42f, 61, 205n44
Yang Yi, 29f
Yang Zhu, 171
Yang Zijian, 61
yanwai (beyond words), 216n4
Yan Youyi, 45
Yan Yu, 48
Yan Zhitui, 94
Yiqiejing yiyi, 111
Yi Yin, 150
Yiyuan, 157
Yokoyama Iseo, 131f, 151, 158, 171, 224n32
yong dian (allusion to the Classics), 154
yong shi (historical allusion), 153
yong wu (poems on objects), 126–30 *passim*, 170
Yoshikawa Kōjirō, 47f, 81, 204n28
Young, Edward, 8–13 *passim*, 17, 21
Yuan qi (Primal Qi), 182f, 186
Yuanyou poets and poetics, 30, 33
Yu Cheng, 186
Yu, Pauline R., 213n10
Yu Xin, 28
Yuzhao, 203n12

Zao hua (cosmic transformation), 183, 185
Zen, 137–42 *passim*
Zeng Gong, 61
Zeng You, 174
Zhang Bangji, 211n18
Zhang Dun, 96
Zhang Heng, 154
Zhang Hua, 123
Zhang Huai, 224n30
Zhang Ji (Eastern Han), 33, 61
Zhang Ji (8th c.), 139
Zhang Lei, 25, 67, 94, 143
Zhang Xu, 70
Zhang Yenyuan, 210n10
Zhang Yi, 28
Zhang Yue, 41
Zhang Zai, 58

Zhao Tingzhi, 196
Zheng Zhanyin, 113
Zhenzhong ji (Story upon a pillow), 159
zhi yin (one who knows the tone), 79, 212*n*35
Zhong Rong, 154. *See also Shipin*
Zhong Ziqi, 79f, 109, 169
Zhou Fang, 31
Zhou Zizhi, 207*n*20
Zhuangzi, 28, 33, 50f, 55, 61, 69, 84f, 111f, 122ff, 139, 152, 161, 167ff, 171, 177, 185, 205*n*41

Zhu Dongrun, 204*n*34
Zhuge Liang, 150f
Zhuo Qi, 110
Zhuo Wangsun, 163
Zhu Zeqing, 78
Zichang, 92
Ziqi, 85
Ziyou, 85
Zuo Qiuming, 61
Zuozhuan, 113, 133
Zuxin, 55

Library of Congress Cataloging-in-Publication Data

Palumbo-Liu, David.
    The poetics of appropriation : the literary theory and practice of Huang Tingjian / David Palumbo-Liu.
    p. cm.
Includes bibliographical references and index.
ISBN 0-8047-2126-2 (alk. paper) :
    1. Huang, T'ing-chien, 1045–1105.—Criticism and interpretation.
PL2681.Z5P35   1993   92-22990
895.1′142—dc20   CIP

∞ This book is printed on acid-free paper

OHIO UNIVERSITY LIBRARY
Please return this book as soon as you have finished with it. In order to avoid a fine it must be returned by the latest date stamped below... all after two